ATS-77   ADMISSION TEST SERIES

This is your
PASSBOOK for...

California Basic Educational Skills Test (CBEST)

Test Preparation Study Guide
Questions & Answers

COPYRIGHT NOTICE

This book is SOLELY intended for, is sold ONLY to, and its use is RESTRICTED to individual, bona fide applicants or candidates who qualify by virtue of having seriously filed applications for appropriate license, certificate, professional and/or promotional advancement, higher school matriculation, scholarship, or other legitimate requirements of education and/or governmental authorities.

This book is NOT intended for use, class instruction, tutoring, training, duplication, copying, reprinting, excerption, or adaptation, etc., by:

1) Other publishers
2) Proprietors and/or Instructors of "Coaching" and/or Preparatory Courses
3) Personnel and/or Training Divisions of commercial, industrial, and governmental organizations
4) Schools, colleges, or universities and/or their departments and staffs, including teachers and other personnel
5) Testing Agencies or Bureaus
6) Study groups which seek by the purchase of a single volume to copy and/or duplicate and/or adapt this material for use by the group as a whole without having purchased individual volumes for each of the members of the group
7) Et al.

Such persons would be in violation of appropriate Federal and State statutes.

PROVISION OF LICENSING AGREEMENTS – Recognized educational, commercial, industrial, and governmental institutions and organizations, and others legitimately engaged in educational pursuits, including training, testing, and measurement activities, may address request for a licensing agreement to the copyright owners, who will determine whether, and under what conditions, including fees and charges, the materials in this book may be used them. In other words, a licensing facility exists for the legitimate use of the material in this book on other than an individual basis. However, it is asseverated and affirmed here that the material in this book CANNOT be used without the receipt of the express permission of such a licensing agreement from the Publishers. Inquiries re licensing should be addressed to the company, attention rights and permissions department.

All rights reserved, including the right of reproduction in whole or in part, in any form or by any means, electronic or mechanical, including photocopying, recording, or by any information storage and retrieval system, without permission in writing from the Publisher.

Copyright © 2024 by
National Learning Corporation

212 Michael Drive, Syosset, NY 11791
(516) 921-8888 • www.passbooks.com
E-mail: info@passbooks.com

PASSBOOK® SERIES

THE *PASSBOOK® SERIES* has been created to prepare applicants and candidates for the ultimate academic battlefield – the examination room.

At some time in our lives, each and every one of us may be required to take an examination – for validation, matriculation, admission, qualification, registration, certification, or licensure.

Based on the assumption that every applicant or candidate has met the basic formal educational standards, has taken the required number of courses, and read the necessary texts, the *PASSBOOK® SERIES* furnishes the one special preparation which may assure passing with confidence, instead of failing with insecurity. Examination questions – together with answers – are furnished as the basic vehicle for study so that the mysteries of the examination and its compounding difficulties may be eliminated or diminished by a sure method.

This book is meant to help you pass your examination provided that you qualify and are serious in your objective.

The entire field is reviewed through the huge store of content information which is succinctly presented through a provocative and challenging approach – the question-and-answer method.

A climate of success is established by furnishing the correct answers at the end of each test.

You soon learn to recognize types of questions, forms of questions, and patterns of questioning. You may even begin to anticipate expected outcomes.

You perceive that many questions are repeated or adapted so that you can gain acute insights, which may enable you to score many sure points.

You learn how to confront new questions, or types of questions, and to attack them confidently and work out the correct answers.

You note objectives and emphases, and recognize pitfalls and dangers, so that you may make positive educational adjustments.

Moreover, you are kept fully informed in relation to new concepts, methods, practices, and directions in the field.

You discover that you are actually taking the examination all the time: you are preparing for the examination by "taking" an examination, not by reading extraneous and/or supererogatory textbooks.

In short, this PASSBOOK®, used directedly, should be an important factor in helping you to pass your test.

CALIFORNIA BASIC EDUCATIONAL SKILLS TEST (CBEST)

INTRODUCTION
The CALIFORNIA BASIC EDUCATIONAL SKILLS TEST (CBEST) was developed to meet requirements of laws relating to credentialing and employment.

WHO MUST TAKE THE TEST
Applicants for a first teaching credential or a service credential must demonstrate proficiency in basic reading, writing, and mathematics skills in English by passing the CALIFORNIA BASIC EDUCATIONAL SKILLS TEST. The test is also required for the issuance or renewal of an Emergency Credential unless the applicant already holds a valid California teaching credential for which a baccalaureate degree is required.

TEST DESCRIPTION
The purpose of the CALIFORNIA BASIC EDUCATIONAL SKILLS TEST is to provide a general measure of basic proficiency in reading, writing, and mathematics. Although separate scores are provided for each of these three areas, the scores provide only an overall indication of your strength or weakness in each of the three skill areas. The test is not a measure of teaching skills or abilities.

Reading Section
The Reading section of the CBEST assesses your ability to comprehend written and graphically presented materials. The materials used in the test will vary in difficulty and complexity and are drawn from a variety of fields, such as the social sciences, the humanities, and health and consumer affairs. None of the questions require outside knowledge; all of the questions related to a particular passage can be answered on the basis of the information given in the passage. Some of the passages are long, consisting of approximately 200 words; some are shorter, of approximately 100 words; and others are short statements of one or two sentences.
The questions you will be asked come from three skill categories: literal comprehension, logical comprehension, and critical comprehension.

Mathematics Section
This portion of the test is intended to assess your cumulative knowledge of mathematics from having studied it all through elementary school, in high school, and possibly in college. The questions are selected to test the kinds of mathematics that all teachers may need, whether or not they are assigned to teach mathematics. The following broad categories are covered:
Processes Used in Problem Solving
Solution of Applied Problems
Mathematical Concepts and Relationships

A small number of questions (no more than 10 percent in a given test) fall into a fourth category that tests functional transfer of knowledge. Questions in this category are based on such things as logical thinking and the interpretation of graphs.

Overall, on any given form, no more than 40 percent of the questions in the first three categories will test arithmetic concepts and skills, and at least 20 percent of the questions from these three categories will test geometric concepts and skills. None of the questions test straight computation; instead, computation is embedded in applications, such as measurement, the calculation of interest, and so forth. Some of the mathematical concepts with which you should be familiar before taking the Mathematics test are:

- Arithmetic
- Algebra
- Measurement and Geometry

Writing Section

The Writing Section is intended to test your ability to write effectively in a limited period of time. You are given 60 minutes to write on the two topics that are printed in the test book. All examinees who take the test at the same time write on the same two topics. One of the topics asks you to analyze a situation or statement; the other asks you to write about a personal experience. You are not expected to demonstrate specialized knowledge, such as an understanding of the history of education or of particular theories of learning.

HOW TO TAKE A TEST

You have studied long, hard and conscientiously.

With your official admission card in hand, and your heart pounding, you have been admitted to the examination room.

You note that there are several hundred other applicants in the examination room waiting to take the same test.

They all appear to be equally well prepared.

You know that nothing but your best effort will suffice. The "moment of truth" is at hand: you now have to demonstrate objectively, in writing, your knowledge of content and your understanding of subject matter.

You are fighting the most important battle of your life—to pass and/or score high on an examination which will determine your career and provide the economic basis for your livelihood.

What extra, special things should you know and should you do in taking the examination?

I. YOU MUST PASS AN EXAMINATION

A. WHAT EVERY CANDIDATE SHOULD KNOW
Examination applicants often ask us for help in preparing for the written test. What can I study in advance? What kinds of questions will be asked? How will the test be given? How will the papers be graded?

B. HOW ARE EXAMS DEVELOPED?
Examinations are carefully written by trained technicians who are specialists in the field known as "psychological measurement," in consultation with recognized authorities in the field of work that the test will cover. These experts recommend the subject matter areas or skills to be tested; only those knowledges or skills important to your success on the job are included. The most reliable books and source materials available are used as references. Together, the experts and technicians judge the difficulty level of the questions.
Test technicians know how to phrase questions so that the problem is clearly stated. Their ethics do not permit "trick" or "catch" questions. Questions may have been tried out on sample groups, or subjected to statistical analysis, to determine their usefulness.
Written tests are often used in combination with performance tests, ratings of training and experience, and oral interviews. All of these measures combine to form the best-known means of finding the right person for the right job.

II. HOW TO PASS THE WRITTEN TEST

A. BASIC STEPS

1) Study the announcement

How, then, can you know what subjects to study? Our best answer is: "Learn as much as possible about the class of positions for which you've applied." The exam will test the knowledge, skills and abilities needed to do the work.

Your most valuable source of information about the position you want is the official exam announcement. This announcement lists the training and experience qualifications. Check these standards and apply only if you come reasonably close to meeting them. Many jurisdictions preview the written test in the exam announcement by including a section called "Knowledge and Abilities Required," "Scope of the Examination," or some similar heading. Here you will find out specifically what fields will be tested.

2) Choose appropriate study materials

If the position for which you are applying is technical or advanced, you will read more advanced, specialized material. If you are already familiar with the basic principles of your field, elementary textbooks would waste your time. Concentrate on advanced textbooks and technical periodicals. Think through the concepts and review difficult problems in your field.

These are all general sources. You can get more ideas on your own initiative, following these leads. For example, training manuals and publications of the government agency which employs workers in your field can be useful, particularly for technical and professional positions. A letter or visit to the government department involved may result in more specific study suggestions, and certainly will provide you with a more definite idea of the exact nature of the position you are seeking.

3) Study this book!

III. KINDS OF TESTS

Tests are used for purposes other than measuring knowledge and ability to perform specified duties. For some positions, it is equally important to test ability to make adjustments to new situations or to profit from training. In others, basic mental abilities not dependent on information are essential. Questions which test these things may not appear as pertinent to the duties of the position as those which test for knowledge and information. Yet they are often highly important parts of a fair examination. For very general questions, it is almost impossible to help you direct your study efforts. What we can do is to point out some of the more common of these general abilities needed in public service positions and describe some typical questions.

1) General information

Broad, general information has been found useful for predicting job success in some kinds of work. This is tested in a variety of ways, from vocabulary lists to questions about current events. Basic background in some field of work, such as sociology or economics, may be sampled in a group of questions. Often these are principles which have become familiar to most persons through exposure rather than through formal training. It is difficult to advise you how to study for these questions; being alert to the world around you is our best suggestion.

2) Verbal ability

An example of an ability needed in many positions is verbal or language ability. Verbal ability is, in brief, the ability to use and understand words. Vocabulary and grammar tests are typical measures of this ability. Reading comprehension or paragraph interpretation questions are common in many kinds of civil service tests. You are given a paragraph of written material and asked to find its central meaning.

IV. KINDS OF QUESTIONS

1. Multiple-choice Questions

Most popular of the short-answer questions is the "multiple choice" or "best answer" question. It can be used, for example, to test for factual knowledge, ability to solve problems or judgment in meeting situations found at work.

A multiple-choice question is normally one of three types:
- It can begin with an incomplete statement followed by several possible endings. You are to find the one ending which best completes the statement, although some of the others may not be entirely wrong.
- It can also be a complete statement in the form of a question which is answered by choosing one of the statements listed.
- It can be in the form of a problem – again you select the best answer.

Here is an example of a multiple-choice question with a discussion which should give you some clues as to the method for choosing the right answer:

When an employee has a complaint about his assignment, the action which will best help him overcome his difficulty is to
- A. discuss his difficulty with his coworkers
- B. take the problem to the head of the organization
- C. take the problem to the person who gave him the assignment
- D. say nothing to anyone about his complaint

In answering this question, you should study each of the choices to find which is best. Consider choice "A" – Certainly an employee may discuss his complaint with fellow employees, but no change or improvement can result, and the complaint remains unresolved. Choice "B" is a poor choice since the head of the organization probably does not know what assignment you have been given, and taking your problem to him is known as "going over the head" of the supervisor. The supervisor, or person who made the assignment, is the person who can clarify it or correct any injustice. Choice "C" is, therefore, correct. To say nothing, as in choice "D," is unwise. Supervisors have and interest in knowing the problems employees are facing, and the employee is seeking a solution to his problem.

2. True/False

3. Matching Questions

Matching an answer from a column of choices within another column.

V. RECORDING YOUR ANSWERS

Computer terminals are used more and more today for many different kinds of exams.

For an examination with very few applicants, you may be told to record your answers in the test booklet itself. Separate answer sheets are much more common. If this separate answer sheet is to be scored by machine – and this is often the case – it is highly important that you mark your answers correctly in order to get credit.

VI. BEFORE THE TEST

YOUR PHYSICAL CONDITION IS IMPORTANT

If you are not well, you can't do your best work on tests. If you are half asleep, you can't do your best either. Here are some tips:

1) Get about the same amount of sleep you usually get. Don't stay up all night before the test, either partying or worrying—DON'T DO IT!
2) If you wear glasses, be sure to wear them when you go to take the test. This goes for hearing aids, too.
3) If you have any physical problems that may keep you from doing your best, be sure to tell the person giving the test. If you are sick or in poor health, you relay cannot do your best on any test. You can always come back and take the test some other time.

Common sense will help you find procedures to follow to get ready for an examination. Too many of us, however, overlook these sensible measures. Indeed, nervousness and fatigue have been found to be the most serious reasons why applicants fail to do their best on civil service tests. Here is a list of reminders:

- Begin your preparation early – Don't wait until the last minute to go scurrying around for books and materials or to find out what the position is all about.
- Prepare continuously – An hour a night for a week is better than an all-night cram session. This has been definitely established. What is more, a night a week for a month will return better dividends than crowding your study into a shorter period of time.
- Locate the place of the exam – You have been sent a notice telling you when and where to report for the examination. If the location is in a different town or otherwise unfamiliar to you, it would be well to inquire the best route and learn something about the building.
- Relax the night before the test – Allow your mind to rest. Do not study at all that night. Plan some mild recreation or diversion; then go to bed early and get a good night's sleep.
- Get up early enough to make a leisurely trip to the place for the test – This way unforeseen events, traffic snarls, unfamiliar buildings, etc. will not upset you.
- Dress comfortably – A written test is not a fashion show. You will be known by number and not by name, so wear something comfortable.
- Leave excess paraphernalia at home – Shopping bags and odd bundles will get in your way. You need bring only the items mentioned in the official notice you received; usually everything you need is provided. Do not bring reference books to the exam. They will only confuse those last minutes and be taken away from you when in the test room.

- Arrive somewhat ahead of time – If because of transportation schedules you must get there very early, bring a newspaper or magazine to take your mind off yourself while waiting.
- Locate the examination room – When you have found the proper room, you will be directed to the seat or part of the room where you will sit. Sometimes you are given a sheet of instructions to read while you are waiting. Do not fill out any forms until you are told to do so; just read them and be prepared.
- Relax and prepare to listen to the instructions
- If you have any physical problem that may keep you from doing your best, be sure to tell the test administrator. If you are sick or in poor health, you really cannot do your best on the exam. You can come back and take the test some other time.

VII. AT THE TEST

The day of the test is here and you have the test booklet in your hand. The temptation to get going is very strong. Caution! There is more to success than knowing the right answers. You must know how to identify your papers and understand variations in the type of short-answer question used in this particular examination. Follow these suggestions for maximum results from your efforts:

1) Cooperate with the monitor

The test administrator has a duty to create a situation in which you can be as much at ease as possible. He will give instructions, tell you when to begin, check to see that you are marking your answer sheet correctly, and so on. He is not there to guard you, although he will see that your competitors do not take unfair advantage. He wants to help you do your best.

2) Listen to all instructions

Don't jump the gun! Wait until you understand all directions. In most civil service tests you get more time than you need to answer the questions. So don't be in a hurry. Read each word of instructions until you clearly understand the meaning. Study the examples, listen to all announcements and follow directions. Ask questions if you do not understand what to do.

3) Identify your papers

Civil service exams are usually identified by number only. You will be assigned a number; you must not put your name on your test papers. Be sure to copy your number correctly. Since more than one exam may be given, copy your exact examination title.

4) Plan your time

Unless you are told that a test is a "speed" or "rate of work" test, speed itself is usually not important. Time enough to answer all the questions will be provided, but this does not mean that you have all day. An overall time limit has been set. Divide the total time (in minutes) by the number of questions to determine the approximate time you have for each question.

5) Do not linger over difficult questions

If you come across a difficult question, mark it with a paper clip (useful to have along) and come back to it when you have been through the booklet. One caution if you do this – be sure to skip a number on your answer sheet as well. Check often to be sure that you have not lost your place and that you are marking in the row numbered the same as the question you are answering.

6) Read the questions

Be sure you know what the question asks! Many capable people are unsuccessful because they failed to read the questions correctly.

7) Answer all questions

Unless you have been instructed that a penalty will be deducted for incorrect answers, it is better to guess than to omit a question.

8) Speed tests

It is often better NOT to guess on speed tests. It has been found that on timed tests people are tempted to spend the last few seconds before time is called in marking answers at random – without even reading them – in the hope of picking up a few extra points. To discourage this practice, the instructions may warn you that your score will be "corrected" for guessing. That is, a penalty will be applied. The incorrect answers will be deducted from the correct ones, or some other penalty formula will be used.

9) Review your answers

If you finish before time is called, go back to the questions you guessed or omitted to give them further thought. Review other answers if you have time.

10) Return your test materials

If you are ready to leave before others have finished or time is called, take ALL your materials to the monitor and leave quietly. Never take any test material with you. The monitor can discover whose papers are not complete, and taking a test booklet may be grounds for disqualification.

VIII. EXAMINATION TECHNIQUES

1) Read the general instructions carefully. These are usually printed on the first page of the exam booklet. As a rule, these instructions refer to the timing of the examination; the fact that you should not start work until the signal and must stop work at a signal, etc. If there are any special instructions, such as a choice of questions to be answered, make sure that you note this instruction carefully.

2) When you are ready to start work on the examination, that is as soon as the signal has been given, read the instructions to each question booklet, underline any key words or phrases, such as least, best, outline, describe and the like. In this way you will tend to answer as requested rather than discover on reviewing your paper that you listed without describing, that you selected the worst choice rather than the best choice, etc.

3) If the examination is of the objective or multiple-choice type – that is, each question will also give a series of possible answers: A, B, C or D, and you are called upon to select the best answer and write the letter next to that answer on your answer paper – it is advisable to start answering each question in turn. There may be anywhere from 50 to 100 such questions in the three or four hours allotted and you can see how much time would be taken if you read through all the questions before beginning to answer any. Furthermore, if you

come across a question or group of questions which you know would be difficult to answer, it would undoubtedly affect your handling of all the other questions.

4) If the examination is of the essay type and contains but a few questions, it is a moot point as to whether you should read all the questions before starting to answer any one. Of course, if you are given a choice – say five out of seven and the like – then it is essential to read all the questions so you can eliminate the two that are most difficult. If, however, you are asked to answer all the questions, there may be danger in trying to answer the easiest one first because you may find that you will spend too much time on it. The best technique is to answer the first question, then proceed to the second, etc.

5) Time your answers. Before the exam begins, write down the time it started, then add the time allowed for the examination and write down the time it must be completed, then divide the time available somewhat as follows:
    - If 3-1/2 hours are allowed, that would be 210 minutes. If you have 80 objective-type questions, that would be an average of 2-1/2 minutes per question. Allow yourself no more than 2 minutes per question, or a total of 160 minutes, which will permit about 50 minutes to review.
    - If for the time allotment of 210 minutes there are 7 essay questions to answer, that would average about 30 minutes a question. Give yourself only 25 minutes per question so that you have about 35 minutes to review.

6) The most important instruction is to read each question and make sure you know what is wanted. The second most important instruction is to time yourself properly so that you answer every question. The third most important instruction is to answer every question. Guess if you have to but include something for each question. Remember that you will receive no credit for a blank and will probably receive some credit if you write something in answer to an essay question. If you guess a letter – say "B" for a multiple-choice question – you may have guessed right. If you leave a blank as an answer to a multiple-choice question, the examiners may respect your feelings but it will not add a point to your score. Some exams may penalize you for wrong answers, so in such cases only, you may not want to guess unless you have some basis for your answer.

7) Suggestions
   a. Objective-type questions
      1. Examine the question booklet for proper sequence of pages and questions
      2. Read all instructions carefully
      3. Skip any question which seems too difficult; return to it after all other questions have been answered
      4. Apportion your time properly; do not spend too much time on any single question or group of questions
      5. Note and underline key words – all, most, fewest, least, best, worst, same, opposite, etc.
      6. Pay particular attention to negatives
      7. Note unusual option, e.g., unduly long, short, complex, different or similar in content to the body of the question
      8. Observe the use of "hedging" words – probably, may, most likely, etc.

9. Make sure that your answer is put next to the same number as the question
10. Do not second-guess unless you have good reason to believe the second answer is definitely more correct
11. Cross out original answer if you decide another answer is more accurate; do not erase until you are ready to hand your paper in
12. Answer all questions; guess unless instructed otherwise
13. Leave time for review

b. Essay questions
1. Read each question carefully
2. Determine exactly what is wanted. Underline key words or phrases.
3. Decide on outline or paragraph answer
4. Include many different points and elements unless asked to develop any one or two points or elements
5. Show impartiality by giving pros and cons unless directed to select one side only
6. Make and write down any assumptions you find necessary to answer the questions
7. Watch your English, grammar, punctuation and choice of words
8. Time your answers; don't crowd material

8) Answering the essay question

Most essay questions can be answered by framing the specific response around several key words or ideas. Here are a few such key words or ideas:

M's: manpower, materials, methods, money, management
P's: purpose, program, policy, plan, procedure, practice, problems, pitfalls, personnel, public relations

a. Six basic steps in handling problems:
1. Preliminary plan and background development
2. Collect information, data and facts
3. Analyze and interpret information, data and facts
4. Analyze and develop solutions as well as make recommendations
5. Prepare report and sell recommendations
6. Install recommendations and follow up effectiveness

b. Pitfalls to avoid
1. Taking things for granted – A statement of the situation does not necessarily imply that each of the elements is necessarily true; for example, a complaint may be invalid and biased so that all that can be taken for granted is that a complaint has been registered
2. Considering only one side of a situation – Wherever possible, indicate several alternatives and then point out the reasons you selected the best one
3. Failing to indicate follow up – Whenever your answer indicates action on your part, make certain that you will take proper follow-up action to see how successful your recommendations, procedures or actions turn out to be
4. Taking too long in answering any single question – Remember to time your answers properly

EXAMINATION SECTION

READING COMPREHENSION
UNDERSTANDING AND INTERPRETING
WRITTEN MATERIAL

COMMENTARY

The ability to read and understand written materials—texts, publications, newspapers, orders, directions, expositions—is a skill basic to a functioning democracy and to an efficient business or viable government.

That is why almost all examinations—for beginning, middle, and senior levels—test reading comprehension, directly or indirectly.

The reading test measures how well you understand what you read. This is how it is done: You read a short paragraph and five statements. From the five statements, you choose the one statement, or answer, that is BEST supported by, or best matches, what is said in the paragraph.

SAMPLE QUESTIONS

DIRECTIONS: Each question has five suggested answers, lettered A, B, C, D, and E. Decide which one is the BEST answer. *PRINT THE LETTER OF THE CORRECT ANSWER IN THE SPACE AT THE RIGHT.*

1. The prevention of accidents makes it necessary not only that safety devices be used to guard exposed machinery but also that mechanics be instructed in safety rules which they must follow for their own protection and that the light in the plant be adequate.
   The paragraph BEST supports the statement that industrial accidents
   A. are always avoidable
   B. may be due to ignorance
   C. usually result from inadequate machinery
   D. cannot be entirely overcome
   E. result in damage to machinery

1.____

ANALYSIS

Remember what you have to do:
- First - Read the paragraph
- Second - Decide what the paragraph means
- Third - Read the five suggested answers.
- Fourth - Select the one answer which BEST matches what the paragraph says or is BEST supported by something in the paragraph. (Sometimes you may have to read the paragraph again in order to be sure which suggested answer is best.

This paragraph is talking about three steps that should be taken to prevent industrial accidents
1. Use safety devices on machines
2. Instruct mechanics in safety rules
3. provide adequate lighting

SELECTION

With this in mind, let's look at each suggested answer. Each one starts with "Industrial accidents…"

SUGGESTED ANSWER A
Industrial accidents (A) are always avoidable.
(The paragraph talks about how to avoid accidents, but does not say that accidents are always avoidable.)

SUGGESTED ANSWER B
Industrial accidents (B) may be due to ignorance.
(One of the steps given in the paragraph to prevent accidents is to instruct mechanics on safety rules. This suggests that lack of knowledge or ignorance of safety rules causes accidents. This suggested answer sounds like a good possibility for being the right answer.)

SUGGESTED ANSWER C
Industrial accidents (C) usually result from inadequate machinery.
(The paragraph does suggest that exposed machines cause accidents, but it doesn't say that it is the usual cause of accidents. The word usually makes this a wrong answer.)

SUGGESTED ANSWER D
Industrial accidents (D) cannot be entirely overcome.
(You may know from your own experience that this is a true statement. But that is not what the paragraph is talking about. Therefore, it is NOT the correct answer.)

SUGGESTED ANSWER E
Industrial accidents (E) result in damage to machinery.
(This is a statement that may or may not be true, but in any case it is NOT covered by the paragraph.)

Looking back, you see that the one suggested answer of the five given that BEST matches what the paragraph says is: Industrial accidents (B) may be due to ignorance.

The CORRECT answer then is B.

Be sure to read ALL the possible answers before you make your choice. You may think that none of the five answers is really good, but choose the BEST one of the five.

---

2. Probably few people realize, as they drive on a concrete road, that steel is used to keep the surface flat in spite of the weight of the busses and trucks. Steel bars, deeply embedded in the concrete, provide sinews to take the stresses so that the stresses cannot crack the slab or make it wavy.
   The paragraph BEST supports the statement that a concrete road
   A. is expensive to build
   B. usually cracks under heavy weights
   C. looks like any other road
   D. is used only for heavy traffic
   E. is reinforced with other material

2.____

ANALYSIS

This paragraph is commenting on the fact that
   1. few people realize, as they drive on a concrete road, that steel is deeply embedded
   2. steel keeps the surface flat
   3. steel bars enable the road to take the stresses without cracking or becoming wavy

SELECTION

Now read and think about the possible answers:
   A. A concrete road is expensive to build. (Maybe so but that is not what the paragraph is about.)
   B. A concrete road usually cracks under heavy weights. (The paragraph talks about using steel bars to prevent heavy weights from cracking concrete roads. It says nothing about how usual it is for the roads to crack. The word usually makes this suggested answer wrong.)
   C. A concrete road looks like any other road. (This may or may not be true. The important thing to note is that it has nothing to do with what the paragraph is about.)
   D. A concrete road is used only for heavy traffic. (This answer at least has something to do with the paragraph—concrete roads are used with heavy traffic—but it does not say "used only.")
   E. A concrete road is reinforced with other material. (This choice seems to be the correct one on two counts: First, the paragraph does suggest that concrete roads are made

stronger by embedding steel bars in them. This is another way of saying "concrete roads are reinforced with steel bars." Second, by the process of elimination, the other four choices are ruled out as correct answers simply because they do not apply.)

You can be sure that not all the reading questions will be so easy as these.

HINTS FOR ANSWERING READING QUESTIONS

1. Read the paragraph carefully. Then read each suggested answer carefully. Read every word, because often one word can make the difference between a right and a wrong answer.

2. Choose that answer which is supported in the paragraph itself. Do not choose an answer which is a correct statement unless it is based on information in the paragraph.

3. Even though a suggested answer has many of the words used in the paragraph, it may still be wrong.

4. Look out for words—such as *always*, *never*, *entirely*, or *only*—which tend to make a suggested answer wrong.

5. Answer first those questions which you can answer most easily. Then work on the other questions.

6. If you can't figure out the answer to the question, guess.

READING COMPREHENSION
UNDERSTANDING AND INTERPRETING WRITTEN MATERIAL

STRATEGIES

SURVEYING PASSAGES, SENTENCES AS CUES

While individual readers develop unique reading styles and skills, there are some known strategies which can assist any reader in improving his or her reading comprehension and performance on the reading subtest. These strategies include understanding how single paragraphs and entire passages are structured, how the ideas in them are ordered, and how the author of the passage has connected these ideas in a logical and sequential way for the reader.

The section that follows highlights the importance of reading a passage through once for meaning, and provides instruction on careful reading for context cues within the sentences before and after the missing word.

SURVEY THE ENTIRE PASSAGE

To get a sense of the topic and the organization of ideas in a passage, it is important to survey each passage initially in its entirety and to identify the main idea. (The first sentence of a paragraph usually states the main idea.) Do not try to fill in the blanks initially. The purpose or surveying a passage is to prepare for the more careful reading which will follow. You need a sense of the big picture before you start to fill in the details; for example, a quick survey of the passage on page 11 indicate that the topic is the early history of universities. The paragraphs are organized to provide information on the origin of the first universities, the associations formed by teachers and students, the early curriculum, and graduation requirements.

READ PRECEDING SENTENCES CAREFULLY

The missing words in a passage cannot be determined by reading and understanding only the sentences in which the deletions occur. Information from the sentences which precede or follow can provide important cues to determine the correct choice. For example, if you read the first sentence from the passage about universities which contains a blank, you will notice that all the alternatives make sense if this one sentence is read in isolation:

Nobody actually _____ them.
- A. started
- B. guarded
- C. blamed
- D. compared
- E. remembered

The only way that you can make the correct word choice is to read the preceding sentences. In the excerpt below, notice that the first sentence tells the reader what the passage will be about: how universities developed. A key word in the first sentence is *emerged*, which is closely related in meaning to one of the five choices for the first blank. The second sentence explains the key word *emerged*, by pointing out that we have no historical record of a decree or a date indicating when the first university was established. Understanding the ideas in the first two sentences makes it possible to select the correct word for the blank. Look at the sentence with the deleted word in the context of the preceding sentences and think about why you are now able to make the correct choice.

> The first universities emerged at the end of the 11th century and beginning of the 12th. These institutions were not founded on any particular date or created by any formal action. Nobody actually _____ them.
>   A. started   B. guarded   C. blamed
>   D. compared   E. remembered

Started is the best choice because it fits the main idea of the passage and is closely related to the key word *emerged*.

READ THE SENTENCE WHICH FOLLOWS TO VERIFY YOUR CHOICE

The sentences which follow the one from which a word has been deleted may also provide cues to the correct choice. For example, look at an excerpt from the passage about universities again, and consider how the sentence which follows the one with the blank helps to reinforce the choice of the word *started*.

> The first universities emerged at the end of the 11th century and the beginning of the 12th. These institutions were not founded on any particular date or created by any formal action. Nobody actually _____ them. Instead, they developed gradually in places like Paris, Oxford, and Bologna, where scholars had long been teaching students.
>   A. started   B. guarded   C. blamed
>   D. compared   E. remembered

The words *developed gradually* mean the same as the key word *emerged*. The signal word *instead* helps to distinguish the difference between starting on a specific date as a result of some particular act or event and emerging over a period of time as a result of various factors.

Here is another example of how the sentence which follows the one from which a word is deleted might help you decide which of two good alternatives is the correct choice. This excerpt is from the practice passage about bridges (page 10).

> Bridges are built to allow a continuous flow of highway and railway traffic across water lying in their paths. But engineers cannot forget that river traffic, too, is essential to our economy. The role of _____ is important. To keep these vessels moving freely, bridges are built big enough, when possible, to let them pass underneath.
>   A. wind   B. boats   C. weight
>   D. wires   E. experience

After the first two sentences, the reader may be uncertain about the direction the writer intended to take in the rest of the paragraph. If the writer intended to continue the paragraph with information concerning how engineers make choices about the relative importance and requirements of land traffic and rive traffic, *experience* might be the appropriate choice for the missing word. However, the sentence following the one in which the deletion occurs makes it clear that *boats* is the correct choice. It provides the synonym *vessels*, which in the noun phrase *these vessels* must refer back to the previous sentence or sentences. The phrase *to let them pass underneath* also helps make it clear that *boats* is the appropriate choice. *Them* refers back to *these vessels* which, in turn, refers back to *boats* when the word *boats* is placed in the previous sentence. Thus, the reader may use these cohesive ties (the pronoun referents) to verify the final choice.

Even when the text following a sentence with a deletion is not necessary to choose the best alternative, it may be helpful in other ways. Specifically, complete sentences provide important transitions into a related topic which is developed in the rest of the paragraph or in the next paragraph of the same passage. For example, the first paragraph in the passage about universities ends with a sentence which introduces the term *guilds*: *But, over time, they joined together to form guilds.* Prior to this sentence, information about the slow emergence of universities and about how independently scholars had acted was introduced. The next paragraph begins with two sentences about guilds in general. Someone who had not read the last sentence in the first paragraph might have missed the link between guilds and scholars and universities and, thus, might have been unnecessarily confused.

COHESIVE TIES AS CUES

Sentences in a paragraph may be linked together by several devices called cohesive ties. Attention to these ties may provide further cues about missing words. This section will describe the different types of cohesive ties and show how attention to them can help you to select the correct word.

PERSONAL PRONOUNS

Personal pronouns (e.g., he, she, they, it, its) are often used in adjoining sentences to refer back to an already mentioned person, place, thing, or idea. The word to which the pronoun refers is called the antecedent.

> Tools used in farm work changed very slowly from ancient times to the eighteenth century, and the changes were minor. Since the eighteenth century *they* have changed quickly and dramatically.

The word *they* refers back to *tools* in the example above.

In the examination reading subtest, a deleted word sometimes occurs in a sentence in which the sentence subject is a pronoun that refers back to a previously mentioned noun. You must correctly identify the referent for the particular pronoun in order to interpret the sentence and select the correct answer. Here is an example from the passage about bridges.

> An ingenious engineer designed the bridge so that it did not have to be raised above traffic. Instead it was _____.
> A. burned   B. emptied   C. secured
> D. shared   E. lowered

Q. What is the antecedent of *it* in both cases in the example?
A. The antecedent, of course, is *bridge*.

DEMONSTRATIVE PRONOUNS

Demonstrative pronouns (e.g., this, that, these) are also used to refer to a specific, previously mentioned noun. They may occur alone as noun replacements, or they may accompany and modify nouns.

I like jogging, swimming, and tennis. *These* are the only sports I enjoy.

In the sentence above, the word *these* is a replacement noun. However, demonstrative pronouns may also occur as adjectives modifying nouns.

I like jogging, swimming, and tennis. *These* sports are the only ones I enjoy.

The word *these* in the example above is an adjective modifier. The word *these* in each of the two previous examples refers to *jogging, swimming,* and *tennis.*

Here is an example from the passage about universities on page 11.

Undergraduates took classes in Greek philosophy, Latin grammar, arithmetic, music, and astronomy. These were the only _____ available.
  A. rooms   B. subjects   C. clothes
  D. pens   E. company

Q. Which word is a noun replacement?
A. The word *these* is the replacement for *Greek philosophy, Latin grammar, arithmetic, music,* and *astronomy.*

Here is another example from the same passage.

The concept of a fixed program of study leading to a degree first evolved in Medieval Europe. This _____ had not appeared before.
  A. idea   B. desk   C. library   D. capital

Q. What is the antecedent of *this*?
A. The antecedent is *the concept of a fixed program of study leading to a degree.*

COMPARATIVE ADJECTIVES AND ADVERBS

When comparative adjectives and adverbs (e.g., so, such, better, more) occur, they refer to something else in the passage, otherwise a comparison could not be made.

The hotels in the city were all full; so were the motels and boarding houses.

Q. To what in the first sentence does the word *so* refer?
A. So tells us to compare the *motels* and *boarding houses* to the *hotels in the city.*

Q. In what way are the *hotels, motels,* and *boarding houses* similar to each other?
A. The *hotels, motels,* and *boarding houses* are similar in that they were all *full.*

Look at an example from the passage about universities.

Guilds were groups of tradespeople, somewhat akin to modern trade unions. In the Middle Ages, all the crafts had such
   A. taxes   B. secrets   C. products
   D. problems   E. organizations

Q. To what in the first sentence does the word *such* refer?
A. *Such* refers to *groups of tradespeople*.

SUBSTITUTIONS

Substitution is another form of cohesive tie. A substitution occurs when one linguistic item (e.g., a noun) is replaced by another. Sometimes the substitution provides new or contrasting information. The substitution is not identical to the original, or antecedent, idea. A frequently occurring substitution involves the use of *one*. A noun substitution may involve another member of the same class as the original one.

My car is falling apart. I need a new one.

Q. What in the first sentence is replaced in the second sentence with *one*?
A. *One* is a substitute for the specific car mentioned in the first sentence. The contrast comes from the fact that the *new one* isn't the writer's current car.

The substitution may also pinpoint a specific member of a general class.

1. There are many unusual courses available at the university this summer. The *one* I am taking is called *Death and Dying.*
2. There are many unusual courses available at the university this summer. *Some* have never been offered before.

Q. In these examples, what is the general class in the first sentence that is replaced by *one* and by *some*?
A. In both cases the words *one* and *some* replace *many unusual* courses.

SYNONYMS

Synonyms are words that have similar meaning. In the examination reading subtest, a synonym of a deleted word is sometimes found in one of the sentences before and/or after the sentence with the deletion. Examine the following excerpt from the passage about bridges again.

But engineers cannot forget that river traffic, too, is essential to our economy. The role of _____ is important. To keep these vessels moving freely, bridges are built high enough, when possible, to let them pass underneath.
   A. wind   B. boats   C. weight
   D. wires   E. experience

Q. Can you identify synonyms in the sentences, before and after the sentence containing the deletion, which are cues to the correct deleted word?
A. If you identified the correct words, you probably noticed that *river traffic* is not exactly a synonym since it is a slightly more general term than the word *boats* (the correct choice). But the word *vessels* is a direct synonym. Demonstrative pronouns (this, that, these, those) are sometimes used as modifiers for synonymous nouns in sentences which follow those containing deletions. The word *these* in *these vessels* is the demonstrative pronoun (modifier) for the synonymous noun *vessels*.

ANTONYMS

Antonyms are words of opposite meaning. In the examination reading subtest passages, antonyms may be cues for missing words. A contrasting relationship, which calls for the use of an antonym, is often signaled by the connective words *instead*, *however*, *but*, etc. Look at an excerpt from the passage about bridges.

An ingenious engineer designed the bridges so that it did not have to be raised above traffic. Instead it was
 A. burned   B. emptied   C. secured
 D. shared   E. lowered

Q: Can you identify an antonym in the first sentence for one of the five alternatives?
A. The word *raised* is an antonym for the word *lowered*.

SUBORDINATE-SUBORDINATE WORDS

In the examination reading subtest, a passage sometimes contains a general term which provides a cue that a more specific term is the appropriate alternative. At other times, the passage may contain a specific term which provides cues that a general term is the appropriate alternative for a particular deletion. The general and more specific words are said to have superordinate-subordinate relationships.

Look at Example 1 below. The more specific word *boy* in the first sentence serves as the antecedent for the more general word *child* in the second sentence. In Example 2, the relationship is reversed. In both examples, the words *child* and *boy* reflect a superordinate-subordinate relationship.

1. The *boy* climbed the tree. Then the *child* fell.
2. The *child* climbed the tree. Then the *boy* fell.

In the practice passage about bridges on Page 11, the phrase *river traffic* is a general term that is superordinate to the alternative *boats* (Item 1). Later in the passage about bridges the following sentences also contain superordinate-subordinate words:

A lift bridge was desired, but there were wartime shortages of steel and machinery needed for the towers. It was hard to find enough _____.
 A. work   B. material   C. time
 D. power   E. space

Q. Can you identify two words in the first sentence that are specific examples for the correct response in the second sentence?
A. Of course, the words *steel* and *machinery* are the specific examples for the more general term *material*.

WORDS ASSOCIATED BY ENTAILMENT

Sometimes the concept described by one word within the context of the passage entails, or implies, the concept described by another word. For example, consider again Item 7 in the practice passage about bridges. Notice how the follow-up sentence to Item 7 provides a cue to the correct response.

An ingenious engineer designed the bridge so that it did not have to be raised above traffic. Instead it was _____. It could be submerged seven meters below the surface of the river.
  A. burned   B. emptied   C. secured
  D. shared   E. lowered

Q. What word in the sentence after the blank implies the concept of an alternative?
A. *Submerged* implies *lowered*. The concept of submerging something implies the idea of lowering the object beneath the surface of the water.

WORDS ASSOCIATED BY PART-WHOLE RELATIONSHIPS

Words may be related because they involve part of a whole and the whole itself; for example, *nose* and *face*. Words may also be related because they involve two parts of the same whole; for example, *radiator* and *muffler* both refer to parts of a car.

The captain of the ship was nervous. The storm was becoming worse and worse. The hardened man paced the _____.
  A. floor   B. hall   C. deck   D. court

Q. Which choice has a part-whole relationship with a word in the sentences above?
A. A *deck* is a part of a *ship*. Therefore, *deck* has a part-whole relationship with *ship*.

CONJUNCTIVE AND CONNECTIVE WORDS AND PHRASES

Conjunctions or connectives are words or phrases that connect parts of sentences or parts of a passage to each other. Their purpose is to help the reader understand the logical and conceptual relationships between ideas and events within a passage. Examples of these words and phrases include coordinate conjunctions (e.g., and, but, yet), subordinate conjunctions (e.g., because, although, since, after), and other connective words and phrases (e.g., too, also, on the other hand, as a result).

Listed below are types of logical relationships expressed by conjunctive, or connective words. Also listed are examples of words used to cue relationships to the reader.

Additive and comparative words and phrases: and, in addition to, too, also, furthermore, similarly.

Adversative and contrastive words and phrases: yet, though, only, but, however, instead, rather, on the other hand, conversely.

Causal words or phrases: so, therefore, because, as a result, if...then, unless, except, in that case, under the circumstances.

Temporal words and phrases: before, after, when, while, initially, lastly, finally, until.

Examples

1. I enjoy fast-paced sports like tennis and volleyball, but my brother prefers _____ sports.
    A. running   B. slower   C. team   D. active

    Q. What is the connective word that tells you to look for a contrast relationship between the two parts of the sentence?
    A. The connective word *but* signals that a contrast relationship exists between the two parts of the sentence.

    Q. Of the four options, what is the best choice for the blank?
    A. The word *slower* is the best response here.

2. The child stepped to close to the edge of the brook. As a result, he _____ in.
    A. fell   B. waded   C. ran   D. jumped

    Q. What is the connective phrase that links the two sentences?
    A. The connective phrase *as a result* links the two sentences.

    Q. Of the four relationships of words and phrases listed previously, what kind of relationship between the two sentences does the connective phrase in the example signal to the reader?
    A. The phrase *as a result* signals that a cause and effect relationship exists between the two sentences.

    Q. Identify the correct response which makes the second sentence reflect and cause and effect relationship.
    A. The correct response is *fell*.

Understanding connectives is very important to success on the examination reading subtest. Sentences with deletions are often very closely related to adjacent sentences in meaning, and the relationships often signaled by connective words or phrases. Here is an example from the practice passage about universities.

At first, these tutors had not been associated with one another. Rather, they had been _____. But, over time, they joined together to form guilds.
    A. curious   B. poor   C. religious
    D. ready   E. independent

Q. Identify the connective and contrastive words and phrases in the example.
A. *At first* and *over time* are connective phrases that set up temporal progression. *Rather* and *but* are contrastive items. The use of *rather* in the sentence with the deletion tells the reader that the missing word has to convey a meaning in contrast to *associated with one another*. (Notice also that *rather* occurs after a negative statement.) The use of *but* in the sentence after the one with the deletion indicates that the deleted word in the previous sentence has to reflect a meaning that contrasts with *joined together*. Thus, the reader is given two substantial cues to the meaning of the missing word. *Independent* is the only choice that meets the requirement for contrastive meaning.

SAMPLE QUESTIOINS

DIRECTIONS: There are two passages on the following pages. In each passage some words are missing. Wherever a word is missing, there is a blank line with a number on it. Below the passage you will find the same number and five words. Choose the word that makes the best sense in the blank. You may not be sure of the answer to a question until you read the sentences that come after the blank, so be sure to read enough to answer the questions. As you work on these passages, you will find that the second passage is harder to read than the first. Answer as many questions as you can.

Bridges are built to allow a continuous flow of highway and railway traffic across water lying in their paths. But engineers cannot forget that river traffic, too, is essential to our economy. The role of __1__ is important. To keep these vessels moving freely, bridges are built high enough, when possible, to let them pass underneath. Sometimes, however, channels must accommodate very tall ships. It may be uneconomical to build a tall enough bridge. The __2__ would be too high. To save money, engineers build movable bridges.

In the swing bridge, the middle part pivots or swings open. When the bridge is closed, this section joins the two ends of the bridge, blocking tall vessels. But this section __3__. When swung open, it is perpendicular to the ends of the bridge, creating two free channels for river traffic. With swing bridges channel width is limited by the bridge's piers. The largest swing bridge provides only a 75-meter channel. Such channels are sometimes __4__. In such cases, a bascule bridge may be built.

Bascule bridges are drawbridges with two arms that swing upward. They provide an opening as wide as the span. They are also versatile. These bridges are not limited to being fully opened or fully closed. They can be __5__ in many ways. They can be fixed at different angles to accommodate different vessels.

In vertical lift bridges, the center remains horizontal. Towers at both ends allow the center to be lifted like an elevator. One interesting variation of this kind of bridge was built during World War II. A lift bridge was desired, but there were wartime shortages of the steel and machinery needed for the towers. It was hard enough to find enough __6__. An ingenious engineer designed the bridge so that it did not have to be raised above traffic. Instead it was __7__. It could be submerged seven meters below the surface of the river. Ships sailed over it.

1. A. wind B. boats C. experience 1.____
   D. wires E. experience

2. A. levels B. cost C. standards 2.____
   D. waves E. deck

3. A. stands B. floods C. wears 3.____
   D. turns E. supports

4. A. narrow B. rough C. long 4.____
   D. deep E. straight

5. A. crossed B. approached C. lighted 5.____
   D. planned E. positioned

6. A. work   B. material   C. time   6.____
   D. power   E. space

7. A. burned   B. emptied   C. secured   7.____
   D. shared   E. lowered

The first universities emerged at the end of the 11th century and beginning of the 12th. These institutions were not founded on any particular date or created by any formal action. Nobody actually __8__ them. Instead, they developed gradually in places like Paris, Oxford, and Bologna, where scholars had long been teaching students. At first, these tutors had not been associated with one another. Rather, they had been __9__. But, over time, they joined together to form guilds.

Guilds were groups of tradespeople, somewhat akin to modern unions. In the Middle Ages, all the crafts had such __10__. The scholars' guilds built school buildings and evolved an administration which charged fees and set standards for the curriculum. It set prices for members' services and fixed requirements for entering the profession.

Professors were not the only schoolpeople forming associations. In Italy, students joined guilds to which teachers had to swear obedience. The students set strict rules, fining professors for beginning class a minute late. Teachers had to seek their students' permission to marry, and such permission was not always granted. Sometimes the students __11__. Even if they said yes, the teacher got only one day's honeymoon.

Undergraduates took classes in Greek philosophy, Latin grammar, arithmetic, music, and astronomy. These were the only __12__ available. More advanced study was possible in law, medicine, and theology, but one could not earn such postgraduate degrees quickly. It took a long time to __13__. Completing the requirements in theology, for example, took at least 13 years.

The concept of a fixed program of study leading to a degree first evolved in medieval Europe. This __14__ had not appeared before, in earlier academic settings, notions about *meeting requirements meeting requirements* and *graduating* had been absent. Since the middle ages, though, we have continued to view education as a set curriculum culminating in a degree.

8. A. started   B. guarded   C. blamed   8.____
   D. compared   E. remembered

9. A. curious   B. poor   C. religious   9.____
   D. ready   E. independent

10. A. taxes   B. secrets   C. products   10.____
    D. problems   E. organizations

11. A. left   B. copied   C. refused   11.____
    D. paid   E. prepared

12. A. rooms   B. subjects   C. clothes   12.____
    D. pens   E. markets

13. A. add   B. answer   C. forget   13.____
    D. finish   E. travel

14. A. idea B. desk C. library 14.____
    D. capital E. company

KEY (CORRECT ANSWERS)

1.	B	6.	B	11.	C
2.	B	7.	E	12.	B
3.	D	8.	A	13.	D
4.	A	9.	E	14.	A
5.	E	10.	E		

READING COMPREHENSION
UNDERSTANDING WRITTEN MATERIALS
COMMENTARY

The ability to read and understand written materials—texts, publications, newspapers, orders, directions, expositions—is a skill basic to a functioning democracy and to an efficient business or viable government.

That is why almost all examinations—for beginning, middle, and senior levels—test reading comprehension, directly or indirectly.

The reading test measures how well you understand what you read. This is how it is done: You read a passage followed by several statements. From these statements, you choose the one statement, or answer, that is BEST supported by, or BEST matches, what is said in the paragraph. PRINT THE LETTER OF THE CORRECT ANSWER IN THE SPACE AT THE RIGHT.

SAMPLE QUESTIONS

DIRECTIONS: Answer Questions 1 and 2 ONLY according to the information given in the following passage.

1. When a fingerprint technician inks and takes rolled impressions of a subject's fingers, the degree of downward pressure the technician applies is important. The correct pressure may best be determined through experience and observation. It is quite important, however, that the subject be cautioned to relax and not help the fingerprint technician by also applying pressure, as this prevents the fingerprint technician from gaging the amount needed. A method which is helpful in getting the subject to relax his hand is to instruct him to look at some distant object and not to look at his hands.

1. According to this passage, the technician tries to relax the subject's hands by
    A. instructing him to let his hands hang loosely
    B. telling him that being fingerprinted is painless
    C. asking him to look at this hand instead of some distant object
    D. asking him to look at something other than his hand

2. The subject is asked NOT to press down on his fingers while being fingerprinted because
    A. the impressions taken become rolled
    B. the subject may apply too little downward pressure and spoil the impressions
    C. the technician cannot tell whether he is applying the right degree of pressure
    D. he doesn't have the experience to apply the exact amount of pressure

CORRECT ANSWERS
1. D
2. C

EXAMINATION SECTION

TEST 1

DIRECTIONS: Questions 1 through 3 are to be answered on the basis of the following reading passage. *PRINT THE LETTER OF THE CORRECT ANSWER IN THE SPACE AT THE RIGHT.*

Thermostats should be tested in hot water for proper opening. A bucket should be filled with sufficient water to cover the thermostat and fitted with a thermometer suspended in the water so that the sensitive bulb portion does not rest directly on the bucket. The water is then heated on a stove. As the temperature of the water passes the 160-165° range, the thermostat should start to open and should be completely opened when the temperature has risen to 185-190°. Lifting the thermostat into the air should cause a pronounced closing action and the unit should be closed entirely within a short time.

1. The thermostat described above is a device which opens and closes with changes in the
    A. position   B. pressure   C. temperature   D. surroundings

1.____

2. According to the above passage, the closing action of the thermostat should be tested by
    A. working the thermostat back and forth
    B. permitting the water to cool gradually
    C. adding cold water to the bucket
    D. removing the thermostat from the bucket

2.____

3. The bulb of the thermometer should not rest directly on the bucket because
    A. the bucket gets hotter than the water
    B. the thermometer might be damaged in that position
    C. it is difficult to read the thermometer in that position
    D. the thermometer might interfere with operation of the thermostat

3.____

KEY (CORRECT ANSWERS)

1. C
2. D
3. A

TEST 2

DIRECTIONS: Questions 1 through 3 are to be answered on the basis of the following reading passage. *PRINT THE LETTER OF THE CORRECT ANSWER IN THE SPACE AT THE RIGHT.*

All idle pumps should be turned daily by hand, and should be run under power at least once a week. Whenever repairs are made on a pump, a record should be kept so that it will be possible to judge the success with which the pump is performing its functions. If a pump fails to deliver liquid, there may be an obstruction in the suction line, the pump's parts may be badly worn, or the packing defective.

1. According to the above passage, pumps 1._____
   A. in use should be turned by hand every day
   B. which are not in use should be run under power every day
   C. which are in daily use should be run under power several times a week
   D. which are not in use should be turned by hand every day

2. According to the above passage, the reason for keeping records of repairs made on pumps is to 2._____
   A. make certain that proper maintenance is being performed
   B. discover who is responsible for improper repairs
   C. rate the performance of the pumps
   D. know when to replace worn parts

3. The one of the following causes of pump failure which is NOT mentioned in the above passage is 3._____
   A. excessive suction lift   B. clogged lines
   C. bad packing   D. worn parts

KEY (CORRECT ANSWERS)

1. A
2. C
3. A

TEST 3

DIRECTIONS: Questions 1 through 5 are to be answered on the basis of the following reading passage. *PRINT THE LETTER OF THE CORRECT ANSWER IN THE SPACE AT THE RIGHT.*

Floors in warehouses, storerooms, and shipping rooms must be strong enough to stay level under heavy loads. Unevenness of floors may cause boxes of materials to topple and fall. Safe floor load capacities and maximum heights to which boxes may be stacked should be posted conspicuously so all can notice it. Where material in boxes, containers, or cartons of the same weight is regularly stored, it is good practice to paint a horizontal line on the wall indicating the maximum height to which the material may be piled. A qualified expert should determine floor load capacity from the building plans, the age and condition of the floor supports, the type of floor, and other related information.

Working aisles are those from which material is placed into and removed from storage. Working aisles are of two types: transportation aisles, running the length of the building, and cross aisles, running across the width of the building. Deciding on the number, width, and location of working aisles is important. While aisles are necessary and determine boundaries of storage areas, they reduce the space actually used for storage.

1. According to the above passage, how should safe floor load capacities be made known to employees? They should be
   A. given out to each employee
   B. given to supervisors only
   C. printed in large red letters
   D. posted so that they are easily seen

   1.____

2. According to the above passage, floor load capacities should be determined by
   A. warehouse supervisors   B. the fire department
   C. qualified experts   D. machine operators

   2.____

3. According to the above passage, transportation aisles
   A. run the length of the building
   B. run across the width of the building
   C. are wider than cross aisles
   D. are shorter than cross aisles

   3.____

4. According to the above passage, working aisles tend to
   A. take away space that could be used for storage
   B. add to space that could be used for storage
   C. slow down incoming stock
   D. speed up outgoing stock

   4.____

5. According to the above passage, unevenness of floors may cause
   A. overall warehouse deterioration   B. piles of stock to fall
   C. materials to spoil   D. many worker injuries

   5.____

KEY (CORRECT ANSWERS)

1. D
2. C
3. A
4. A
5. B

TEST 4

DIRECTIONS: Questions 1 through 3 are to be answered on the basis of the following reading passage. *PRINT THE LETTER OF THE CORRECT ANSWER IN THE SPACE AT THE RIGHT.*

In a retail establishment, any overweight means a distinct loss to the merchant, and even an apparently inconsequential overweight on a single package or sale when multiplied by the total number of transactions, could run into large figures. In addition to the use of reliable scales and weights, and their maintenance in proper condition, there must be proper supervision of the selling force. Such supervision is a difficult matter, particularly on the score of carelessness, as the depositing of extra amounts of material on the scale and failure to remove the same when it overbalances the scale may become a habit. In case of underweight, either in the weighing or by the use of fraudulent scales and weights, the seller soon will hear of it, but there is no reason why the amount weighed out should be in excess of what the customer pays for. Checking sales records against invoices and inventories can supply some indication of the tendency of the sales force to become careless in this field.

1. Of the following, the MOST valid implication of the above passage is that 1.____
    A. all overweights which occur in retail stores are in small amounts
    B. even-arm and uneven-arm balances and weights which are unreliable lead more often to underweights than to overweights
    C. overweights due to errors of salesclerks necessarily lead to large losses by a retailer
    D. supervision to prevent overweights is more important to a retailer than remedial measures after their occurrence

2. Of the following, the MOST valid implication of the above passage is that 2.____
    A. depositing of insufficient amounts of commodities on scales and failure to add to them may become a habit with salesclerks
    B. salesclerks should be trained in understanding and maintenance of scale mechanisms
    C. supervision of salesclerks to prevent careless habits in weighing must depend upon personal observation

3. According to the above passage, the MOST accurate of the following statements 3.____
   is:
    A. For the most part, the ideas expressed in the passage do not apply to wholesale establishments.
    B. Inventories of commodities prepacked in the store are the only ones which can be used in checking losses due to overweight.
    C. Invoices which give the value and weight of merchandise received are useful in checking losses due to overweights.
    D. The principal value of inventories is to indicate losses due to overweights.

KEY (CORRECT ANSWERS)

1. D
2. C
3. C

TEST 5

DIRECTIONS: Questions 1 through 5 are to be answered on the basis of the following reading passage. *PRINT THE LETTER OF THE CORRECT ANSWER IN THE SPACE AT THE RIGHT.*

TITANIC AIR COMPRESSOR

Valves: The compressors are equipped with Titanic plate valves which are automatic in operation. Valves are so constructed that an entire valve assembly can readily be removed from the head. The valves provide large port areas with short lift and are accurately guided to insure positive seating.

Starting Unloader: Each compressor (or air end) is equipped with a centrifugal governor which is bolted directly to the compressor crank shaft. The governor actuates cylinder relief valves so as to relieve pressure from the cylinders during starting and stopping. The motor is never required to start the compressor tinder load.

Air Strainer: Each cylinder air inlet connection is fitted with a suitable combination air strainer and muffler.

Pistons: Pistons are lightweight castings, ribbed internally to secure strength, and are accurately turned and ground. Each piston is fitted with four (4) rings, two of which are oil control rings. Piston pins are hardened and tempered steel of the full floating type. Bronze bushings are used between piston pin and piston

Connecting Rods: Connecting rods are of solid bronze designed for maximum strength, rigidity, and wear. Crank pins are fitted with renewable steel bushings. Connecting rods are of the one-piece type, there being no bolts, nuts, or cotter pins which can come loose. With this type of construction, wear is reduced to a negligible amount, and adjustment of wrist pin and crank pin bearings is unnecessary.

Main Bearings: Main bearings are of the ball type and are securely held in position by spacers. This type of bearing entirely eliminates the necessity of frequent adjustment or attention. The crank shaft is always in perfect alignment.

Crank Shaft: The crank shaft is a one-piece heat-treated forging of best quality open-hearth steel, of rugged design and of sufficient size to transmit the motor power and any additional stresses which may occur in service. Each crank shaft is counter-balanced (dynamically balanced to reduce vibration to a minimum, and is accurately machined to properly receive the ball-bearing races, crank pin bushing, flexible coupling, and centrifugal governor. Suitable provision is made to insure proper lubrication of all crank shaft bearings and bushings with the minimum amount of attention.

Coupling: Compressor and motor shafts are connected through a Morse Chain Company all-metal enclosed flexible coupling. This coupling consists of two sprockets, one mounted on, and keyed to, each shaft; the sprockets are wrapped by a single Morse Chain, the entire assembly being enclosed in a split aluminum grease-packed cover.

1. The crank pin of the connecting rod is fitted with a renewable bushing made of   1.____
   A. solid bronze   B. steel
   C. a lightweight casting   D. ball bearings

25

2. When the connecting rod is of the one-piece type,
   A. the wrist pins require frequent adjustment
   B. the crank pins require frequent adjustment
   C. the cotter pins frequently will come loose
   D. wear is reduced to a negligible amount

3. The centrifugal governor is bolted directly to the
   A. compressor crank shaft   B. main bearing
   C. piston pin   D. muffler

4. The number of oil control rings required for each piston is
   A. one   B. two   C. three   D. four

5. The compressor and motor shafts are connected through a flexible coupling. These couplings are _____ to the shafts.
   A. keyed   B. brazed   C. soldered   D. press-fit

KEY (CORRECT ANSWERS)

1. B
2. D
3. A
4. B
5. A

TEST 6

DIRECTIONS: Questions 1 through 6 are to be answered on the basis of the following reading passage. *PRINT THE LETTER OF THE CORRECT ANSWER IN THE SPACE AT THE RIGHT.*

Perhaps the strongest argument the mass transit backer has is the advantage in efficiency that mass transit has over the automobile in the urban traffic picture. It has been estimated that given comparable location and construction conditions, the subway can carry four times as many passengers per hour and cost half as much to build as urban highways. Yet public apathy regarding the mass transportation movement in the 1960's resulted in the building of more roads. Planned to provide 42,000 miles of highways in the period from 1956-72, including 7,500 miles within cities, the Federal Highway System project is now about two-thirds completed. The Highway Trust Fund supplies 90 percent of the cost of the system, with state and local sources putting up the rest of the money. By contrast, a municipality as had to put up the bulk of the cost of a rapid transit system. Although the system and its Trust Fund have come under attack in the past few years from environmentalists and groups opposed to the continued building of urban freeways—considered to be the most expensive, destructive, and inefficient segments of the system—a move by them to get the Trust Fund transformed into a general transportation fund at the expiration of the present program in 1972 seems to be headed nowhere.

1. Given similar building conditions and locations, a city that builds a subway instead of a highway can expect to receive for each dollar spent _____ as much transport value.
   A. half   B. twice   C. four times   D. eight times

2. The general attitude of the public in the past ten years toward the mass transportation movement has been
   A. favorable   B. indifferent   C. enthusiastic   D. unfriendly

3. The number of miles of highways still to be completed in the Federal Highway System project is MOST NEARLY
   A. 2,500   B. 5,000   C. 14,000   D. 28,000

4. What do certain groups who object to some features of the Federal Highway System program want to do with the Highway Trust Fund after 1972?
   A. Extend it in order to complete the project
   B. Change it so that the money can be used for all types of transportation
   C. End it even if the project is not completed
   D. Change it so that the money will be used only for urban freeways

5. Which one of the following statements is a VALID conclusion based on the facts in the above passage?
   A. The advantage of greater efficiency is the only argument that supporters of the mass transportation movement can offer.
   B. It was easier for cities to build roads rather than mass transit systems in the last 15 years because of the large financial contribution made by the Federal Government.

27

C. Mass transit systems cause as much congestion and air pollution in cities as automobiles.
D. In 1972, the Highway Trust Fund becomes a general transportation fund.

6. The MAIN idea or theme of the above passage is that the
   A. cost of the Federal Highway System is shared by the federal, state, and local governments
   B. public is against spending money for building mass transportation facilities in the cities
   C. cities would benefit more from expansion and improvement of their mass transit systems than from the building of more highways
   D. building of mass transportation facilities has been slowed by the Highway Trust Fund

6._____

KEY (CORRECT ANSWERS)

1. D
2. B
3. C
4. B
5. B
6. C

TEST 7

DIRECTIONS: Questions 1 through 5 are to be answered on the basis of the following reading passage. *PRINT THE LETTER OF THE CORRECT ANSWER IN THE SPACE AT THE RIGHT.*

The use of role-playing as a training technique was developed during the past decade by social scientists, particularly psychologists, who have been active in training experiments. Originally, this technique was applied by clinical psychologists who discovered that a patient appears to gain understanding of an emotionally disturbing situation when encouraged to act out roles in that situation. As applied in government and business organizations, the purpose of role-playing is to aid employees to understand certain work problems involving interpersonal relations and to enable observers to evaluate various reactions to them. Thus, for example, on the problem of handling grievances, two individuals from the group might be selected to act out extemporaneously the parts of subordinate and supervisor. When this situation is enacted by various pairs among the class and the techniques and results are discussed, the members of the group are presumed to reach conclusions about the most effective means of handling similar situations. Often the use or role reversal, where participants take parts different from their actual work roles, assists individuals to gain more insight into other people's problems and viewpoints. Although role-playing can be a rewarding training device, the trainer must be aware of his responsibilities. If this technique is to be successful, thorough briefing of both actors and observers as to the situation in question, the participants' roles, and what to look for, is essential.

1. The role-playing technique was FIRST used for the purpose of 1.____
   A. measuring the effectiveness of training programs
   B. training supervisors in business organizations
   C. treating emotionally disturbed patients
   D. handling employee grievances

2. When role-playing is used in private business as a training device, the CHIEF aim is to 2.____
   A. develop better relations between supervisor and subordinate in the handling of grievances
   B. come up with a solution to a specific problem that has arisen
   C. determine the training needs of the group
   D. increase employee understanding of the human-relation factors in work situations

3. From the above passage, it is MOST reasonable to conclude that when role-playing is used, it is preferable to have the roles acted out by 3.____
   A. only one set of actors
   B. no more than two sets of actors
   C. several different sets of actors
   D. the trainer or trainers of the group

4. It can be inferred from the above passage that a limitation of role-playing as a training method is that
   A. many work situations do not lend themselves to role-play
   B. employees are not experienced enough as actors to play the roles realistically
   C. only trainers who have psychological training can use it successfully
   D. participants who are observing and not acting do not benefit from it

5. To obtain *good* results from the use of role-play in training, a trainer should give participants
   A. a minimum of information about the situation so that they can act spontaneously
   B. scripts which illustrate the best method for handling the situation
   C. a complete explanation of the problem and the roles to be acted out
   D. a summary of work problems which involve interpersonal relations

KEY (CORRECT ANSWERS)

1. C
2. D
3. C
4. A
5. C

READING COMPREHENSION
UNDERSTANDING AND INTERPRETING
WRITTEN MATERIAL

EXAMINATION SECTION

TEST 1

DIRECTIONS: Each question or incomplete statement is followed by several suggested answers or completions. Select the one that BEST answers the question or completes the statement. *PRINT THE LETTER OF THE CORRECT ANSWER IN THE SPACE AT THE RIGHT.*

In its current application to art, the term *"primitive"* is as vague and unspecific as the term "heathen" is in its application to religion. A heathen sect is simply one which is not affiliated with one or another of three or four organized systems of theology. Similarly, a primitive art is one which flourishes outside the small number of cultures which we have chosen to designate as civilizations. Such arts differ vastly and it is correspondingly difficult to generalize about them. Any statements which will hold true for such diverse aesthetic experiences as the pictographs of the Australians, the woven designs of the Peruvians, and the abstract sculptures of the African tribes must be of the broadest and simplest sort. Moreover, the problem is complicated by the meaning attached to the term "primitive" in its other uses. It stands for something simple, undeveloped, and, by implication, ancestral to more evolved forms. Its application to arts and cultures other than our own is an unfortunate heritage from the nineteenth-century scientists who laid the foundations of anthropology. Elated by the newly enunciated doctrines of evolution, these students saw all cultures as stages in a single line of development and assigned them to places in this series on the simple basis of the degree to which they differed from European culture, which was blandly assumed to be the final and perfect flower of the evolutionary process. This idea has long since been abandoned by anthropologists, but before its demise it diffused to other social sciences and became a part of the general body of popular misinformation. It still tinges a great deal of the thought and writing about the arts of non-European peoples and has been responsible for many misunderstandings.

1. The MAIN purpose of the passage is to
   A. explain the various definitions of the term "primitive"
   B. show that the term "primitive" can be applied validly to art
   C. compare the use of the term "primitive" to the use of the term "heathen"
   D. deprecate the use of the term "primitive" as applied to art
   E. show that "primitive" arts vary greatly among themselves

1.____

2. The nineteenth-century scientists believed that the theory of evolution
   A. could be applied to the development of culture
   B. was demonstrated in all social sciences
   C. was substantiated by the diversity of "primitive" art
   D. could be applied only to European culture
   E. disproved the idea that some arts are more "primitive" than others

2.____

3. With which of the following would the author agree? 3._____
   A. The term "primitive" is used only by the misinformed.
   B. "Primitive" arts may be as highly developed as "civilized" arts.
   C. The arts of a culture often indicated how advanced that culture was.
   D. Australian, Peruvian, and African tribal arts are much like the ancestral forms from which European art evolved.
   E. A simple culture is likely to have a simple art.

4. According to the author, many misunderstandings have been caused by the belief that 4._____
   A. most cultures are fundamentally different
   B. inferior works of art in any culture are "primitive" art
   C. "primitive" arts are diverse
   D. non-European arts are diverse
   E. European civilization is the final product of the evolutionary process

KEY (CORRECT ANSWERS)

1. D
2. A
3. B
4. E

TEST 2

DIRECTIONS: Each question or incomplete statement is followed by several suggested answers or completions. Select the one that BEST answers the question or completes the statement. *PRINT THE LETTER OF THE CORRECT ANSWER IN THE SPACE AT THE RIGHT.*

One of the ways the intellectual *avant-garde* affects the technical intelligentsia is through the medium of art, and art is, if only implicitly, a critique of experience. The turning upon itself of modern culture in the forms of the new visual art, the utilization of the detritus of daily experience to mock that experience, constitutes a mode of social criticism. Pop art, it is true, does not go beyond the surface of the visual and tactile experience of an industrial (and a commercialized) culture. Dwelling on the surface, it allows its consumers to mock the elements of their daily life, without abandoning it. Indeed, the consumption of art in the organized market for leisure serves at times to encapsulate the social criticism of the *avant-garde*. However, the recent engagement of writers, artists, and theater people in contemporary issues suggests that this sort of containment may have begun to reach its limits.

In an atmosphere in which the intellectually dominant group insists on the contradictions inherent in daily experience, the technical intelligentsia will find it difficult to remain unconscious of those contradictions. The technical intelligentsia have until now avoided contradictions by accepting large rewards for their expertise. As expertise becomes increasingly difficult to distinguish from ordinary service on the one hand, and merges on the other with the change of the social environment, the technical intelligentsia's psychic security may be jeopardized. Rendering of labor services casts it back into spiritual proletarianization; a challenge to the social control exercised by elites, who use the technical intelligentsia's labor power, pushes it forward to social criticism and revolutionary politics. That these are matters, for the moment, of primarily spiritual import does not diminish their ultimate political significance. A psychological precondition for radical action is usually far more important than an "objectively" revolutionary situation—whatever that may be.

The chances for a radicalization of the technical intelligentsia, thus extending the student revolt cannot be even approximated. I believe I have shown there is a chance.

1. It may be *inferred* that the technical intelligentsia are
   I. The executives and employers in society
   II. Critics of *avant-garde* art
   III. Highly skilled technical workers
   The CORRECT answer is:
   A. I only
   B. I and III
   C. I, II, and III
   D. III only
   E. I and II

2. The engagement of the intellectual *avant-garde* in contemporary issues
   A. indicates that people tire of questioning the contradictions inherent in day-to-day living
   B. indicates that the technical intelligentsia are close to the point where they will rebel against the *avant-garde*
   C. could cause a challenge to the social control of the elites
   D. could cause the public to become more leisure-oriented
   E. could cause an increase in the consumption of art in the organized market for leisure services

3. The *possible* effect of the intellectual *avant-garde* on the technical intelligentsia is that
    A. the intellectual *avant-garde* makes the technical intelligentsia conscious of society's contradictions
    B. rapid curtailment of large rewards for expertise will result
    C. it may cause a strong likelihood of a radicalization of the technical intelligentsia
    D. the *avant-garde* will replace the employment of the technical intelligentsia in contemporary issues
    E. the rendering of labor services will be eliminated

4. If it is assumed that the technical intelligentsia becomes fully aware of the contradictions of modern life, it is the author's position that
    A. revolution will result
    B. the technical intelligentsia may refuse to perform manual labor
    C. the technical intelligentsia will be pushed forward to social criticism and revolutionary politics
    D. the technical intelligentsia will experience some psychic dislocation
    E. ordinary service will replace technical expertise

5. According to the author,
    A. the state of mind of a particular group may have more influence on its action than the effect of environmental factors
    B. the influence of art will often cause social upheaval
    C. matters of primarily spiritual import necessarily lack political significance
    D. the detritus of day-to-day living should be mocked by the intellectual *avant-garde*
    E. the technical intelligentsia can only protect their psychic security by self-expression through art

6. With which of the following would the author agree?
    I. As contradictions are less contained, the psychic security of all members of the working class would be jeopardized.
    II. The expertise of the technical intelligentsia evolved from the ownership and management of property.
    III. The technical intelligentsia is not accustomed to rendering labor services.
    The CORRECT answer is:
    A. I only   B. III only   C. I and III
    D. II only   E. None of the above

7. The MAIN purpose of the passage is to
    A. discuss the influence of the *avant-garde* art form on the expertise of the technical intelligentsia
    B. discuss the effect of the intellectual *avant-garde* on the working classes
    C. discuss the social significance of the technical intelligentsia
    D. discuss the possible effects of the de-encapsulation of *avant-garde* social criticism
    E. point out that before a change psychological preconditions are first established

KEY (CORRECT ANSWERS)

1. D
2. C
3. A
4. D
5. A
6. B
7. D

TEST 3

DIRECTIONS: Each question or incomplete statement is followed by several suggested answers or completions. Select the one that BEST answers the question or completes the statement. *PRINT THE LETTER OF THE CORRECT ANSWER IN THE SPACE AT THE RIGHT.*

Turbulent flow over a boundary is a complex phenomenon for which there is no really complete theory even in simple laboratory cases. Nevertheless, a great deal of experimental data has been collected on flows over solid surfaces, both in the laboratory and in nature, so that, from an engineering point of view at least, the situation is fairly well understood. The force exerted on a surface varies with the roughness of that surface and approximately with the square of the wind speed at some fixed height above it. A wind of 10 meters per second (about 20 knots, or 22 miles per hour) measured at a height of 10 meters will produce a force of some 30 tons per square kilometer on a field of mown grass or of about 70 tons per square kilometer on a ripe wheat field. On a really smooth surface, such as glass, the force is only about 10 tons per square kilometer.

When the wind blows over water, the whole thing is much more complicated. The roughness of the water is not a given characteristic of the surface but depends on the wind itself. Not only that, the elements that constitute the roughness—the waves—themselves move more or less in the direction of the wind. Recent evidence indicates that a large portion of the momentum transferred from the air into the water goes into waves rather than directly into making currents in the water; only as the waves break, or otherwise lose energy, does their momentum become available to generate currents, or produce Ekman layers. Waves carry a substantial amount of both energy and momentum (typically about as much as is carried by the wind in a layer about one wavelength thick), and so the wave-generation process is far from negligible. A violently wavy surface belies its appearance by acting, as far as the wind is concerned, as though it were very smooth. At 10 meters per second, recent measurements seem to agree, the force on the surface is quite a lot less than the force over mown grass and scarcely more than it is over glass; some observations in light winds of two or three meters per second indicate that the force on the wavy surface is less than it is on a surface as smooth as glass. In some way the motion of the waves seems to modify the airflow so that air slips over the surface even more freely than it would without the waves. This seems not to be the case at higher wind speeds, above about five meters per second, but the force remains strikingly low compared with that over other natural surfaces.

One serious deficiency is the fact that there are no direct observations at all in those important cases in which the wind speed is greater than about 12 meters per second and has had time and fetch (the distance over water) enough to raise substantial waves. The few indirect studies indicate that the apparent roughness of the surface increases somewhat under high-wind conditions, so that the force on the surface increases rather more rapidly than as the square of the wind speed.

Assuming that the force increases at least as the square of the wind speed, it is evident that high-wind conditions produce effects far more important than their frequency of occurrence would suggest. Five hours of 60-knot storm winds will put more momentum into the water than a week of 10-knot breezes. If it should be shown that, for high winds, the force on the surface increases appreciably more rapidly than as the square of the wind speed, then the transfer of momentum to the ocean will turn out to be dominated by what happens during the occasional storm rather than by the long-term average winds.

2 (#3)

1. According to the passage, several hours of storm winds (60 miles per hour) over the ocean would
   A. be similar to the force exerted by light winds for several hours over glass
   B. create an ocean roughness which reduces the force exerted by the high winds
   C. have proved to be more significant in creating ocean momentum than light winds
   D. create a force not greater than 6 times the force of a 10-mile-per-hour wind
   E. eventually affect ocean current

2. According to the passage, a rough-like ocean surface
   A. is independent of the force of the wind
   B. has the same force exerted against it by high and light winds
   C. is more likely to have been caused by a storm than by continuous light winds
   D. nearly always allows airflow to be modified so as to cause the force of the wind to be less than on glass
   E. is a condition under which the approximate square of wind speed can never be an accurate figure in measuring the wind force

3. The author indicates that, where a hurricane is followed by light winds of 10 meters per second or less,
   I. ocean current will be unaffected by the light winds
   II. ocean current will be more affected by the hurricane winds than the following light winds
   III. the force of the light winds on the ocean would be less than that exerted on a wheat field.
   The CORRECT combination is:
   A. I only   B. III only   C. II and III   D. I and III   E. II only

4. The MAIN purpose of the passage is to discuss
   A. oceanic momentum and current
   B. turbulent flow of wind over water
   C. wind blowing over water as related to causing tidal flow
   D. the significance of high wind conditions on ocean momentum
   E. experiments in wind force

5. The author would be incorrect in concluding that the transfer of momentum to the ocean is dominated by the occasional storm if
   A. air momentum went directly into making ocean current
   B. high speed winds slipped over waves as easily as low speed winds
   C. waves did not move in the direction of wind
   D. the force exerted on a wheat field was the same as on mown grass
   E. the force of wind under normal conditions increased as the square of wind speed

6. A wind of 10 meters per second measured at a height of 10 meters will produce   6.____
   a force close to 30 tons per square mile on which of the following?
   A. Unmown grass   B. Mown grass   C. Glass
   D. Water   E. A football field

KEY (CORRECT ANSWERS)

1. E
2. C
3. C
4. B
5. B
6. A

TEST 4

DIRECTIONS: Each question or incomplete statement is followed by several suggested answers or completions. Select the one that BEST answers the question or completes the statement. *PRINT THE LETTER OF THE CORRECT ANSWER IN THE SPACE AT THE RIGHT.*

Political scientists, as practitioners of a negligibly formalized discipline, tend to be accommodating to formulations and suggested techniques developed in related behavioral sciences. They even tend, on occasion, to speak of psychology, sociology, and anthropology as "hard core sciences." Such a characterization seems hardly justified. The disposition to uncritically adopt into political science non-indigenous sociological and general systems concepts tends, at times, to involve little more than the adoption of a specific, and sometimes barbarous, academic vocabulary which is used to redescribe reasonably well-confirmed or intuitively-grasped low-order empirical generalizations.

At its worst, what results in such instances is a runic explanation, a redescription in a singular language style, i.e., no explanation at all. At their best, functional accounts as they are found in the contemporary literature provide explanation sketches, the type of elliptical explanation characteristic of historical and psychoanalytic accounts. For each such account there is an indeterminate number of equally plausible ones, the consequence of either the complexity of the subject matter, differing perspectives, conceptual vagueness, the variety of sometimes mutually exclusive empirical or quasi-empirical generalizations employed, or syntactical obscurity, or all of them together.

Functional explanations have been most reliable in biology and physiology (where they originated) and in the analysis of servo mechanical and cybernetic systems (to which they have been effectively extended). In these areas we possess a well-standardized body of lawlike generalizations. Neither sociology nor political science has as yet the same resource of well-confirmed lawlike statements. Certainly sociology has few more than political science. What passes for functional explanation in sociology is all too frequently parasitic upon suggestive analogy and metaphor, trafficking on our familiarity with goal-directed systems.

What is advanced as "theory" in sociology is frequently a non-theoretic effort at classification or "codification," the search for an analytic conceptual schema which provides a typology or a classificatory system serviceable for convenient storage and ready retrieval of independently established empirical regularities. That such a schema takes on a hierarchic and deductive character, imparting to the collection of propositions a *prima facie* theoretical appearance, may mean no more than that the terms employed in the high-order propositions are so vague that they can accommodate almost any inference and consequently can be made to any conceivable state of affairs.

1. The author *implies* that, when the political scientist is at his best, his explanations   1._____
   A. are essentially a retelling of events
   B. only then form the basis of an organized discipline
   C. plausibly account for past occurrences
   D. are prophetic of future events
   E. are confirmed principles forming part of the political scientist's theory

2. With which of the following would the author probably agree?
   I. Because of an abundance of reasonable explanations for past conduct, there is the possibility of contending schools within the field of political science developing.
   II. Political science is largely devoid of predictive power.
   III. Political science has very few verified axioms.
   The CORRECT answer is:
   A. III only   B. I and III   C. I and II   D. I, II, III   E. I only

3. The passage *implies* that many sociological theories
   A. are capable of being widely applied to various situations
   B. do not even appear to be superficially theoretical in appearance
   C. contrast with those of political science in that there are many more confirmed lawlike statements
   D. are derived from deep analysis and exhaustive research
   E. appear theoretical but are really very well proved

4. The author's thesis would be UNSUPPORTABLE if
   A. the theories of the political scientist possessed predictive power
   B. political science did not consist of redescription
   C. political scientists were not restricted to "hard core sciences"
   D. political science consisted of a body of theories capable of application to any situation
   E. none of the above

5. The author believe that sociology as a "hard core science," contains reliable and functional explanations
   A. is never more than a compilation of conceptual schema
   B. is in nearly every respect unlike political science
   C. is a discipline which allows for varied inferences to be drawn from its general propositions
   D. is a science indigenous *prima facie* theoretical appearance containing very little codification posing as theory

KEY (CORRECT ANSWERS)

1. C
2. D
3. A
4. A
5. D

TEST 5

DIRECTIONS: Each question or incomplete statement is followed by several suggested answers or completions. Select the one that BEST answers the question or completes the statement. *PRINT THE LETTER OF THE CORRECT ANSWER IN THE SPACE AT THE RIGHT.*

James' own prefaces to his works were devoted to structural composition and analytics and his approach in those prefaces has only recently begun to be understood. One of his contemporary critics, with the purest intention to blame, wrote what might be recognized today as sophisticated praise when he spoke of the later James as "an impassioned geometer" and remarked that "what interested him was not the figures but their relations, the relations which alone make pawns significant." James's explanations of his works often are so bereft of interpretation as to make some of our own austere defenses against interpretation seem almost embarrassingly rich with psychological meanings. They offer, with a kind of brazen unselfconsciousness, an astonishingly artificial, even mechanical view of novelistic invention. It's not merely that James asserts the importance of technique; more radically, he tends to discuss character and situation almost entirely as functions of technical ingenuities. The very elements in a Jamesian story which may strike us as requiring the most explanation are presented by James either as a *solution* to a problem of compositional harmony or else as the *donnee* about which it would be irrelevant to ask any questions at all.

James should constantly be referred to as a model of structuralist criticism. He consistently redirects our attention from the referential aspect of a work of art (its extensions into "reality") to its own structural coherence as the principal source of inspiration.

What is most interesting about James's structurally functional view of character is that a certain devaluation of what we ordinarily think of as psychological interest is perfectly consistent with an attempt to portray reality. It's as if he came to feel that a kind of autonomous geometric pattern, in which the parts appeal for their value to nothing but their contributive place in the essentially abstract pattern, is the artist's most successful representation of life. Thus, he could perhaps even think that verisimilitude—a word he liked—has less to do with the probability of the events the novelist describes than with those processes, deeply characteristic of life, by which he creates sense and coherence from any event. The only faithful picture of life in art is not in the choice of a significant subject (James always argues against the pseudo realistic prejudice), but rather in the illustration of sense- or design-making processes. James proves the novel's connection with life by deprecating its derivation from life; and it's when he is most abstractly articulating the growth of a structure that James is almost most successfully defending the mimetic function of art (and of criticism). His deceptively banal position that only execution matters means most profoundly that verisimilitude, properly considered, is the grace and the truth of a formal unity.

1. The author suggests that James, in explanations of his own art, 1.____
   A. was not bound by formalistic strictures but concentrated on verisimilitude
   B. was deeply psychological and concentrated on personal insight
   C. felt that his art had a one-to-one connection with reality
   D. was basically mechanical and concentrated on geometrical form
   E. was event-and-character-oriented rather than technique-oriented

2. The passage indicates that James's method of approaching reality was
   A. that objective reality did not exist and was patterned only by the mind
   B. that formalism and pattern were excellent means of approaching reality
   C. not to concentrate on specific events but rather on character development
   D. that the only objective reality is the psychological processes of the mind
   E. that in reality events occur which are not structured but rather as random occurrences

3. The MAIN purpose of the paragraph is to
   A. indicate that James's own approach to his work is only now beginning to be understood
   B. deprecate the geometrical approach towards the novel
   C. question whether James's novels were related to reality
   D. indicate that James felt that society itself could be seen as a geometric structure
   E. discuss James's explanation of his works

4. In discussing his own works, James
   I. talks of people and events as a function of technique to the exclusion of all else
   II. is quick to emphasize the referential aspect of the work
   III. felt that verisimilitude could be derived not from character but rather from the ordering of event
   The CORRECT answer is:
   A. I only   B. II only   C. III only   D. I and III   E. I and II

5. The author
   A. *approves* of James's explanations of his work but *disapproves* his lack of discussion into the psychological makings of his characters
   B. *disapproves* of James's explanation of his own work and his lack of discussion into the psychological makings of his characters
   C. *approves* of James's explanations of his works in terms of structure as being well-rated to life
   D. *disapproves* of James's explanation of his works in terms of structure as lacking verisimilitude
   E. *approves* of James's explanation of his works because of the significance of the subjects chosen

6. The following is NOT true of James's explanation of his own works: He
   A. did not explain intriguing elements of a story except as part of a geometric whole
   B. felt the artist could represent life by its patterns rather than its events
   C. defended the imitative function of art by detailing the growth of a structure
   D. attempted to give the reader insight into the psychology of his characters by insuring that his explanation followed a strict geometrical pattern
   E. was able to devalue psychological interest and yet be consistent with an attempt to truly represent life

7. James believed it to be *essential* to
   A. carefully choose a subject which would lend itself to processes by which sense and cohesion is achieved
   B. defend the mimetic function of art by emphasizing verisimilitude
   C. emphasize the manner in which different facets of a story could fit together
   D. explain character in order to achieve literary harmony
   E. be artificial and unconcerned with representing life

KEY (CORRECT ANSWERS)

1.	D	5.	C
2.	B	6.	D
3.	E	7.	C
4.	C		

TEST 6

DIRECTIONS: Each question or incomplete statement is followed by several suggested answers or completions. Select the one that BEST answers the question or completes the statement. *PRINT THE LETTER OF THE CORRECT ANSWER IN THE SPACE AT THE RIGHT.*

    The popular image of the city as it is now is a place of decay, crime, of fouled streets, and of people who are poor or foreign or odd. But what is the image of the city of the future? In the plans for the huge redevelopment projects to come, we are being shown a new image of the city. Gone are the dirt and the noise—and the variety and the excitement and the spirit. That it is an ideal makes it all the worse; these bleak new utopias are not bleak because they have to be; they are the concrete manifestation—and how literally—of a deep, and at times arrogant, misunderstanding of the function of the city.
    Being made up of human beings, the city is, of course, a wonderfully resilient institution. Already it has reasserted itself as an industrial and business center. Not so many years ago, there was much talk of decentralizing to campus-like offices, and a wholesale exodus of business to the countryside seemed imminent. But a business pastoral is something of a contradiction in terms, and for the simple reason that the city is the center of things because it is a center, the suburban heresy never came off. Many industrial campuses have been built, but the overwhelming proportion of new office building has been taking place in the big cities. But the rebuilding of downtown is not enough; a city deserted at night by its leading citizens is only half a city. If it is to continue as the dominant cultural force in American life, the city must have a core of people to support its theatres and museums, its shops and its restaurants—even a Bohemia of sorts can be of help. For it is the people who like living in the city who make it an attraction to the visitors who don't. It is the city dwellers who support its style; without them there is nothing to come downtown to.
    The cities have a magnificent opportunity. There are definite signs of a small but significant move back from suburbia. There is also evidence that many people who will be moving to suburbia would prefer to stay in the city—and it would not take too much more in amenities to make them stay. But the cities seem on the verge of muffing their opportunity and muffing it for generations to come. In a striking failure to apply marketing principles and an even more striking failure of aesthetics, the cities are freezing on a design for living ideally calculated to keep everybody in suburbia. These vast, barracks-like superblocks are not designed for people who like cities, but for people who have no other choice. A few imaginative architects and planners have shown that redeveloped blocks don't have to be repellent to make money, but so far their ideas have had little effect. The institutional approach is dominant, and, unless the assumptions embalmed in it are re-examined, the city is going to be turned into a gigantic bore.

1. The author would NOT be pleased with   1._____
    A. a crowded, varied, stimulating city
    B. the dedication of new funds to the reconstruction of the cities
    C. a more detailed understanding of the poor
    D. the elimination of assumptions which do not reflect the function of the city
    E. the adoption of a laissez-faire attitude by those in charge of redevelopment

2. "The rebuilding of downtown" (1st sentence, 3rd paragraph) refers to
   A. huge redevelopment projects to come
   B. the application of marketing and aesthetic principles to rejuvenating the city
   C. keeping the city as the center of business
   D. attracting a core of people to support the city's functions
   E. the doing away with barracks-like structures

3. According to the author the city, in order to better itself, *must*
   A. increase its downtown population
   B. attract an interested core of people to support its cultural institutions
   C. adhere to an institutional approach rather than be satisfied with the status quo
   D. erect campus-like business complexes
   E. establish an ideal for orderly future growth

4. The MAIN purpose of the passage is to
   A. show that the present people inhabiting the city do not make the city viable
   B. discuss the types of construction which should and should not take place in the city's future
   C. indicate that imaginative architects and planners have shown that redeveloped areas don't have to be ugly to make money
   D. discuss the human element in the city
   E. point out the lack of understanding by many city planners of the city's functions

5. The author's thesis would be LESS supportable if
   I. city planners presently understood that stereotyped reconstruction is doomed to ultimate failure
   II. the institutional approach referred to in the passage was based upon assumptions which took into account the function of the city
   III. there were signs that a shift back to the city from suburbia were occurring
   The CORRECT answer is:
   A. II only   B. II and III   C. I and II   D. I only   E. III only

KEY (CORRECT ANSWERS)

1. D
2. C
3. B
4. E
5. C

TEST 7

DIRECTIONS: Each question or incomplete statement is followed by several suggested answers or completions. Select the one that BEST answers the question or completes the statement. *PRINT THE LETTER OF THE CORRECT ANSWER IN THE SPACE AT THE RIGHT.*

    In estimating the child's conceptions of the world, the first question is to decide whether external reality is as external and objective for the child as it is for adults. In other words, can the child distinguish the self from the external world? So long as the child supposes that everyone necessarily thinks like himself, he will not spontaneously seek to convince others, nor to accept common truths, nor, above all, to prove or test his opinions. If his logic lacks exactitude and objectivity, it is because the social impulses of mature years are counteracted by an innate egocentricity. In studying the child's thought, not in this case in relation to others but to things, one is faced at the outset with the analogous problem of the child's capacity to dissociate thought from self in order to form an objective conception of reality.
    The child, like the uncultured adult, appears exclusively concerned with things. He is indifferent to the life of thought and the originality of individual points of view escape him. His earliest interests, his first games, his drawings are all concerned solely with the imitation of what is. In short, the child's thought has every appearance of being exclusively realistic.
    But realism is of two types, or, rather, objectivity must be distinguished from realism. Objectivity consists in so fully realizing the countless intrusions of the self in everyday thought and the countless illusions which result—illusions of sense, language, point of view, value, etc.—that the preliminary step to every judgment is the effort to exclude the intrusive self. Realism, on the contrary, consists in ignoring the existence of self and thence regarding one's own perspective as immediately objective and absolute. Realism is thus anthropocentric illusion, finality—in short, all those illusions which teem in the history of science. So long as thought has not become conscious of self, it is a prey to perpetual confusions between objective and subjective, between the real and the ostensible; it values the entire content of consciousness on a single lane in which ostensible realities and the unconscious interventions of the self are inextricably mixed. It is thus not futile, but, on the contrary, indispensable to establish clearly and before all else the boundary the child draws between the self and the external world.

1. The result of a child's not learning that others think differently than he does is that   1.____
   A. the child will not be able to function as an adult
   B. when the child has matured, he will be innately egocentric
   C. when the child has matured, his reasoning will be poor
   D. upon maturity, the child will not be able to distinguish thought from objects
   E. upon maturity, the child will not be able to make non-ego-influenced value

2. Objectivity is the ability to   2.____
   A. distinguish ego from the external world
   B. dissociate oneself from others
   C. realize that others have a different point of view
   D. dissociate ego from thought

3. When thought is not conscious of self,
   A. one is able to draw the correct conclusions from his perceptions
   B. the apparent may not be distinguishable from the actual
   C. conscious thought may not be distinguishable from the unconscious
   D. the ego may influence the actual
   E. ontogeny recapitulates phylogony

4. The MAIN purpose of the passage is to
   A. argue that the child should be made to realize that others may not think like he does
   B. estimate the child's conception of the world
   C. explain the importance of distinguishing the mind from external objects
   D. emphasize the importance of non-ego-influenced perspective
   E. show how the child establishes the boundary between himself and the external world

5. The author *implies* that, if an adult is to think logically,
   A. his reasoning, as he matures, must be tempered by other viewpoints
   B. he must be able to distinguish one physical object from another
   C. he must be exclusively concerned with thought instead of things
   D. he must be able to perceive reality without the intrusions of the self
   E. he must not value the content of consciousness on a single plain

6. Realism, according to the passage, is
   A. the realization of the countless intrusions of the self
   B. final and complete objectivity
   C. a desire to be truly objective and absolute
   D. the ability to be perceptive and discerning
   E. none of the above

7. The child who is exclusively concerned with things
   A. thinks only objectivity
   B. is concerned with imitating the things he sees
   C. must learn to distinguish between realism and anthropomorphism
   D. has no innate ability
   E. will, through interaction with others, often prove his opinions

KEY (CORRECT ANSWERS)

1. C
2. E
3. B
4. D
5. A
6. E
7. B

TEST 8

DIRECTIONS: Each question or incomplete statement is followed by several suggested answers or completions. Select the one that BEST answers the question or completes the statement. *PRINT THE LETTER OF THE CORRECT ANSWER IN THE SPACE AT THE RIGHT.*

Democracy is not logically antipathetic to most doctrines of natural rights, fundamental or higher law, individual rights, or any similar ideals—but merely asks citizens to take note of the fact that the preservation of these rights rests with the majority, in political processes, and does not depend upon a legal or constitutional Maginot line. Democracy may, then, be supported by believers in individual rights providing they believe that rights—or any transcendental ends—are likely to be better safeguarded under such a system. Support for democracy on such instrumental ground may, of course, lead to the dilemma of loyalty to the system vs. loyalty to a natural right—but the same kind of dilemma may arise for anyone, over any prized value, and in any political system, and is insoluble in advance.

There is unanimous agreement that—as a matter of fact and law, not of conjecture—no single right can be realized, except at the expense of other rights and claims. For that reason their absolute status, in some philosophic sense, is of little political relevance. Political policies involve much more than very generable principles or rights. The main error of the older natural rights school was not that it had an absolute right, but that it had too many absolute rights. There must be compromise, and, as any compromise destroys the claim to absoluteness, the natural outcome of experience was the repudiation of all of them. And now the name of "natural right" can only creep into sight with the reassuring placard, "changing content guaranteed." Nor is it at all easy to see how many doctrine of inalienable, natural, individual rights can be reconciled with a political doctrine of common consent—except in an anarchist society, or one of saints. Every natural right ever put forward, and the lists are elusive and capricious, is every day invaded by governments, in the public interest and with widespread public approval.

To talk of relatively attainable justice or rights in politics is not to plump for a moral relativism—in the sense that all values are equally good. But while values may be objective, the specific value judgments and policies are inevitably relative to a context, and is only when a judgment divorces context from general principle that it looks like moral relativism. Neither, of course, does the fact of moral diversity invalidate all moral rules.

Any political system, then, deals only with relatively attainable rights, as with relative justice and freedoms. Hence, we may differ in given instances on specific policies, despite agreement on broad basic principles such as a right or a moral "ought"; and, per contra, we may agree on specific policies while differing on fundamental principles or long-range objectives or natural rights. Politics and through politics, law and policies, give these rights—and moral principles—their substance and limits. There is no getting away from the political nature of this or any other prescriptive ideal in a free society.

1. With which of the following would the author *agree*? 1._____
    A. Natural and individual rights can exist at all only under a democracy.
    B. While natural rights may exist, they are only relatively attainable.
    C. Civil disobedience has no place in a democracy where natural rights have no philosophic relevance.
    D. Utilitarianism, which draws its criteria from the happiness and welfare of individuals, cannot logically be a goal of a democratic state.
    E. Some natural rights should never be compromised for the sake of political policy.

2. It can be *inferred* that a democratic form of government
   A. can be supported by natural rightists as the best pragmatic method of achieving their aims
   B. is a form of government wherein fundamental or higher law is irrelevant
   C. will inn time repudiate all inalienable rights
   D. forces a rejection of moral absolutism
   E. will soon exist in undeveloped areas of the world

3. The MAIN purpose of the passage is to
   A. discuss natural rights doctrine
   B. compare and contrast democracy to individual rights
   C. discuss the reconciliation of a doctrine of inalienable natural rights with a political system
   D. discuss the safeguarding of natural rights in a democratic society
   E. indicate that moral relativism is antipathetic to democracy

4. The author indicates that natural rights
   I. are sometimes difficult to define
   II. are easily definable but at times unreconcilable with a system of government predicated upon majority rule
   III. form a basis for moral relativism
   The CORRECT answer is:
   A. I only   B. II only   C. I and II   D. III only   E. II and III

5. The fact that any political system deals with relatively attainable rights
   A. shows that all values are equally good or bad
   B. is cause for divorcing political reality from moral rules
   C. shows that the list of natural rights is elusive and capricious
   D. is inconsistent with the author's thesis
   E. does not necessarily mean that natural rights do not exist

6. The passage indicates that an important conflict which can exist in a democracy is the rights of competing groups, i.e., labor versus management
   A. adherence to the democratic process versus non-democratic actions by government
   B. difficulty in choosing between two effective compromises
   C. adherence to the democratic process versus the desire to support a specific right
   D. difficulty in reconciling conflict by natural rights

KEY (CORRECT ANSWERS)

1. B   4. A
2. A   5. E
3. C   6. D

READING COMPREHENSION
UNDERSTANDING AND INTERPRETING WRITTEN MATERIAL
EXAMINATION SECTION
TEST 1

DIRECTIONS: Each question or incomplete statement is followed by several suggested answers or completions. Select the one that BEST answers the question or completes the statement. *PRINT THE LETTER OF THE CORRECT ANSWER IN THE SPACE AT THE RIGHT.*

1. Most managers make the mistake of using absolutes as signals of trouble or its absence. A quality problem emerges—that means trouble; a test is passed—we have no problems. Outside of routine organizations, there are always going to be such signals of trouble or success, but they are not very meaningful. Many times everything looks good, but the roof is about to cave in because something no one thought about and for which there is no rule, procedure, or test has been neglected. The specifics of such problems cannot be predicted, but they are often signaled in advance by changes in the organizational system: Managers spend less time on the project; minor problems proliferate; friction in the relationships between adjacent work groups or departments increases; verbal progress reports become overly glib, or overly reticent; change occur in the rate at which certain events happen, not in whether or not they happen. And they are monitored by random probes into the organization—seeing how things are going.
According to the above paragraph,
   A. managers do not spend enough time managing
   B. managers have a tendency to become overly glib when writing reports
   C. managers should be aware that problems that exist in the organization may not exhibit predictable signals of trouble
   D. managers should attempt to alleviate friction in the relationship between adjacent work groups by monitoring random probes into the organization's problems

1.____

2. *Lack of challenge* and *excessive zeal* are opposite villains. You cannot do your best on a problem unless you are motivated. Professional problem solvers learn to be motivated somewhat by money and future work that may come their way if they succeed. However, challenge must be present for at least some of the time, or the process ceases to be rewarding. On the other hand, an excessive motivation to succeed, especially to succeed quickly, can inhibit the creative process. The tortoise-and-the-hare phenomenon is often apparent in problem solving. The person who thinks up the simple elegant solution, although he or she may take longer in doing so, often wins. As in the race, the tortoise depends upon an inconsistent performance from the rabbit. And if the rabbit spends so little time on conceptualization that the rabbit merely chooses the first answers that occur, such inconsistency is almost guaranteed.

2.____

According to the above paragraph,
- A. excessive motivation to succeed can be harmful in problem solving
- B. it is best to spend a long time on solving problems
- C. motivation is the most important component in problem solving
- D. choosing the first solution that occurs is a valid method of problem solving

3. Virginia Woolf's approach to the question of women and fiction, about which she wrote extensively, polemically, and in a profoundly feminist way, was grounded in a general theory of literature. She argued that the writer was the product of her or his historical circumstances and that material conditions were of crucial importance. Secondly, she claimed that these material circumstances had a profound effect on the psychological aspects of writing, and that they could be seen to influence the nature of the creative work itself. According to this paragraph,
    - A. the material conditions and historical circumstances in which male and female writers find themselves greatly influence their work
    - B. a woman must have an independent income to succeed as a writer
    - C. Virginia Woolf preferred the writings of female authors, as their experiences more clearly reflected hers
    - D. male writers are less likely than women writers to be influenced by material circumstances

3.____

4. A young person's first manager is likely to be the most influential person in his or her career. If this manager is unable or unwilling to develop the skills the young employee needs to perform effectively, the latter will set lower personal standards than he or she is capable of achieving, that person's self-image will be impaired, and he or she will develop negative attitudes toward the job, the employer—in all probability—his or her career. Since the chances of building a successful career with the employer will decline rapidly, he or she will leave, if that person has high aspirations, in hope of finding a better opportunity. If, on the other hand, the manager helps the employee to achieve maximum potential, he or she will build a foundation for a successful career.
According to the above paragraph,
    - A. If an employee has negative attitudes towards his or her job, the manager is to blame
    - B. managers of young people often have a great influence upon their careers
    - C. good employees will leave a job they like if they are not given a chance to develop their skills
    - D. managers should develop the full potential of their young employees

4.____

5. The reason for these difference is not that the Greeks had a superior sense of form or an inferior imagination or joy in life, but that they thought differently. Perhaps an illustration will make this clear. With the historical plays of Shakespeare in mind, let the reader contemplate the only extant Greek play on a historical subject, the Persians of Aeschylus, a play written less than ten years after the event which it deals with, and performed before the Athenian people who had played so notable a part in the struggle—incidentally,

5.____

immediately below the Acropolis which the Persians had sacked and defiled. Any Elizabethan dramatist would have given us a panorama of the whole war, its moments of despair, hope, and triumph; we should see on the stage the leaders who planned and some of the soldiers who won the victory. In the Persians we see nothing of the sort. The scene is laid in the Persian capital, one action is seen only through Persian eyes, the course of the war is simplified so much that the naval battle of Artemisium is not mentioned, nor even the heroic defense of Thermopylae, and not a single Greek is mentioned by name. The contrast could hardly be more complete.

Which sentence is BEST supported by the above paragraph?
- A. Greek plays are more interesting than Elizabethan plays.
- B. Elizabethan dramatists were more talented than Greek dramatists.
- C. If early Greek dramatists had the same historical material as Shakespeare had, the final form the Greek work would take would be very different from the Elizabethan work.
- D. Greeks were historically more inaccurate than Elizabethans.

6. The problem with present planning systems, public or private, is that accountability is weak. Private planning systems in the global corporations operate on a set of narrow incentives that frustrate sensible public policies such as full employment, environmental protection, and price stability. Public planning is Olympian and confused because there is neither a clear consensus on social values nor political priorities. To accomplish anything, explicit choices must be made, but these choices can be made effectively only with the active participation of the people most directly involved. This, not nostalgia for small-town times gone forever, is the reason that devolution of political power to local communities is a political necessity. The power to plan locally is a precondition for sensible integration of cities, regions, and countries into the world economy. According to the author,
   - A. people most directly affected by issues should participate in deciding those issues
   - B. private planning systems are preferable to public planning systems
   - C. there is no good system of government
   - D. county governments are more effective than state governments

Questions 7-11.

DIRECTIONS: Questions 7 through 11 are to be answered SOLELY on the basis of the following passage.

The ideal relationship for the interview is one of mutual confidence. To try to pretend, to put on a front of cordiality and friendship is extremely unwise for the interviewer because he will certainly convey, by subtle means, his real feelings. It is the interviewer's responsibility to take the lead in establishing a relationship of mutual confidence.

As the interviewer, you should help the interviewee to feel at ease and ready to talk. One of the best ways to do this is to be at ease yourself. If you are, it will probably be evident; if you are not, it will almost certainly be apparent to the interviewee. Begin the interview with topics for discussion which are easy to talk about and non-menacing. This interchange can be like the conversation of people when they are waiting for a bus, at the ballgame, or discussing the weather. However, do not prolong this warm-up too long since the interviewee knows as well as you do that these are not the things he came to discuss. Delaying too long in betting down too business may suggest to him that you are reluctant to deal with the topic.

Once you get onto the main topics, do all that you can to get the interviewee to talk freely with a little prodding from you as possible. This will probably require that you give him some idea of the area and of ways of looking at it. Avoid, however, prejudicing or coloring his remarks by what you say; especially, do not in any way indicate that there are certain things you want to hear, others which you do not want to hear. It is essential that he feel free to express his own ideas unhampered by your ideas, your values and preconceptions.

Do not appear to dominate the interview, nor have even the suggestion of a patronizing attitude. Ask some questions which will enable the interviewee to take pride in his knowledge. Take the attitude that the interviewee sincerely wants the interview to achieve its purpose. This creates a warm, permissive atmosphere that is most important in all interviews.

7. Of the following, the BEST title for the above passage is
   A. PERMISSIVENESS IN INTERVIEWING
   B. INTERVIEW TECHNIQUES
   C. THE FACTOR OF PRETENSE IN THE INTERVIEW
   D. THE CORDIAL INTERVIEW

8. Which of the following recommendations on the conduct of an interview is made by the above passage?
   A. Conduct the interview as if it were an interchange between people discussing the weather.
   B. The interview should be conducted in a highly impersonal manner.
   C. Allow enough time for the interview so that the interviewee does not feel rushed.
   D. Start the interview with topics which are not threatening to the interviewee.

9. The above passage indicates that the interviewer should
   A. feel free to express his opinions
   B. patronize the interviewee and display a permissive attitude
   C. permit the interviewee to give the needed information in his own fashion
   D. provide for privacy when conducting the interview

10. The meaning of the word *unhampered*, as it is used in the last sentence of the fourth paragraph of the above passage, is MOST NEARLY
    A. unheeded   B. unobstructed   C. hindered   D. aided

11. It can be INFERRED from the above passage that
    A. interviewers, while generally mature, lack confidence
    B. certain methods in interviewing are more successful than others in obtaining information
    C. there is usually a reluctance on the part of interviewers to deal with unpleasant topics
    D. it is best for the interviewer not to waiver from the use of hard and fast rules when dealing with clients

Questions 12-19.

DIRECTIONS: Questions 12 through 19 are to be answered SOLELY on the basis of the following passage.

Disabled cars pose a great danger to bridge traffic at any time, but during rush hours it is especially important that such vehicles be promptly detected and removed. The term *disable car* is an all-inclusive label referring to cars stalled due to a flat tire, mechanical failure, an accident, or locked bumpers. Flat tires are the most common reason why cars become disabled. The presence of disabled vehicles caused 68% of all traffic accidents last year. Of these, 75% were serious enough to require hospitalization of at least one of the vehicle's occupants.

The basic problem in the removal of disabled vehicles is detection of the car. Several methods have been proposed to aid detection. At a 1980 meeting of traffic experts and engineers, the idea of sinking electronic eyes into roadways was first suggested. Such *eyes* let officers know when traffic falls below normal speed and becomes congested. The basic argument against this approach is the high cost of installation of these eyes. One Midwestern state has, since 1978, employed closed circuit television to detect the existence and locations of stalled vehicles. When stalled vehicles are seen on the closed circuit television screen, the information is immediately communicated by radio to units stationed along the roadway, thus enabling the prompt removal of these obstructions to traffic. However, many cities lack the necessary manpower and equipment to use this approach. For the past five years, several east-coast cities have used the method known as *safety chains*, consisting of mobile units which represent the links at the *safety chain*. These mobile units are stationed as posts one or two miles apart along roadways to detect disabled cars. Standard procedure is for the units in the *safety chain* to have roof blinker lights turned on to full rotation. The officer, upon spotting a disabled car, at once assumes a post that gives him the most control in directing traffic around the obstruction. Only after gaining such control does he investigate and decide what action should be taken.

12. From the above passage, The PERCENTAGE of accidents caused by disabled cars in which hospitalization was required by at least one of the occupants of a vehicle last year was
    A. 17% B. 51% C. 68% D. 75%

13. According to the above passage, vehicles are MOST frequently disabled because of
    A. flat tires
    B. locked bumpers
    C. brake failure
    D. overheated motors

14. According to the above passage, in the electronic eye method of detection, the *eyes* are placed
    A. on lights along the roadway
    B. on patrol cars stationed along the roadway
    C. in booths spaced two miles apart
    D. into the roadway

15. According to the above passage, the factor COMMON to both the *safety chain* method and the *closed circuit television* method of detecting disabled vehicles is that both
    A. require the use of *electronic eyes*
    B. may be used where there is a shortage of officers
    C. employ units that are stationed along the highway
    D. require the use of trucks to move the heavy equipment used

15._____

16. The one of the following which is NOT discussed in the above passage as a method that may be used to detect disabled vehicles is
    A. closed circuit television   B. radar
    C. electronic eyes   D. safety chains

16._____

17. One DRAWBACK mentioned by the above passage to the use of the closed circuit television method for detection of disabled cars is that this technique
    A. cannot be used during bad weather
    B. does not provide for actual removal of the cars
    C. must be operated by a highly skilled staff of traffic engineers
    D. requires a large amount of manpower and equipment

17._____

18. The NEWEST of the methods discussed in the above passage for detection of disabled vehicles is
    A. electronic eyes   B. the mobile unit
    C. the safety chain   D. closed circuit television

18._____

19. When the *safety chain* method is being used, an officer who spots a disabled vehicle should FIRST
    A. turn off his roof blinker lights
    B. direct traffic around the disabled vehicle
    C. send a ratio message to the nearest mobile unit
    D. conduct an investigation

19._____

20. The universe is 15 billion years old, and the geological underpinnings of the earth were formed long before the first sea creature slithered out of the slime. But it is only in the last 6,000 years or so that men have descended into mines to chop and scratch at the earth's crust. Human history is, as Carl Sagan has put it, the equivalent of a few seconds in the 15 billion year life of the earth. What alarms those who keep track of the earth's crust is that since 1950 human beings have managed to consume more minerals than were mined in all previous history, a splurge of a millisecond in geologic time that cannot be long repeated without using up the finite riches of the earth.
    Of the following, the MAIN idea of this paragraph is:
    A. There is true cause for concern at the escalating consumption of the earth's minerals in recent years.
    B. Human history is the equivalent of a few seconds in the 15 billion year life of the earth
    C. The earth will soon run out of vital mineral resources

20._____

21. The authors of the Economic Report of the President are collectively aware, despite their vision of the asset-rich household, of the real economy in which millions of Americans live. There are glimpses, throughout the Report, of the underworld in which about 23 million people do not have public or private health insurance; in which the number of people receiving unemployment compensation was 41 percent of the total unemployed, in which the average dole for the compensated unemployed is about one-half of take-home pay. The authors understand, for example, that a worker may become physically disabled and that individuals generally do not like the risk of losing their ability to earn income. But such realities justify no more than the most limited interference in the (imperfect) market for disability insurance. There is only, as far as I can tell, one moment of genuine emotion in the entire Report when the authors' passions are stirred beyond market principles. They are discussing the leasing provisions of the 1981 Tax Act (conditions which so reduce tax revenues that they are apparently opposed in their present form by the Business Roundtable, the American Business Conference, and the National Association of Manufacturers).

    In the dark days before the 1981 ACT, according to the Report, (*firms with temporary tax losses* (a condition especially characteristic of new enterprises) were often unable to take advantage of investment tax incentives. The reason was that temporarily unprofitable companies had no taxable income against which to apply the investment tax deduction. It was a piteous contingency for the truly needy entrepreneur. But all was made right with the Tax Act. Social Security for the disabled incompetent corporation: the compassionate soul of Reagan's new economy.

    According to the above passage,
    - A. the National Association of Manufacturers and those companies that are temporarily unprofitable oppose the leasing provisions of the 1981 Tax Act
    - B. the authors of the Report are willing to ignore market principles in order to assist corporations unable to take advantage of tax incentives
    - C. the authors of the Report feel the National Association of Manufacturers and the Business Roundtable are wrong in opposing the leasing provisions of the 1981 Tax Act
    - D. the authors of the Report have more compassion for incompetent corporations than for disabled workers

22. Much of the lore of management in the West regards ambiguity as a symptom of a variety of organizational ills whose cure is larger doses of rationality, specificity, and decisiveness. But is ambiguity sometimes desirable? Ambiguity may be thought of as a shroud of the unknown surrounding certain events. The Japanese have a word for it, *ma*, for which there is no English translation. The word is valuable because it gives an explicit place to the unknowable aspect of things. In English, we may refer to an empty space between the chair and the table; the Japanese don't say the space is empty but *full of nothing*. However amusing the illustration, it goes to the core of the issue. Westerners speak of what is unknown primarily in reference to what is known (like the space between the chair and the table, while most eastern languages give honor to the unknown in its own right.

Of course, there are many situations that a manager finds himself in where being explicit and decisive is not only helpful but necessary. There is considerable advantage, however, in having a dual frame of reference—recognizing the value of both the clear and the ambiguous. The point to bear in mind is that in certain situations, ambiguity may serve better than absolute clarity.

Which sentence is BEST supported by the above passage?
- A. We should cultivate the art of being ambiguous.
- B. Ambiguity may sometimes be an effective managerial tool,
- C. Westerners do not have a dual frame of reference.
- D. It is important to recognize the ambiguous aspects of all situations.

23. Everyone ought to accustom himself to grasp in his thought at the same time facts that are at once so few and so simple, that he shall never believe that he has knowledge of anything which he does not mentally behold with a distinctiveness equal to that of the objects which he knows most distinctly of all. It is true that some people are born with a much greater aptitude for such discernment than others, but the mind can be made much more expert at such work by art and exercise. But there is one fact which I should here emphasize above all others; and that is everyone should firmly persuade himself that none of the sciences, however abstruse, is to be deduced from lofty and obscure matters, but that they all proceed only from what is easy and more readily understood.

    According to the author,
    - A. people should concentrate primarily on simple facts
    - B. intellectually gifted people have a great advantage over others
    - C. even difficult material and theories proceed from what is readily understood
    - D. if a scientist cannot grasp a simple theory, he or she is destined to fail

24. Goethe's casual observations about language contain a profound truth. Every word in every language is a part of a system of thinking unlike any other. Speakers of different languages live in different worlds; or rather, they live in the same world but can't help looking at it in different ways. Words stand for patterns of experience. As one generation hand its language down to the next, it also hands down a fixed pattern of thinking, seeing, and feeling. When we go from one language to another, nothing stays put; different peoples carry different nerve patterns in their brains, and there's no point where they fully match.

    According to the above passage,
    - A. language differences and their ramifications are a major cause of tensions between nations
    - B. it is not a good use of one's time to read novels that have been translated from another language because of the tremendous differences in interpretation
    - C. differences in languages reflect the different experiences of people the world over
    - D. language students should be especially careful to retain awareness of the subtleties of their native language

Questions 25-27.

DIRECTIONS: Questions 25 through 27 are to be answered SOLELY on the basis of the following passage.

The context of all education is twofold—individual and social. Its business is to make us more and more ourselves, too cultivate in each of us our own distinctive genius, however modest it may be, while showing us how this genius may be reconciled with the needs and claims of the society of which we are a part. Thought it is not education's aim to cultivate eccentrics, that society is richest, most flexible, and most humane that best uses and most tolerates eccentricity. Conformity beyond a point breeds sterile minds and, therefore, a sterile society.

The function of secondary—and still more of higher education is to affect the environment. Teachers are not, and should not be, social reformers. But they should be the catalytic agents by means of which young minds are influenced to desire and execute reform. To aspire to better things is a logical and desirable part of mental and spiritual growth.

25. Of the following, the MOST suitable title for the above passage is 25.____
    A. EDUCATION'S FUNCTION IN CREATING INDIVIDUAL DIFFERENCES
    B. THE NEED FOR EDUCATION TO ACQUAINT US WITH OUR SOCIAL ENVIRONMENT
    C. THE RESPONSIBILITY OF EDUCATION TOWARD THE INDIVIDUAL AND SOCIETY
    D. THE ROLE OF EDUCATION IN EXPLAINIING THE NEEDS OF SOCIETY

26. On the basis of the above passage, it may be inferred that 26.____
    A. conformity is one of the forerunners of totalitarianism
    B. education should be designed to create at least a modest amount of genius in everyone
    C. tolerance of individual differences tends to give society opportunities for improvement
    D. reforms are usually initiated by people who are somewhat eccentric

27. On the basis of the above passage, it may be inferred that 27.____
    A. genius is likely to be accompanied by a desire for social reform
    B. nonconformity is an indication of the inquiring mind
    C. people who are not high school or college graduates are not able to affect the environment
    D. teachers may or may not be social reformers

Questions 28-30.

DIRECTIONS: Questions 28 through 30 are to be answered SOLELY on the basis of the following passage.

Disregard for odds and complete confidence in one's self have produced many of our great successes. But every young man who wants to go into business for himself should appraise himself as a candidate for the one percent to survive. What has he to offer that is new or better? Has he special talents, special know-how, a new invention or service, or more capital than the average competitor? Has he the most important qualification of all, a willingness to work harder than anyone else? A man who is working for himself without limitation of hours or personal sacrifice can run circles around any operation that relies on paid help. But he must forget the eight-hour day, the forty-hour week, and the annual vacation. When he stops work, his income stops unless he hires a substitute. Most small operations have their busiest day on Saturday, and the owner uses Sunday to catch up on his correspondence, bookkeeping, inventorying, and maintenance chores. The successful self-employed man invariably works harder and worries more than the man on a salary. His wife and children make corresponding sacrifices of family unity and continuity; they never know whether their man will be home or in a mood to enjoy family activities.

28. The title that BEST expresses the ideas of the above passage is 28.____
   A. OVERCOMING OBSTACLES
   B. RUNNING ONE'S OWN BUSINESS
   C. HOW TO BECOME A SUCCESS
   D. WHY SMALL BUSINESSES FAIL

29. The above passage suggests that 29.____
   A. small businesses are the ones that last
   B. salaried workers are untrustworthy
   C. a willingness to work will overcome loss of income
   D. working for one's self may lead to success

30. The author of the above passage would MOST likely believe in 30.____
   A. individual initiative   B. socialism
   C. corporations   D. government aid to small business

KEY (CORRECT ANSWERS)

1.	C	11.	B	21.	D
2.	A	12.	B	22.	B
3.	A	13.	A	23.	C
4.	B	14.	D	24.	C
5.	C	15.	C	25.	C
6.	A	16.	B	26.	D
7.	B	17.	D	27.	D
8.	D	18.	A	28.	B
9.	C	19.	B	29.	D
10.	B	20.	A	30.	A

READING COMPREHENSION
UNDERSTANDING AND INTERPRETING WRITTEN MATERIAL
EXAMINATION SECTION
TEST 1

DIRECTIONS: Each question or incomplete statement is followed by several suggested answers or completions. Select the one that BEST answers the question or completes the statement. *PRINT THE LETTER OF THE CORRECT ANSWER IN THE SPACE AT THE RIGHT.*

1. The question *Who shall now teach Hegel?* is shorthand for the question *Who is going to teach this genre—all the so-called Continental philosophers?* The obvious answer to this question is *Whoever cares to study them.* This is also the right answer, but we can only accept it whole heartedly if we clear away a set of factitious questions. On such question is: *Are these Continental philosophers really philosophers?* Analytic philosophers, because they identify philosophical ability with argumentative skill and notice that there is nothing they would consider an argument in the bulk of Heidegger or Foucault, suggest that these must be people who tried to be philosophers and failed-incompetent philosophers. This is as silly as saying that Plato was an incompetent sophist, or that a hedgehog is an incompetent fox. Hegel knew what he thought about philosophers who imitated the method and style of mathematics. He thought they were incompetent. These reciprocal charges of incompetence do nobody any good. We should just drop the questions of what philosophy really is or who really counts as a philosopher.
Which sentence is BEST supported by the above paragraph?
   A. The study of Hegel's philosophy is less popular now than in the past.
   B. Philosophers must stop questioning the competence of other philosophers.
   C. Philosophers should try to be as tolerant as Foucault and Heidegger.
   D. Analytic philosophers tend to be more argumentative than other philosophers.

1.____

2. It is an interesting question: the ease with which organizations of different kinds at different stages in their history can continue to function with ineffectual leadership at the top, or even function without a clear system of authority. Certainly, the success of some experiments in worker self-management shows that bosses are not always necessary, as some contemporary Marxists argue. Indeed, sometimes the function of those at the top is merely to symbolize organizational accountability, especially in dealing with outside authorities, but not to guide the actions of those within the organization. A vice president of a large insurance company remarked to us that *Presidents are powerless; no one needs them. They should all be sent off to do public relations for the company.* While this is clearly a self-serving statement from someone next in line to command, it does give meaning to the expression being kicked upstairs. According to the author,

2.____

A. organizations function very smoothly without bosses
B. the function of those at the top is sometimes only to symbolize organizational accountability
C. company presidents are often inept at guiding the actions of those within the organization
D. presidents of companies have less power than one might assume they have

3. The goal of a problem is a terminal expression one wishes to cause to exist in the world of the problem. There are two types of goals: specified goal expressions in proof problems and incompletely specified goal expressions in find problems. For example, consider the problem of finding the value of X, given the expression 4X+5 = 17. In this problem, one can regard the goal expression as being of the form X = _____, the goal expression. The goal expression in a find problem of this type is incompletely specified. If the goal expression were specified completely—for example, X = 3—then the problem would be a proof problem, with only the sequence of operations to be determined in order to solve the problem. Of course, if one were not guaranteed that the goal expression X = 3 was true, then the terminal goal expression should really be considered to be incompletely specified—something like the statement X = 3 (true or false).
According to the preceding paragraph,
A. the goal of the equation 4X+5 = 17 is true, not false
B. if the goal expression was specified as being equal to 3, the problem 4X+5 = 17 would be a proof problem
C. if the sequence of operations of the problem given in the paragraph is predetermined, the goal of the problem becomes one of terminal expression, or the number 17
D. X cannot be found unless X is converted into a proof problem

4. We have human psychology and animal psychology, but no plant psychology. Why? Because we believe that plants have no perceptions or intentions. Some plants exhibit *behavior* and have been credited with *habits*. If you stroke the midrib of the compound leaf of a sensitive plant, the leaflets close. The sunflower changes with the diurnal changes in the source of light. The lowest animals have not much more complicated forms of behavior. The sea anemone traps and digests the small creatures that the water brings to it; the pitcher plant does the same thing and even more, for it presents a cup of liquid that attracts insects, instead of letting the surrounding medium drift them into its trap. Here as everywhere in nature where the great, general classes of living things diverge, the lines between them are not perfectly clear. A sponge is an animal; the pitcher plant is a flowering plant, but it comes nearer to *feeding itself* than the animal. Yet the fact is that we credit all animals, and only the animals, with some degree of feeling.
Of the following, the MAIN idea expressed in the above paragraph is:
A. The classification of plants has been based on beliefs about their capacity to perceive and feel
B. Many plants are more evolved than species considered animals

C. The lines that divide the classes of living things are never clear.
D. The abilities and qualities of plants are undervalued.

5. Quantitative indexes are not necessarily adequate measures of true economic significance or influence. But even the raw quantitative data speak loudly of the importance of the new transnationalized economy. The United Nations estimated value added in this new sector of the world economy at $500 billion in 2001, mounting to one-fifth of total GNP of the non-socialist world and exceeding the GNP of any one other country except the United States. Furthermore, all observers agree that the share of this sector in the world economy is growing rapidly. At least since 1980, its annual rate of growth has been high and remarkably steady at 10 percent compared to 4 percent for noninternationalized output in the Western developed countries.
One spokesman for the new system franklin envisages that within a generation some 400 to 500 multinational corporations will own close to two-thirds of the world's fixed assets.
According to the author, all of the following are true EXCEPT
   A. Quantitative indexes are not necessarily adequate measures of actual economic influence.
   B. The transnational sector of the world economy is growing rapidly.
   C. Since 1980, the rate of growth of transnationals has been 10% compared to 4% for internationalized output in the Western developed countries.
   D. Continued growth for multinational corporations is likely.

5.____

6. A bill may be sent to the Governor when it has passed both houses. During the session, he is given ten days to act on bills that reach his desk. Bills sent to him within ten days of the end of the session must be acted on within 30 days after the last day of the session. If the Governor takes no action on a ten day bill, it automatically becomes a law. If he disapproves or vetoes a ten day bill, it can become law only if it is re-passed by two-thirds vote in each house. If he fails to act on a 30 day bill, the bill is said to have received a *pocket veto*. It is customary for the Governor to act, however, on all bills submitted to him, and give his reason in writing for approving or disapproving important legislation.
According to the above paragraph, all of the following are true EXCEPT:
   A. Bills sent to the Governor in the last ten days of the session must be acted on within thirty days after the last day of the session,
   B. If the Governor takes no action on a 10 day bill, it is said to have received a *pocket veto*.
   C. It is customary for the Governor to act on all bills submitted to him.
   D. If the Governor vetoes a ten day bill, it can become law only if passed by a two-thirds vote of the Legislature.

6.____

7. It is particularly when I see a child going through the mechanical process of manipulating numbers without any intuitive sense of what it is all about that I recall the lines of Lewis Carroll: *Reeling and Writhing, of course, to begin with…and then the different branches of Arithmetic-Ambition, Distraction, Uglification, and Derision.* Or, as Max Beberman has put it, much more gently: *Somewhat related to the notion of discovery in teaching is our insistence that*

7.____

the student become aware of a concept before a name has been assigned to the concept. I am quite aware that the issue of intuitive understanding is a very live one among teachers of mathematics, and even a casual reading of the yearbook of the National Council of Teachers of Mathematics makes it clear that they are also very mindful of the gap that exists between proclaiming the importance of such understanding and actually producing it in the classroom.
The MAIN idea expressed in the above paragraph is:
- A. Math teachers are concerned about the difficulties inherent in producing an understanding of mathematics in their students.
- B. It is important that an intuitive sense in approaching math problems be developed, rather than relying on rote, mechanical learning.
- C. Mathematics, by its very nature, encourages rote, mechanical learning.
- D. Lewis Carroll was absolutely correct in his assessment of the true nature of mathematics.

8. Heisenberg's *Principle of Uncertainty*, which states that events at the atomic level cannot be observed with certainty, can be compared to this: In the world of everyday experience, we can observe any phenomenon and measure its properties without influencing the phenomenon in question to any significant extent. To be sure, if we try to measure the temperature of a demitasse with a bathtub thermometer, the instrument will absorb so much heat from the coffee that it will change the coffee's temperature substantially. But with a small chemical thermometer, we may get a sufficiently accurate reading. We can measure the temperature of a living cell with a miniature thermometer, which has almost negligible heat capacity. But in the atomic world, we can never overlook the disturbance caused by the introduction of the measuring apparatus.
Which sentence is BEST supported by the above paragraph?
- A. There is little we do not alter by the mere act of observation.
- B. It is always a good idea to use the smallest measuring device possible.
- C. Chemical thermometers are more accurate than bathtub thermometers.
- D. It is not possible to observe events at the atomic level and be sure that the same events would occur if we were not observing them.

8._____

9. It is a myth that American workers are pricing themselves out of the market, relative to workers in other industrialized countries of the world. The wages of American manufacturing workers increased at a slower rate in the 1990s than those of workers in other major western countries. In terms of American dollars, between 1990 and 2000, hourly compensation increased 489 percent in Japan and 464 percent in Germany, compared to 128 percent in the United States. Even though these countries experienced faster productivity growth, their unit labor costs still rose faster than in the United States, according to the Bureau of Labor Statistics. During the 1990s, unit labor costs rose 192 percent in Japan, 252 percent in Germany, and only 78 percent in the United States.
According to the above passage,
- A. unit labor costs in the 1990s were higher in Japan than they were in Germany or the United States
- B. the wages of American workers need to be increased to be consistent with other countries

9._____

C. American worker are more productive than Japanese or German workers
D. the wages of American workers in manufacturing increased at a slower rate in the 1990s than the wages of workers in Japan or Germany

10. No people have invented more ways to enjoy life than the Chinese, perhaps to balance floods, famines, warlords, and other ills of fate. The clang of gongs, clashing cymbals, and beating of drums sound through their long history. No month is without fairs and theatricals when streets are hung with fantasies of painted lanterns and crowded with *carriages that flow like water, horses like roaming dragons*. Night skies are illumined by firecrackers—a Chinese invention—bursting in the form of flowerpots, peonies, fiery devils. The ways of pleasure are myriad. Music plays in the air through bamboo whistles of different pitch tied to the wings of circling pigeons. To skim a frozen lake in an ice sleigh with a group of friends on a day when the sun is warm is rapture, like *moving in a cup of jade*. What more delightful than the ancient festival called *Half an Immortal*, when everyone from palace officials to the common man took a ride on a swing? When high in the air, one felt like an Immortal, when back to earth once again human—no more than to be for an instant a god.
According to the above passage,
   A. if the Chinese hadn't had so many misfortunes, they wouldn't have created so many pleasurable past times
   B. the Chinese invented flowerpots
   C. every month the Chinese have fairs and theatricals
   D. pigeons are required to play the game *Half an Immortal*

10.____

11. In our century, instead, poor Diphilus is lost in the crowd of his peers. We flood one another. No one recognizes him as he loads his basket in the supermarket. What grevious fits of melancholy have I not suffered in one of our larger urban bookstores, gazing at the hundreds, thousands, tens of thousands of books on shelve and tables? And what are they to the hundreds of thousands, the millions that stand in our research libraries? More books than Noah saw raindrops. How many readers will read a given one of them—mine, yours—in their lifetimes? And how will it be in the distant future? Incomprehensible masses of books, Pelion upon Ossa, hordes of books, each piteously calling for attention, respect, love, in competition with the vast disgorgements of the past and with one another in the present. Neither is it at all helpful that books can even now be reduced to the size of a postage stamp. Avanti! Place the Bible on a pinhead! Crowding more books into small spaces does not cram more books into our heads. Here I come to the sticking point that unnerves the modern Diphilus. The number of books a person can read in a given time is, roughly speaking, a historical constant. It does not change significantly even when the number of books available for reading does. Constants are pitted against variables to confound both writer and reader.
Of the following, the MAIN idea in this passage is:
   A. It is difficult to attain immortality because so many books are being published.
   B. Too many books are being published, so fewer people are reading them.

11.____

C. Because so many books are being published, the quality of the writing is poorer.
D. Because so many books are available, but only a fixed amount of time to read them, frustration results for both the reader and the writer.

12. Until recently, consciousness of sexual harassment has been low. But workers have become aware of it as more women have arrived at levels of authority in the workplace, feminist groups have focused attention on rape and other violence against women, and students have felt freer to report perceived abuse by professors. In the last 5 years, studies have shown that sexual misconduct at the workplace is a big problem. For example, in a recently published survey of federal employees, 42% of 694,000 women and 15% of 1,168,000 men said they had experienced some form of harassment. According to the author,   12._____
    A. the awareness of sexual harassment at the workplace is increasing
    B. the incidence of harassment is higher in universities than workplaces
    C. sexual harassment is much more commonly experienced by women than men
    D. it is rare for men to experience sexual harassment

Questions 13-17.

DIRECTIONS: Questions 13 through 17 are to be answered SOLELY on the basis of the following paragraph.

Since discounts are in common use in the commercial world and apply to purchases made by government agencies as well as business firms, it is essential that individuals in both public and private employment who prepare bills, check invoices, prepare payment vouchers, or write checks to pay bills have an understanding of the terms used. These include cash or time discount, trade discount, and discount series. A cash or time discount offers a reduction in price to the buyer for the prompt payment of the bill and is usually expressed as a percentage with a time requirement, stated in days, within which the bill must be paid in order to earn the discount. An example would be 3/10, meaning a 3% discount may be applied to the bill if the payment is forwarded to the vendor within 10 days. On an invoice, the cash discount terms are usually followed by the net terms, which is the time in days allowed for ordinary payment of the bill. Thus, 3/10, Net 30 means that full payment is expected in thirty days if the cash discount of 3% is not taken for having paid the bill within ten days. When the expression Terms Net Cash is listed on a bill, it means that no deduction for early payment is allowed. A trade discount is normally applied to list prices by a manufacturer to show the actual price to retailers so that they may know their cost and determine markups that will allow them to operate competitively and at a profit. A trade discount is applied by the seller to the list price and is independent of a cash or time discount. Discounts may also be used by manufacturers to adjust prices charged to retailers without changing list prices. This is usually done by series discounting and is expressed as a series of percentages. To compute a series discount, such as 40%, 20%, 10%, first apply the 40% discount to the list price, then apply the 20% discount to the remainder, and finally apply the 10% discount to the second remainder.

13. According to the above paragraph, trade discounts are   13.____
    A. applied by the buyer
    B. independent of cash discounts
    C. restricted to cash sales
    D. used to secure rapid payment of bills

14. According to the above paragraph, if the sales terms 5/10, Net 60 appear on a   14.____
    bill in the amount of $100 dated December 5 and the buyer submits his
    payment on December 15, his PROPER payment should be
    A. $60   B. $90   C. $95   D. $100

15. According to the above paragraph, if a manufacturer gives a trade discount of   15.____
    40% for an item with a list price of $250 and the terms are Net Cash, the price
    a retail merchant is required to pay for this item is
    A. $250   B. $210   C. $150   D. $100

16. According to the above paragraph, a series discount of 25%, 20%, 10% applied   16.____
    to a list price of $200 results in an ACTUAL price to the buyer of
    A. $88   B. $90   C. $108   D. $110

17. According to the above paragraph, if a manufacturer gives a trade discount   17.____
    of 50% and the terms are 6/10, Net 30, the cost to a retail merchant of an item
    with a list price of $500 and for which he takes the time discount, is
    A. $220   B. $235   C. $240   D. $250

Questions 18-22.

DIRECTIONS: Questions 18 through 22 are to be answered SOLELY on the basis of the
              following paragraph.

   The city may issue its own bonds or it may purchase bonds as an investment. Bonds may
be issued in various denominations, and the face value of the bond is its par value. Before
purchasing a bond, the investor desires to know the rate of income that the investment will yield.
In computing the yield on a bond, it is assumed that the investor will keep the bond until the date
of maturity, except for callable bonds which are not considered in this paragraph. To compute
exact yield is a complicated mathematical problem, and scientifically prepared tables are
generally used to avoid such computation. However, the approximate yield can be computed
much more easily. In computing approximate yield, the accrued interest on the date of
purchase should be ignored, because the buyer who pays accrued interest to the seller receives
it again at the next interest date. Bonds bought at a premium (which cost more) yield a lower
rate of income than the same bonds bought at par (face value), and bonds bought at a discount
(which cost less) yield a higher rate of income than the same bonds bought at par.

18. An investor bought a $10,000 city bond paying 6% interest.   18.____
    Which of the following purchase prices would indicate that the bond was
    bought at a PREMIUM?
    A. $9,000   B. $9,400   C. $10,000   D. $10,600

19. During the year, a particular $10,000 bond paying 74% sold at fluctuating prices.
    Which of the following prices would indicate that the bond was bought at a DISCOUNT?
    A. $9,800	B. $10,000	C. $10,200	D. $10,750

    19._____

20. A certain group of bonds was sold in denominations of $5,000, $10,000, $20,000 and $50,000.
    In the following list of four purchase prices, which one is MOST likely to represent a bond sold at par value?
    A. $10,500	B. $20,000	C. $22,000	D. $49,000

    20._____

21. When computing the approximate yield on a bond, it is DESIRABLE to
    A. assume the bond was purchased at par
    B. consult scientifically prepared tables
    C. ignore accrued interest on the date of purchase
    D. wait until the bond reaches maturity

    21._____

22. Which of the following is MOST likely to be an exception to the information provided in the above paragraph? Bonds
    A. purchased at a premium	B. sold at par
    C. sold before maturity	D. which are callable

    22._____

Questions 23-25

DIRECTIONS: Questions 23 through 25 are to be answered SOLELY on the basis of the following paragraph.

There is one bad habit of drivers that often causes chain collisions at traffic lights. It is the habit of keeping one foot poised over the accelerator pedal, ready to step on the gas the instant the light turns green. A driver who is watching the light, instead of watching the cars in front of him, may *jump the gun* and bump the car in front of him, and this car in turn may bump the next car. If a driver is resting his foot on the accelerator, his foot will be slammed down when he bumps into the car ahead. This makes the collision worse and makes it very likely that cars further ahead in the line are going to get involved in a series of violent bumps.

23. Which of the following conclusions can MOST reasonably drawn from the information given in the above paragraph?
    A. American drivers have a great many bad driving habits.
    B. Drivers should step on the gas as soon as the light turns green.
    C. A driver with poor driving habits should be arrested and fined.
    D. A driver should not rest his foot on the accelerator when the car is stopped for a traffic light.

    23._____

24. From the information given in the above paragraph, a reader should be able to tell that a chain collision may be defined as a collision
    A. caused by bad driving habits at traffic lights
    B. in which one car hits another, this second car hits a third car, and so on

    24._____

C. caused by drivers who fail to use their accelerators
D. that takes place at an intersection where there is a traffic light

25. The above passage states that a driver who watches the light instead of paying attention to traffic may   25.____
    A. be involved in an accident
    B. end up in jail
    C. lose his license
    D. develop bad driving habits

KEY (CORRECT ANSWERS)

1.	B	11.	D
2.	B	12.	A
3.	B	13.	B
4.	A	14.	C
5.	C	15.	C
6.	B	16.	C
7.	B	17.	B
8.	D	18.	D
9.	D	19.	A
10.	C	20.	B

21.	C
22.	D
23.	D
24.	B
25.	A

TEST 2

DIRECTIONS: Each question or incomplete statement is followed by several suggested answers or completions. Select the one that BEST answers the question or completes the statement. *PRINT THE LETTER OF THE CORRECT ANSWER IN THE SPACE AT THE RIGHT.*

Questions 1-4.

DIRECTIONS: Each of the statements in this section is followed by several labeled choices. In the space at the right, write the letter of the sentence which means MOST NEARLY what is stated or implied in the passage.

1. It may be said that the problem in adult education seems to be not the piling up of facts but practice in thinking.
   This statement means MOST NEARLY that
   A. educational methods for adults and young people should differ
   B. adults seem to think more than young people
   C. a well-educated adult is one who thinks but does not have a store of information
   D. adult education should stress ability to think

   1.____

2. Last year approximately 19,000 fatal accidents were sustained in industry. There were approximately 130 non-fatal injuries to each fatal injury.
   According to the above statement, the number of non-fatal accidents was
   A. 146,000   B. 190,000   C. 1,150,000   D. 2,500,000

   2.____

3. No employer expects his stenographer to be a walking encyclopedia, but it is not unreasonable for him to expect her to know where to look for necessary information on a variety of topics.
   The above statement means MOST NEARLY that the stenographer should
   A. be a college graduate
   B. be familiar with standard office reference books
   C. keep a scrapbook of all interesting happenings
   D. go to the library regularly

   3.____

4. For the United States, Canada has become the most important country in the world, yet there are few countries about which Americans know less. Canada is the third largest country in the world; only Russia and China are larger. The area of Canada is more than a quarter of the whole British Empire.
   According to the above statement, the
   A. British Empire is smaller than Russia or China
   B. territory of China is greater than that of Canada
   C. Americans know more about Canada than they do about China or Russia
   D. Canadian population is more than one-quarter the population of the British Empire

   4.____

Questions 5-8.

DIRECTIONS: Questions 5 through 8 are to be answered SOLELY on the basis of the following paragraph.

A few people who live in old tenements have had the bad habit of throwing garbage out of their windows, especially if there is an empty lot near their building. Sometimes the garbage is food; sometimes the garbage is half-empty soda cans. Sometimes the garbage is a little bit of both mixed together. These people just don't care about keeping the lot clean.

5. The above paragraph states that throwing garbage out of windows is a 5.____
   A. bad habit   B. dangerous thing to do
   C. good thing to do   D. good way to feed rats

6. According to the above paragraph, an empty lot next to an old tenement is 6.____
   sometimes used as a place to
   A. hold local gang meetings   B. play ball
   C. throw garbage   D. walk dogs

7. According to the above paragraph, which of the following throw garbage out 7.____
   of their windows?
   A. Nobody   B. Everybody
   C. Most people   D. Some people

8. According to the above paragraph, the kinds of garbage thrown out of windows 8.____
   are
   A. candy and cigarette butts   B. food and half-empty soda cans
   C. fruit and vegetables   D. rice and bread

Questions 9-12.

DIRECTIONS: Questions 9 through 12 are to be answered SOLELY on the basis of the following paragraph.

The game that is recognized all over the world as an all-American game is the game of baseball. As a matter of fact, baseball heroes like Joe DiMaggio, Willie Mays, and Babe Ruth were as famous in their day as movie stars Robert Redford, Paul Newman, and Clint Eastwood are now. All these men have had the experience of being mobbed by fans whenever they put in an appearance anywhere in the world. Such unusual popularity makes it possible for stars like these to earn at least as much money off the job as on the job. It didn't take manufacturers and advertising men long to discover that their sales of shaving lotion, for instance, increased when they got famous stars to advertise their product for them on radio and television.

9. According to the above paragraph, baseball is known everywhere as a(n) _____ 9.____
   game.
   A. all-American   B. fast   C. unusual   D. tough

10. According to the above paragraph, being so well known means that it is possible 10.____
for people like Willie Mays and Babe Ruth to
    A. ask for anything and get it
    B. make as much money off the job as on it
    C. travel anywhere free of charge
    D. watch any game free of charge

11. According to the above paragraph, which of the following are known all over 11.____
the world?
    A. Baseball heroes   B. Advertising men
    C. Manufacturers   D. Basketball heroes

12. According to the above paragraph, it is possible to sell much more shaving lotion 12.____
on television and radio if
    A. the commercials are in color instead of black and white
    B. you can get a prize with each bottle of shaving lotion
    C. the shaving lotion makes you smell nicer than usual
    D. the shaving lotion is advertised by famous stars

Questions 13-15.

DIRECTIONS: Questions 13 through 15 are to be answered SOLELY on the basis of the following passage.

That music gives pleasure is axiomatic. Because this is so, the pleasures of music may seem a rather elementary subject for discussion. Yet the source of that pleasure, our musical instinct, is not at all elementary. It is, in fact, one of the prime puzzles of consciousness. Why is it that we are able to make sense out of these nerve signals so that we emerge from engulfment in the orderly presentation of sound stimuli as if we had lived through an image of life?

If music has impact for the mere listener, it follows that it will have much greater impact for those who sing it or play it themselves with proficiency. Any educated person in Elizabethan times was expected to read musical notation and take part in a madrigalsing. Passive listeners, numbered in the millions, are a comparatively recent innovation.

Everyone is aware that so-called serious music has made great strikes in general public acceptance in recent years, but the term itself still connotes something forbidding and hermetic to the mass audience. They attribute to the professional musician a kind of initiation into secrets that are forever hidden from the outsider. Nothing could be more misleading. We all listen to music, professionals, and non-professionals alike in the same sort of way, in a dumb sort of way, really, because simple or sophisticated music attracts all of us in the first instance, on the primordial level of sheer rhythmic and sonic appeal. Musicians are flattered, no doubt, by the deferential attitude of the layman in regard to what he imagines to be our secret understanding of music. But in all honesty, we musicians know that in the main we listen basically as others do, because music hits us with an immediacy that we recognize in the reactions of the most simple minded of music listeners.

13. A suitable title for the above passage would be
    A. HOW TO LISTEN TO MUSIC
    B. LEARNING MUSIC APPRECIATION
    C. THE PLEASURES OF MUSIC
    D. THE WORLD OF THE MUSICIAN

13._____

14. The author implies that the passive listener is one who
    A. cannot read or play music
    B. does not appreciate serious music
    C. does not keep time to the music by hand or toe tapping
    D. will not attend a concert if he has to pay for the privilege

14._____

15. The author of the above passage is apparently inconsistent when he discusses
    A. the distinction between the listener who pays for the privilege and the one who does not
    B. the historical development of musical forms
    C. the pleasures derived from music by the musician
    D. why it is that we listen to music

15._____

Questions 16-18.

DIRECTIONS: Questions 16 through 18 are to be answered SOLELY on the basis of the following passage.

Who are the clerisy? They are people who like to read books. The use of a word so unusual, so out of fashion, can only be excused on the ground that it has no familiar synonym. The word is little known because what it describes has disappeared, though I do not believe is gone forever. The clerisy are those who read for pleasure, but not for idleness; who read for pastime, but not to kill time; who love books, but do not live by books.

Let us consider the actual business of reading—the interpretive act of getting the words off the age and into your head in the most effective way. The most effective way is not the quickest way of reading; and for those who think that speed is the greatest good, there are plenty of manuals on how to read a book which profess to tell how to strip off the husk and guzzle the milk, like a chimp attacking a coconut. Who among today's readers would whisk through a poem, eyes aflicker, and say that he had read it? The answer to that last question must unfortunately be: far too many. For reading is not respected for the art it is.

Doubtless there are philosophical terms for the attitude of mind of which nasty reading is one manifestation, but here let us call it end-gaining, for its victims put ends before means; they value not reading, but having read. In this, the end-gainers make mischief and spoil all they do; end-gaining is one of the curses of our nervously tense, intellectually flabby civilization. In reading, as in all arts, it is the means, and not the end, which gives delight and brings the true reward. Not straining forward toward the completion, but the pleasure of every page as it comes, is the secret of reading. We must desire to read a book, rather than to have read it. This change in attitude, so simple to describe, is by no means simple to achieve,, if one has lived the life of an end-gainer.

16. A suitable title for the above passage would be 16._____
    A. READING FOR ENLIGHTENMENT
    B. THE ART OF RAPID READING
    C. THE WELL-EDUCATED READER
    D. VALUES IN READING

17. The author does NOT believe that most people read because they 17._____
    A. are bored
    B. have nothing better to do
    C. love books
    D. wish to say that they have read certain books

18. The change in attitude to which the author refers in the last sentence of the above passage implies a change from 18._____
    A. dawdling while reading so that the reader can read a greater number of books
    B. reading light fiction to reading serious fiction and non-fiction
    C. reading works which do not amuse the reader
    D. skimming through a book to reading it with care

Questions 19-22.

DIRECTIONS: Questions 19 through 22 are to be answered SOLELY on the basis of the following passage.

    Violence is not new to literature. The writings of Shakespeare and Cervantes are full of it. But those classic writers did not condone violence. They viewed it as a just retribution for sins against the divine order or as a sacrifice sanctioned by heroism. What is peculiar to the modern literature is violence for the sake of violence. Perhaps our reverence for life has been dulled by mass slaughter, though mass slaughter has not been exceptional in the history of mankind. What is exceptional is the boredom that now alternates with war. The basic emotion in peacetime has become a horror of emptiness: a fear of being alone, of having nothing to do, a neurosis whose symptoms are restlessness, an unmotivated and undirected rage, sinking at times into vapid listlessness. This neurotic syndrome is intensified by the prevailing sense of insecurity. The threat of atomic war has corrupted our faith in life itself.
    This universal neurosis has developed with the progress of technology. It is the neurosis of men whose chief expenditure of energy is to pull a lever or push a button, of men who have ceased to make things with their hands. Such inactivity applies not only to muscles and nerves but to the creative processes that once engaged the mind. If one could contrast visually, by time-and-motion studies, the daily actions of an eighteenth-century carpenter with a twentieth-century machinist, the latter would appear as a <u>confined, repetitive clot</u>, the former as a free and even fantastic pattern. But the most significant contrast could not be visualized—the contrast between a mind suspended aimlessly above an autonomous movement and a mind consciously bent on the shaping of a material substance according to the persistent evidence of the senses.

19. A suitable title for the above passage would be
    A. INCREASING PRODUCTION BY MEANS OF SYSTEMATIZATION
    B. LACK OF A SENSE OF CREATIVENESS AND ITS CONSEQUENCE
    C. TECHNOLOGICAL ACHIEVEMENT IN MODERN SOCIETY
    D. WHAT CAN BE DONE ABOUT SENSELESS VIOLENCE

19.____

20. According to the author, Shakespeare treated violence as a
    A. basically sinful act not in keeping with religious thinking
    B. just punishment of transgressors against moral law
    C. means of achieving dramatic excitement
    D. solution to a problem provided no other solution was available

20.____

21. According to the author, boredom may lead to
    A. a greater interest in leisure-time activities
    B. chronic fatigue
    C. senseless anger
    D. the acceptance of a job which does not provide a sense of creativity

21.____

22. The underlined phrase refers to the
    A. hand movements made by the carpenter
    B. hand movements made by the machinist
    C. relative ignorance of the carpenter
    D. relative ignorance of the machinist

22.____

23. The concentration of women and female-headed families in the city is both cause and consequence of the city's fiscal woes. Women live in cities because it is easier and cheaper for them to do so, but because fewer women are employed, and those that are receive lower pay than men, they do not make the same contribution to the tax base that an equivalent population of men would. Concomitantly, they are more dependent on public resources, such as transportation and housing. For these reasons alone, urban finances would be improved by increasing women's employment opportunities and pay. Yet nothing in our current urban policy is specifically geared to improving women's financial resources. There are some proposed incentives to create more jobs, but not necessarily ones that would utilize the skills women currently have. The most innovative proposal was a tax credit for new hires from certain groups with particularly high unemployment rates. None of the seven targeted groups were women.
    Which sentence is BEST supported by the above paragraph?
    A. Innovative programs are rapidly improving conditions for seven targeted groups with traditionally high unemployment rates.
    B. The contribution of women to a city's tax base reflects their superior economic position.
    C. Improving the economic position of women who live in cities would help the financial conditions of the cities themselves.
    D. Most women in this country live in large cities.

23.____

24. None of this would be worth saying if Descartes had been right in positing a one-to-one correspondence between stimuli and sensations. But we know that nothing of the sort exists. The perception of a given color can be evoked by an infinite number of differently combined wavelengths. Conversely, a given stimulus can evoke a variety of sensations, the image of a duck in one recipient, the image of a rabbit in another. Nor are responses like these entirely innate. One can learn to discriminate colors or patterns which were indistinguishable prior to training. To an extent still unknown, the production of data from stimuli is a learned procedure. After the learning process, the same stimulus evokes a different datum. I conclude that, though data are the minimal elements of our individual experience, they need be shared responses to a given stimulus only within the membership of a relatively homogeneous community: educational, scientific, or linguistic.
Which sentence is BEST supported by the above paragraph?
    A. One stimulus can give rise to a number of different sensations.
    B. There is a one-to-one correspondence between stimuli and sensations.
    C. It is not possible to produce data from stimuli by using a learned procedure.
    D. It is not necessary for a group to be relatively homogeneous in order to share responses to stimuli.

24.____

25. Workers who want to move in the direction of participative structures will need to confront the issues of power and control. The process of change needs to be mutually shared by all involved, or the outcome will not be a really participative model. The demand for a structural redistribution of power is not sufficient to address the problem of change toward a humanistic, as against a technological, workplace. If we are to change our institutional arrangements from hierarchy to participation, particularly in our workplaces, we will need to look to transformations in ourselves as well. As long as we are imbued with the legitimacy of hierarchical authority, with the sovereignty of the status quo, we will never be able to generate the new and original forms that we seek. This means if we are to be equal to the task of reorganizing our workplaces, we need to think about how we can reeducate ourselves and become aware of our assumptions about the nature of our social life together. Unless the issue is approached in terms of these complexities, I fear that all the worker participation and quality of work life efforts will fail.
According to the above paragraph, which of the following is NOT true?
    A. Self-education concerning social roles must go hand in hand with workplace reorganization.
    B. The structural changing of the workplace, alone, will not bring about the necessary changes in the quality of work life.
    C. Individuals can easily overcome their attitudes towards hierarchical authority.
    D. Changing the quality of work life will require the participation of all involved.

25.____

KEY (CORRECT ANSWERS)

1. D
2. D
3. B
4. B
5. A

6. C
7. D
8. B
9. A
10. B

11. A
12. D
13. C
14. A
15. C

16. D
17. C
18. D
19. B
20. B

21. C
22. B
23. C
24. A
25. C

EXAMINATION SECTION
TEST 1

DIRECTIONS: Each question or incomplete statement is followed by several suggested answers or completions. Select the one that BEST answers the question or completes the statement. *PRINT THE LETTER OF THE CORRECT ANSWER IN THE SPACE AT THE RIGHT.*

Questions 1-5.

DIRECTIONS: Each of Questions 1 through 5 consists of a passage which contains one word that is incorrectly used because it is not in keeping with the meaning that the quotation is evidently intended to convey. Determine which word is incorrectly used. Select from the choices lettered A, B, C, and D the word which, when substituted for the incorrectly used word, would BEST to convey the meaning of the quotation.

1. Whatever the method, the necessity to keep up with the dynamics of an organization is the point on which many classification plans go awry. The budgetary approach to "positions," for example, often leads to using for recruitment and pay purposes a position authorized many years earlier for quite a different purpose than currently contemplated—making perhaps the title, the class, and the qualifications required inappropriate to the current need. This happens because executives overlook the stability that takes place in job duties and fail to reread an initial description of the job before saying, as they scan a list of titles, "We should fill this position right away." Once a classification plan is adopted, it is pointless to do anything less than provide for continuous, painstaking maintenance on a current basis, else once different positions that have actually become similar to each other remain in different classes, and some former cognates that have become quite different continue in the same class. Such a program often seems expensive. But to stint too much on this out-of-pocket cost may create still higher hidden costs growing out of lowered morale, poor production, delayed operating programs, excessive pay for simple work, and low pay for responsible work (resulting in poorly qualified executives and professional men)—all normal concomitants of inadequate, hasty, or out-of-date classification.   1.____

   A. evolution   B. personnel   C. disapproved   D. forward

2. At first sight, it may seem that there is little or no difference between the usableness of a manual and the degree of its use. But there is a difference. A manual may have all the qualities which make up the usable manual and still not be used. Take this instance as an example: Suppose you have a satisfactory manual but issue instructions from day to day through the avenue of bulletins, memorandums, and other informational releases. Which will the employee use, the manual or the bulletin which passes over his desk? He will,   2.____

of course, use the latter, for some obsolete material will not be contained in this manual. Here we have a theoretically usable manual which is unused because of the other avenues by which procedural information may be issued.
   A. countermand   B. discard   C. intentional   D. worthwhile

3. By reconcentrating control over its operations in a central headquarters, a firm is able to extend the influence of automation to many, if not all, of its functions—from inventory and payroll to production, sales, and personnel. In so doing, businesses freeze all the elements of the corporate function in their relationship to one another and to the overall objectives of the firm. From this total systems concept, companies learn that computers can accomplish much more than clerical and accounting jobs. Their capabilities can be tapped to perform the traditional applications (payroll processing, inventory control, accounts payable, and accounts receivable) as well as newer applications such as spotting deviations from planned programs (exception reporting), adjusting planning schedules, forecasting business trends, simulating market conditions, and solving production problems. Since the officer manage is a manager of information and each of these applications revolve around the processing of data, he must take an active role in studying and improving the system under his care.
   A. maintaining   B. inclusion   C. limited   D. visualize

4. In addition to the formal and acceptance theories of the source of authority, although perhaps more closely related to the latter, is the belief that authority is generated by personal qualifies of technical competence. Under this heading is the individual who has made, in effect, subordinates of others through sheer force of personality, and the engineer or economist who exerts influence by furnishing answers or sound advice. These may have no actual organizational authority, yet their advice may be so eagerly sought and so unerringly followed that it appears to carry the weight of an order. But, above all, one cannot discount the importance of formal authority with its institutional foundations. Buttressed by the qualities of leadership implicit in the acceptance theory, formal authority is basic to the managerial job. Once abrogated, it may be delegated or withheld, used or misused, and be effective in capable hands or be ineffective in inept hands.
   A. selected   B. delegation   C. limited   D. possessed

5. Since managerial operations in organization, staffing, directing, and controlling are designed to support the accomplishment of enterprise objectives, planning logically precedes the execution of all other managerial functions. Although all the functions intermesh in practice, planning is unique in that it establishes the objectives necessary for all group effort. Besides, plans must be made to accomplish these objectives before the manager knows what kind of organization relationships and personal qualifications are needed, along which course subordinates are to be directed, and what kind of control is to be applied. And, of course, each of the other managerial functions must be planned if they are to be effective.

Planning and control are inseparable—the Siamese twins of management. Unplanned action cannot be controlled, for control involves keeping activities on course by correcting deviations from plans. Any attempt to control without plans would be meaningless, since there are no way anyone can tell whether he is going where he wants to go—the task of control—unless first he knows where he wants to go—the task of planning. Plans thus preclude the standards of control.
    A. coordinating   B. individual   C. furnish   D. follow

Questions 6-7.

DIRECTIONS: Questions 6 and 7 are to be answered SOLELY on the basis of information given in the following paragraph.

In-basket tests are often used to assess managerial potential. The exercise consists of a set of papers that would be likely to be found in the in-basket of an administrator or manager at any given time, and requires the individuals participating in the examination to indicate how they would dispose of each item found in the in-basket. In order to handle the in-basket effectively, they must successfully manage their time, refer and assign some work to subordinates, juggle potentially conflicting appointments and meetings, and arrange for follow-up of problems generated by the items in the in-basket. In other words, the in-basket test is attempting to evaluate the participants' abilities to organize their work, set priorities, delegate control, and make decisions.

6.   According to the above paragraph, to succeed in an in-basket test, an administrator must
    A. be able to read very quickly
    B. have a great deal of technical knowledge
    C. know when to delegate work
    D. arrange a lot of appointments and meetings

7.   According to the above paragraph, all of the following abilities are indications of managerial potential EXCEPT the ability to
    A. organize and control   B. manage time
    C. write effective reports   D. make appropriate decisions

Questions 8-9.

DIRECTIONS: Questions 8 and 9 are to be answered SOLELY on the basis of information given in the following paragraph.

One of the biggest mistakes of government executives with substantial supervisory responsibility is failing to make careful appraisals of performance during employee probationary periods. Many a later headache could have been avoided by prompt and full appraisal during the early months of an employee's assignment. There is not much more to say about this except to emphasize the common prevalence of this oversight, and to underscore that for its consequences, which are many and sad, the offending managers have no one to blame but themselves.

8. According to the above paragraph, probationary periods are
   A. a mistake, and should not be used by supervisors with large responsibilities
   B. not used properly by government executives
   C. used only for those with supervisory responsibility
   D. the consequences of management mistakes

8.____

9. The one of the following conclusions that can MOST appropriately be drawn from the above paragraph is that
   A. management's failure to appraise employees during their probationary period is a common occurrence
   B. there is not much to say about probationary periods, because they are unimportant
   C. managers should blame employees for failing to use their probationary periods properly
   D. probationary periods are a headache to most managers

9.____

Questions 10-12.

DIRECTIONS: Questions 11 and 12 are to be answered SOLELY on the basis of the information given in the following paragraph.

The common sense character of the merit system seems so natural to most Americans that many people wonder why it should ever have been inoperative. After all, the American economic system, the most phenomenal the world has ever known, is also founded on a rugged selective process which emphasizes the personal qualities of capacity, industriousness, and productivity. The criteria may not have always been appropriate and competition has not always been fair, but competition there was, and the responsibilities and the rewards—with exceptions, of course—have gone to those who could measure up in terms of intelligence, knowledge, or perseverance. This has been true not only in the economic area, in the money-making process, but also in achievement in the professions and other walks of life.

10. According to the above paragraph, economic awards in the United States have
    A. always been based on appropriate, fair criteria
    B. only recently been based on a competitive system
    C. not gone to people who compete too ruggedly
    D. usually gone to those people with intelligence, knowledge, and perseverance

10.____

11. According to the above paragraph, a merit system is
    A. an unfair criterion on which to base rewards
    B. unnatural to anyone who is not American
    C. based only on common sense
    D. based on the same principles as the American economic system

11.____

12. According to the above paragraph, it is MOST accurate to say that   12.____
    A. the United States has always had a civil service merit system
    B. civil service employees are very rugged
    C. the American economic system has always been based on a merit objective
    D. competition is unique to the American way of life

Questions 13-15.

DIRECTIONS: The management study of employee absence due to sickness is an effective tool in planning. Questions 13 through 15 are to be answered SOLELY on the data given below.

Number of Days Absent Per Worker (Sickness)	1	2	3	4	5	6	7	8 or Over
Number of Workers	76	23	6	3	1	0	1	0
Total Number of Workers	400							
Period Covered	January 1 – December 31							

13. The total number of man-days lost due to illness was   13.____
    A. 110   B. 137   C. 144   D. 164

14. What percent of the workers had 4 or more days absence due to sickness?   14.____
    A. .25%   B. 2.5%   C. 1.25%   D. 12.5%

15. Of the 400 workers studied, the number who lost no days due to sickness was   15.____
    A. 190   B. 236   C. 290   D. 346

Questions 16-18.

DIRECTIONS: In the graph below, the lines labeled "A" and "B" represent the cumulative progress in the work of two file clerks, each of whom was given 500 consecutively numbered applications to file in the proper cabinets over a five-day work week. Questions 16 through 18 are to be answered SOLELY upon the data provided in the graph.

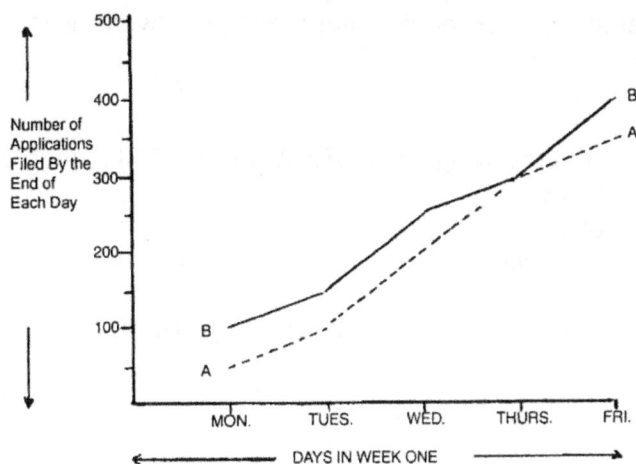

16. The day during which the LARGEST number of applications was filed by both clerks was
    A. Monday   B. Tuesday   C. Wednesday   D. Friday

17. At the end of the second day, the percentage of applications STILL to be filed was
    A. 25%   B. 50%   C. 66%   D. 75%

18. Assuming that the production pattern is the same the following week as the week shown in the chart, the day on which the file clerks will FINISH this assignment will be
    A. Monday   B. Tuesday   C. Wednesday   D. Friday

Questions 19-21.

DIRECTIONS: The following chart shows the differences between the rates of production of employees in Department D in 2009 and 2019. Questions 19 through 21 are to be answered SOLELY on the basis of the information given in the chart.

Number of Employees Producing Work-Units Within Range in 2009	Number of Work-Units Produced	Number of Employees Producing Work-Units Within Range in 2019
7	500 – 1000	4
14	1001 – 1500	11
26	1501 – 2000	28
22	2001 – 2500	36
17	2501 – 3000	39
10	3001 – 3500	23
4	3501 - 4000	9

19. Assuming that within each range of work-units produced the average production was at the mid-point at that range (e.g., category 500 – 1000 = 750), then the AVERAGE number of work-units produced per employee in 2009 fell into the range
    A. 1001 – 1500   B. 1501 – 2000   C. 2001 – 2500   D. 2501 – 3000

20. The ratio of the number of employees producing more than 2000 work-units in 2009 to the number of employees producing more than 2000 work-units in 2019 is MOST NEARLY
    A. 1:2   B. 2:3   C. 3:4   D. 4:5

21. In Department D, which of the following were GREATER in 2019 than in 2009?
    I.   Total number of employees
    II. Total number of work-units produced
    III. Number of employees producing 2000 or fewer work-units
    The CORRECT answer is
    A. I, II, III   B. I, II   C. I, III   D. II, III

22. Unit S's production fluctuated substantially from one year to another. In 2018, Unit S's production was 100% greater than in 2017. In 2019, production decreased by 25% from 2018. In 2020, Unit S's production was 10% greater than in 2019.
On the basis of this information, it is CORRECT to conclude that Unit S's production in 2020 exceeded Unit S's production in 2017 by
 A. 65% B. 85% C. 95% D. 135%

22.____

23. Agency "X" is moving into a new building. It has 1500 employees presently on its staff and does not contemplate much variance from this level. The new building contains 100 available offices, each with a maximum capacity of 30 employees. It has been decided that only 2/3 of the maximum capacity of each office will be utilized.
The TOTAL number of offices that will be occupied by Agency "X" is
 A. 30 B. 66 C. 75 D. 90

23.____

24. One typist completes a form letter every 5 minutes and another typist completes one every 6 minutes.
If the two typists start together, they will again start typing new letters simultaneously _____ minutes later and will have completed _____ letters by that time.
 A. 11; 30 B. 12; 24 C. 24; 12 D. 30; 11

24.____

25. During one week, a machine operator produces 10 fewer pages per hour of work than he usually does.
If it ordinarily takes him six hours to produce a 300-page report, it will take him _____ hours longer to produce that same 300-page report during the week when he produces more slowly.
 A. 1½ B. 1²/₃ C. 2 D. 2¾

25.____

KEY (CORRECT ANSWERS)

		Incorrect Words
1.	A	stability
2.	D	obsolete
3.	D	freeze
4.	D	abrogated
5.	C	preclude

6.	C	16.	C
7.	C	17.	D
8.	B	18.	B
9.	A	19.	C
10.	D	20.	A
11.	D	21.	B
12	C	22.	A
13.	D	23.	C
14.	C	24.	D
15.	C	25.	A

ENGLISH EXPRESSION
CHANGE IN CONSTRUCTION

COMMENTARY

A searching type of multiple-choice question requires the candidate to revise a sentence according to the directions provided for that sentence and choose the word or phrase that will appear in the best revision.

Fundamentally, this question attempts to measure the candidate's ability to re-write or to manipulate a sentence or statement with grammatical correctness, felicity of expression, flexibility in construction, and facility of substitution.

This is actually a subtle method of employing the multiple-choice question to achieve the evaluations ordinarily directly obtained through the traditional essay-writing question.

SAMPLE QUESTIONS

DIRECTIONS: In questions 1 and 2, you are given a complete sentence which you are to rewrite in your mind, starting with the words given just below it.

Make whatever changes the new sentence plan requires, but no others; do not change the overall meaning of the sentence.

Note that you are not correcting a mistake in the original sentence; you are simply changing the construction. The revised sentence should be grammatically correct, but it need not necessarily be a better way of expressing the meaning.

There may be more than one way of recasting the sentence but only one will enable you to answer the question.

Read the directions for each question carefully. They may specify that the missing word or expression appear somewhere in the rewritten sentence; they may ask for the next word in the rewritten sentence, the word following a specific word, etc.

1. Most people acquire about 75 percent of what they learn through the sense of sight.
   REWRITTEN: About 75 percent ....
   Somewhere in the part of the rewritten sentence indicated by dots is the word

   A. them   B. acquired   C. a   D. learning   E. study

   ACCEPTABLY REWRITTEN, the above sentence would read:
   About 75 percent of what most people learn is acquired through the sense of sight.
   You would, therefore, mark B on your answer sheet.

2. Various studies show that a great amount of the absenteeism in factories is caused by preventable accidents.
   REWRITTEN: According to various studies, preventable accidents ...
   The NEXT WORDS in the rewritten sentence are

   A. result from   B. could be   C. are caused by
   D. are related to   E. account for

   ACCEPTABLY REWRITTEN, the above sentence would read:
   According to various studies, preventable accidents account for the great amount of absenteeism in factories.
   You would, therefore, mark E on your answer sheet.

EXAMINATION SECTION
TEST 1

DIRECTIONS: In the following questions, you are given a complete sentence which you are to rewrite in your mind, starting with the words given just below it. Make whatever changes the new sentence plan requires, but no others; do not change the overall meaning of the sentence.

Note that you are not correcting a mistake in the original sentence; you are simply changing the construction. The revised sentence should be grammatically correct, but it need not necessarily be a better way of expressing the meaning. There may be more than one way of recasting the sentence but only one will enable you to answer the question.

Read the directions for each question carefully. They may specify that the missing word or expression appear somewhere in the rewritten sentence; they may ask for the next word in the rewritten sentence, the word following a specific word, etc.

1. As a literary genre, the messianic drama falls into the category of myth or romance, for its central figure conforms to the definitions supplied by Northrup Frye, in THE ANATOMY OF CRITICISM, of the mythic hero.
   REWRITTEN:
     Because its central figure conforms to the definitions of the mythic hero supplied by Northrup Frye, in THE ANATOMY OF CRITICISM, the messianic drama is ....
   The *NEXT* word in the rewritten sentence is

   A. into B. literary C. categorized
   D. categorically E. a

2. In THE EMPEROR JULIAN, the second part of the drama, Ibsen reveals Julian to be a false Messiah.
   REWRITTEN:
     Julian is .....
   Somewhere in the part of the rewritten sentence indicated by dots is the word

   A. reveals B. by C. falsified
   D. in which E. messianic

3. More interesting, because more subtly hidden, is Chekhov's use of melodrama.
   REWRITTEN:
     Because it is more .....
   The *NEXT* word in the rewritten sentence is

   A. subtly B. interesting C. melodramatic
   D. used E. hidden

4. Shaw's response to this is to withdraw, partially, from his public concerns into a more personal, private, and poetic form of expression.
   REWRITTEN:
     Shaw responded to this with a .... .
   Somewhere in the part of the rewritten sentence indicated by dots is the word

   A. partially B. is to C. withdraws
   D. publicly E. withdrawal

5. But life draws him back again, against his will, in the form of uncontrollable instinct.
   REWRITTEN:
   He is ...
   The *NEXT* word in the rewritten sentence is

   A. uncontrollable
   B. instinctive
   C. back
   D. drawn
   E. willful

6. Such destructive criticism accounts, in part, for the unpopularity of this drama, for the modern world wants affirmations.
   REWRITTEN:
   This drama is ....
   The *NEXT* word in the rewritten sentence is

   A. unpopular
   B. accounted
   C. criticized
   D. in part
   E. destructive

7. Shaw is just as unable to accept the concept of a malevolent or determined man as to accept the concept of a determined and mindless universe.
   REWRITTEN:
   It is equally difficult ...
   Somewhere in the part of the rewritten sentence indicated by dots is (are) the word(s)

   A. unable
   B. for him
   C. just
   D. to conceive
   E. to understand

8. We know from his descriptions that Leeuwenhoek saw both plant and animal microorganisms and that among them may have been some bacteria.
   REWRITTEN:
   Among the plant and animal microorganisms which we ...
   The *NEXT* word in the rewritten sentence is

   A. saw
   B. described
   C. know
   D. assume
   E. discovered

9. The Japanese quickly overcame the Russian fleet and then landed troops on the mainland of Asia.
   REWRITTEN:
   The Russian fleet .. .
   Somewhere in the part of the rewritten sentence indicated by dots is(are) the word(s)

   A. overcame
   B. and then
   C. defeated
   D. retreated
   E. who

10. Napoleon would not tolerate such an arrangement and sent an army of twenty thousand men to suppress the movement.
    REWRITTEN:
    The movement .....
    The *NEXT* word in the rewritten sentence is

    A. was
    B. suppressed
    C. would
    D. sent
    E. of

11. To have the program succeed, Marx realized he would need the united support of workingmen all over the world.
    REWRITTEN:
    Marx realized that the success .....
    Somewhere in the part of the rewritten sentence indicated by dots is the word

    A. he			B. would		C. have
    D. required		E. to

12. His beautiful descriptions of nature reflect the poet's deep belief in the closeness of nature to the human soul.
    REWRITTEN:
    One reflection of .....
    The NEXT word(s) in the rewritten sentence is(are)

    A. beauty			B. the poet's		C. poetry
    D. the descriptions	E. closeness

13. The extraordinary play is a chronicle of O'Neill's own spiritual metamorphosis from a messianic into an existential rebel.
    REWRITTEN:
    O'Neill had undergone .....
    The NEXT word in the rewritten sentence is

    A. extraordinary		B. existentialism	C. rebelliousness
    D. spirituality		E. a

14. Considering its great influence, Europe is surprisingly small.
    REWRITTEN:
    The smallness of Europe is surprising when one ...
    The NEXT word in the rewritten sentence is

    A. influences		B. is			C. considers
    D. knows			E. consideration

15. Until late in the 1800's we knew nothing of a remarkable civilization which was old when the Greeks arrived.
    REWRITTEN:
    One remarkable civilization which was old when the Greeks arrived .....
    Somewhere in the part of the rewritten sentence indicated by dots is the word

    A. we			B. unknown		C. knew
    D. nothing		E. of

16. Our knowledge of Aegean civilization comes largely from the work of two men.
    REWRITTEN:
    The work of two men ....
    The NEXT word in the rewritten sentence is

    A. comes			B. teaches		C. acknowledges
    D. enhances		E. contributes

17. Twelve of the most important deities formed a council, which was supposed to meet on snowcapped Mount Olympus, in northern Thessaly.
    REWRITTEN:
    Mount Olympus, in northern Thessaly, was supposed to be the..........
    The NEXT word(s) in the rewritten sentence is (are)

    A. meeting place   B. council   C. most important
    D. epitome   E. deities

18. In the United States the states and local governments regulate the public schools and supply them with funds.
    REWRITTEN:
    Public schools in the United States are .....
    Somewhere in the part of the rewritten sentence indicated by dots is the word

    A. them   B. regulate   C. subsidized
    D. governed   E. supplied

19. The obstacle of distance was partly overcome by the invention of the steamship and the building of the Suez Canal.
    REWRITTEN:
    The invention of the steamship and the building of the Suez Canal helped
    Somewhere in the part of the rewritten sentence indicated by dots is the word

    A. was   B. overcoming   C. overcome
    D. partly   E. shorten

20. Although cotton has been used for cloth since ancient times, It was not known in England until the seventeenth century when the East India Company brought *calico* (named for Calicut) from India.
    REWRITTEN:
    When the East India Company brought *calico* (named for Calicut) from India in the seventeenth century, it was England's first .....
    Somewhere in the part of the rewritten sentence indicated by dots is the word

    A. known   B. knowledge   C. was
    D. although   E. until

21. In the eighteenth century weaving was still done on the hand loom.
    REWRITTEN:
    The hand loom .....
    Somewhere in the part of the rewritten sentence indicated by dots is the word

    A. done   B. on   C. for
    D. remained   E. weaves

22. When rubbed with wool, amber accumulates a charge of static electricity and will then attract small pieces of pith or paper.
    REWRITTEN:
    Small pieces of pith or paper can .....
    The NEXT word in the rewritten sentence is

    A. accumulate   B. be   C. attract
    D. charge   E. then

23. As a result of the Second World War, cities were devastated and millions were left homeless.
    REWRITTEN:
    The Second World War resulted .....
    Somewhere in the part of the rewritten sentence indicated by dots is the word

    A. leaving   B. devastating   C. were
    D. deprivation   E. devastated

24. With the growing urbanization and mechanization of modern life has come increasing recognition of the evils of drunkenness.
    REWRITTEN:
    The evils of drunkenness have become .....
    Somewhere in the part of the rewritten sentence indicated by dots is the word

    A. recognition   B. recognized   C. come
    D. increasing   E. increased

25. Chekhov dilutes the melodramatic pathos by qualifying our sympathy for the victims.
    REWRITTEN:
    The result of Chekhov's .....
    The NEXT word in the rewritten sentence is

    A. dilution   B. diluting   C. melodramatic
    D. qualification E. qualifying

KEYS (CORRECT ANSWERS)

1. C   11. D
2. B   12. B
3. A   13. E
4. E   14. C
5. D   15. B

6. A   16. E
7. B   17. A
8. C   18. E
9. E   19. C
10. A   20. D

21. C
22. B
23. A
24. B
25. E

6 (#1)

ACCEPTABLY REWRITTEN

1. Because its central figure conforms to the definitions of the mythic hero supplied by Northrup Frye, in THE ANATOMY OF CRITICISM, the messianic drama is <u>categorized</u> in the literary genre of myth or romance.

2. Julian is revealed <u>by</u> Ibsen to be a false Messiah, in THE EMPEROR JULIAN, the second part of the drama.

3. Because it is more <u>subtly</u> hidden, Chekhov's use of melodrama is more interesting.

4. Shaw responded to this with a partial <u>withdrawal</u> from his public concerns into a more personal, private, and, poetic form of expression.

5. He is <u>drawn</u> back again by life, against his will, in the form of uncontrollable instinct.

6. This drama is <u>unpopular</u> partly because it receives such destructive criticism when the modern world wants affirmations.

7. It is equally difficult for Shaw to accept the concept of a malevolent or determined man as it is <u>for him</u> to accept the concept of a determined and mindless universe.

8. Among the plant and animal microrganisms which we <u>know</u> that Leewen-hoek saw because of his descriptions, there may have been some bacteria.

9. The Russian fleet was quickly overcome by the Japanese <u>who</u> then landed troops on the mainland of Asia.

10. The movement <u>was</u> suppressed by an army of twenty thousand men sent by Napoleon who would not tolerate such an arrangement.

11. Marx realized that the success of the program <u>required</u> the united support of workingmen all over the world.

12. One reflection of <u>the poet's</u> deep belief in the closeness of nature to the human soul can be found in his beautiful descriptions of nature.

13. O'Neill had undergone <u>a</u> spiritual metamorphosis from a messianic into an existential rebel, of which this play is an extraordinary chronicle.

14. The smallness of Europe is surprising when one <u>considers</u> its great influence.

15. One remarkable civilization which was old when the Greeks arrived was <u>unknown</u> to us until late in the 1800's.

16. The work of two men <u>contributes</u> largely to our knowledge of Aegean civilization.

17. Snowcapped Mount Olympus, in northern Thessaly, was supposed to be the <u>meeting place</u> for a council formed by twelve of the most important deities.

18. Public schools in the United States are regulated and <u>supplied</u> with funds by the states and local government.

19. The invention of the steamship and the building of the Suez Canal helped to <u>overcome</u> the obstacle of distance.

20. When the East India Company brought *calico* (named for Calicut) from India in the seventeenth century, it was England's first introduction to cotton, <u>although</u> it has been used for cloth since ancient times.

21. The hand loom was still used <u>for</u> weaving in the eighteenth century.

22. Small pieces of pith or paper can <u>be</u> attracted by amber if it has been rubbed with wool to accumulate a charge of static electricity.

23. The Second World War resulted in the devastation of cities and the <u>leaving</u> homeless of millions.

24. The evils of drunkenness have become increasingly <u>recognized</u> with the growing urbanization and mechanization of modern life.

25. The result of Chekhov's <u>qualifying</u> our sympathy for the victims is the dilution of the melodramatic pathos.

TEST 2

1. While gazing through his microscope at a drop of water, he saw many kinds of creatures with one or a few cells, which wriggled about and devoured food.
   BEGIN THE SENTENCE WITH
      Many kinds of creatures with one or a few cells wriggling about .....
   Somewhere in the part of the rewritten sentence indicated by dots is (are) the word(s)

      A. he saw   B. and devoured   C. which
      D. by him   E. while gazing

2. The worship of ancestors in China must have arisen in prehistoric times, judging from the reference to it in the most ancient Chinese literature.
   SUBSTITUTE
      ....since the most ancient Chinese literature for judging ...
   The NEXT words in the rewritten sentence are

      A. the references   B. is judged   C. refers it
      D. refers to   E. from the

3. She divided the bread among them, without considering a share for herself.
   BEGIN THE SENTENCE WITH
      She did not .....
   Somewhere in the part of the rewritten sentence indicated by dots is(are) the word(s)

      A. divided   B. when she   C. without
      D. considering   E. dividing

4. Since Smith has been a resident here for twenty years, we should give serious consideration to his suggestions.
   SUBSTITUTE
      ... seriously for give serious
   THE NEXT WORD(S) IN THE REWRITTEN SENTENCE IS (ARE)

      A. to   B. consideration   C. consider
      D. give consideration   E. would

5. In the fight for women's suffrage one judge's decision had little effect, for the most part, upon the ladies' determination.
   CHANGE
      ...effect to effected
   Somewhere in the part of the rewritten sentence indicated by dots is (are) the word(s)

      A. had   B. upon   C. part, upon
      D. had, for   E. part, very little

6. His approach to the committee was certainly not conducive to a cordial reception of his proposals, which were, at best, of doubtful validity.
   BEGIN THE SENTENCE WITH
      He approached .....
   Somewhere in the part of the rewritten sentence Indicated by dots is(are) the word(s)

      A. was certainly   B. which was   C. to the
      D. his   E. committee was

7. When the thirsty horse had drunk its fill, it trotted briskly down the road.
BEGIN THE SENTENCE WITH
   The thirsty horse ......
The NEXT word(s) in the rewritten sentence is (are)

   A. having   B. it trotted   C. when
   D. had   E. had trotted

8. This country must either set up flood controls or be prepared to lose billions of dollars annually.
BEGIN THE SENTENCE WITH
   If......
Somewhere in the part of the rewritten sentence indicated by dots is (are) the word(s)

   A. either   B. must set   C. does not
   D. or   E. country must

9. They are not in Boston now, but I think they're going to that city next week.
BEGIN THE SENTENCE WITH
   I think .....
Somewhere in the part of the rewritten sentence indicated by dots is (are) the word(s)

   A. but I   B. in Boston   C. to Boston
   D. to that   E. now, but

10. Mt.Kinley, in Alaska, is higher than any other mountain in North America.
INSERT THE WORD
   the after is .....
The NEXT word in the rewritten sentence is

   A. highest   B. other   C. any
   D. than   E. higher

11. As a result of the Industrial Revolution, cities grew very rapidly and the demand for food and raw materials increased.
BEGIN THE SENTENCE WITH
   A result .....
Somewhere in the part of the rewritten sentence indicated by dots is (are) the word(s)

   A. grew   B. rapidly   C. the demand
   D. materials increased   E. increased demand

12. Since the late eighteenth century, when the American and French revolutions took place, democracy has had a slow but persistent growth.
SUBSTITUTE
   After for Since .....
Somewhere in the part of the rewritten sentence indicated by dots is (are) the word(s)

   A. slow   B. has had   C. persistently
   D. growth   E. slow but persistent

13. The Treaty of Versailles placed the entire blame for World War I on Germany and her allies.
BEGIN THE SENTENCE WITH
   Germany......
Somewhere in the part of the rewritten sentence indicated by dots is the word

| A. placed | B. on | C. blame |
| D. were | E. entire | |

14. A few years after Harvey's death, other scientists began to study the blood vessels with the aid of microscopes.
    BEGIN THE SENTENCE WITH
    　　Blood vessels .....
    Somewhere in the part of the rewritten sentence indicated by dots is (are) the word(s)

    | A. by | B. began | C. study |
    | D. to | E. the study | |

15. This pamphlet is in response to requests of various groups for a more permanent and usable form of this material.
    BEGIN THE SENTENCE WITH
    　　To provide .....
    Somewhere in the part of the rewritten sentence indicated by dots is (are) the word(s)

    | A. responding to | B. as a response to | C. requested |
    | D. in response to | E. requesting | |

16. The space science events chosen for development illustrate types of experiences in which mathematics and science have a mutually enhancing effect on each other.
    SUBSTITUTE
    　　...are illustrated by for illustrate...
    Somewhere in the part of the rewritten sentence indicated by dots is(are) the word(s)

    | A. have had | B. have | C. had had |
    | D. may be shown to have | E. has | |

17. The criteria will be useful throughout the course in setting up specific objectives, providing learning experiences, and making periodic evaluations.
    SUBSTITUTE
    　　Use the criteria throughout the course for The criteria will be useful throughout the course ...
    The NEXT word in the rewritten sentence is

    | A. in | B. for | C. to | D. with | E. by |

18. The objectives of a training program are achieved by learning experiences designed to help the trainees develop those behaviors and abilities designated in the objectives.
    BEGIN THE SENTENCE WITH
    　　To achieve .....
    Somewhere in the part of the rewritten sentence indicated by dots is (are) the word(s)

    | A. employ | B. to use | C. it will be useful |
    | D. create | E. to create | |

19. Because all of the suggested facilities will not be available in every community, it remains for the teacher to modify or supplement the following suggestions.
    BEGIN THE SENTENCE WITH
    　　The teacher .....
    The word that occurs IMMEDIATELY before the word *modify*, is

    | A. could | B. might | C. would | D. must | E. should |

20. Although teachers differ in their ways or organizing and coordinating important parts of their presentations, they agree that the purpose of a lesson is effective and meaningful classroom instruction.
    BEGIN THE SENTENCE WITH
        Although teachers agree .....
    The FIRST word of the main clause in the rewritten sentence is

    A. the   B. teachers   C. they   D. differing   E. it

21. Many common physical quantities such as temperature, the speed of a moving object, or the displacement of a ship can be expressed as a certain number of units.
    BEGIN THE SENTENCE WITH
        One can express .....
    The NEXT word(s) in the rewritten sentence is (are)

    A. as   B. many   C. in   D. a ship's   E. the

22. A parallel-tuned circuit, on the other hand, offers a very high impedance to currents of its natural, or resonant, frequency and a relatively low impedance to others.
    BEGIN THE SENTENCE WITH
        A very high impedance .....
    The NEXT words in the rewritten sentence are

    A. is offered to   B. offers to   C. is offered for
    D. is offered by   E. on the other hand

23. As the term implies, a voltage feedback amplifier transfers a voltage from the output of the amplifier back to its input.
    CHANGE
        ... transfers to is transferred ...
    The FIRST words of the rewritten sentence are

    A. A voltage
    B. Back to its input
    C. A voltage feedback amplifier
    D. In accordance with the term
    E. From the output

24. Unemployment among youth is a serious problem now, and unless the economy grows much more rapidly in the future than it has during the past decade, today's youngsters will feel the sharp pinch of declining ratios of new employment opportunities to persons seeking work.
    BEGIN THE SENTENCE WITH
        Unless the economy grows, ...
    The LAST CLAUSE in the rewritten sentence begins with

    A. today's   B. unemployment   C. and unless
    D. now   E. since

25. In a great society, talents are evoked and realized, creative minds probe the frontiers of knowledge, expectations of excellence are widely shared.
    BEGIN THE SENTENCE WITH
        A great society .....
    The NEXT words in the rewritten sentence are

A. evokes and realizes
B. talents, creative minds, and expectations of excellence
C. features
D. is characterized by
E. is one in which

KEYS (CORRECT ANSWERS)

1.	D	11.	E
2.	D	12.	C
3.	B	13.	D
4.	C	14.	A
5.	E	15.	D
6.	B	16.	B
7.	A	17.	C
8.	C	18.	A
9.	C	19.	E
10.	A	20.	C

21. A
22. E
23. A
24. E
25. E

ACCEPTABLY REWRITTEN

1. Many kinds of creatures with one or a few cells, wriggling about and devouring food, were seen <u>by him</u> while he was gazing through his microscope at a drop of water.

2. The worship of ancestors in China must have arisen in prehistoric times since the most ancient Chinese literature <u>refers to</u> it.

3. She did not consider a share for herself <u>when she</u> divided the bread among them.

4. Since Smith has been a resident here for twenty years, we should seriously <u>consider</u> his suggestions.

5. In the fight for women's suffrage one judge's decision affected the ladies' decision, for the most <u>part, very little.</u>

6. He approached the committee in a way which was certainly not conducive to a cordial reception of his proposals, which were, at best, of doubtful validity.

7. The thirsty horse, having drunk its fill, trotted briskly down the road.

8. If this country does not set up flood controls, it must be prepared to lose billions of dollars annually.

9. I think they're going to Boston next week, though they're not in that city now.

10. Mt.Kinley, in Alaska, is the highest mountain in North America.

11. A result of the Industrial Revolution was the very rapid growth of cities and the increased-demand for food and raw materials.

12. After the late eighteenth century, when the American and French revolutions took place, democracy grew slowly, but persistently.

13. Germany and her allies were blamed entirely for World War I by the Treaty of Versailles.

14. Blood vessels were studied by other scientists, with the aid of microscopes, a few years after Harvey's death.

15. To provide a more permanent and usable form of this material, in response to the requests of various groups, this pamphlet has been written.

16. The space science events chosen for development are illustrated by types of experiences in which mathematics and science have a mutually enhancing effect on each other.

17. Use the criteria throughout the course to set up specific objectives, provide learning experiences, and make periodic evaluations.

18. To achieve the objectives of a training program employ learning experiences designed to help the trainees develop those behaviors and abilities designated in the objectives.

19. The teacher should modify or supplement the following suggestions because all of the suggested facilities will not be available in every community.

20. Although teachers agree that the purpose of a lesson is effective and meaningful classroom instruction, they differ in their ways of organizing and coordinating important parts of their presentations.

21. One can express as a certain number of units many common physical quantities such as temperature, the speed of a moving object, or the displacement of a ship.

22. A very high impedance, on the other hand, is offered by a parallel-tuned circuit to currents of its natural, or resonant, frequency and a relatively low impedance to others.

23. A voltage is transferred from the output of the amplifier back to its input by a voltage feedback amplifier, as its name implies.

24. Unless the economy grows much more rapidly in the future than it has during the past decade, today's youngsters will feel the sharp pinch of declining ratios of new employment opportunities to persons seeking work <u>since</u> unemployment among youth is a serious problem now.

25. A great society <u>is one in which</u> talents are evoked and realized, creative minds probe the frontiers of knowledge, expectations of excellence are widely shared.

EXAMINATION SECTION

TEST 1

DIRECTIONS: Each question or incomplete statement is followed by several suggested answers or completions. Select the one that BEST answers the question or completes the statement. *PRINT THE LETTER OF THE CORRECT ANSWER IN THE SPACE AT THE RIGHT.*

1. Which of the following fractions is the SMALLEST?
   A. 2/3   B. 4/5   C. 5/7   D. 5/11

2. 40% is equivalent to which of the following?
   A. 4/5   B. 4/6   C. 2/5   D. 4/100

3. How many 100's are in 10,000?
   A. 10   B. 100   C. 10,000   D. 100,000

4. $\frac{6}{7} + \frac{11}{12}$ is approximately
   A. 1   B. 2   C. 17   D. 19

5. The time required to heat water to a certain temperature is directly proportional to the volume of water being heated.
   If it takes 12 minutes to heat 1 ½ gallons of water, how many minutes will it take to heat 2 gallons of water?
   A. 12   B. 16   C. 18   D. 24

6. The cost of an item increased by 25%.
   If the original cost was C dollars, identify the expression which gives the new cost of that item.
   A. C + 0.25   B. 1/4 C   C. 25C   D. 1.25C

7. Given the formula PV = nRT, all of the following are true EXCEPT
   A. T = PV/nR   B. P = nRTN   C. V = P/nRT   D. n = PV/RT

8. If a Fahrenheit (F) temperature reading is 104, find its Celsius (C) equivalent, given that C = i(F-32).
   A. 36   B. 40   C. 72   D. 76

9. If 40% of a graduating class plans to go directly to work after graduation, which of the following must be TRUE?
   A. Less than half of the class plans to go directly to work.
   B. Forty members of the class plan to enter the job market.
   C. Most of the class plans to go directly to work.
   D. Six in ten members of the class are expected not to graduate.

10. Given a multiple-choice test item which has 5 choices, what is the probability of guessing the correct answer if you know nothing about the item content?
    A. 5%   B. 10%   C. 20%   D. 25%

10._____

11.

S	T
0	80
5	75
10	65
15	50
20	30
25	5

Which graph BEST represents the data shown in the above table?

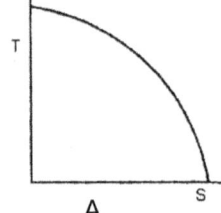
A

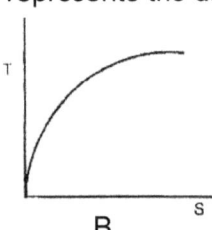
B

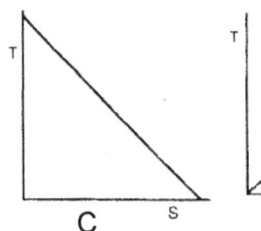
C

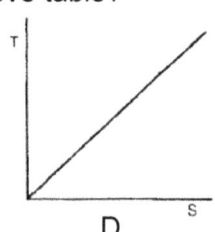
D

11._____

12. If 3(x+5y) = 24, find y when x = 3.
    A. 1   B. 3   C. 33/5   D. 7

12._____

13. The payroll of a grocery store for its 23 clerks is $395,421. Which expression below shows the average salary of a clerk?
    A. 395,421 × 23
    B. 23 ÷ 395,421
    C. (395,421 × 23
    D. 395,421 ÷ 23

13._____

14. If 12.8 pounds of coffee cost $50.80, what is the APPROXIMATE price per pound?
    A. $2.00   B. $3.00   C. $4.00   D. $5.00

14._____

15. A road map has a scale where 1 inch corresponds to 150 miles. A distance of 3 3/4 inches on the map corresponds to what actual distance? _____ miles.
    A. 153.75   B. 375   C. 525   D. 562.5

15._____

16. How many square feet of plywood are needed to construct the back and 4 adjacent sides of the box shown at the right?
    A. 63
    B. 90
    C. 96
    D. 126

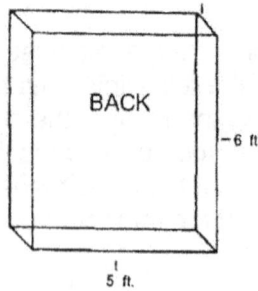

16._____

17. One thirty-pound bag of lawn fertilizer costs $20.00 and will cover 600 square feet of lawn. Terry's lawn is a 96 foot by 75 foot rectangle. How much will it cost Terry to buy enough bags of fertilizer for her lawn?
    Which of the following do you NOT need in order to solve this problem? The
    A. product of 96 and 75
    B. fact that one bag weighs 30 pounds
    C. fact that one bag covers 600 square feet
    D. fact that one bag costs $20.00

    17._____

18. On the graph shown at the right, between which hours was the drop in temperature GREATEST?
    A. 11:00 – Noon
    B. Noon – 1:00
    C. 1:00 – 2:00
    D. 2:00 – 3:00

    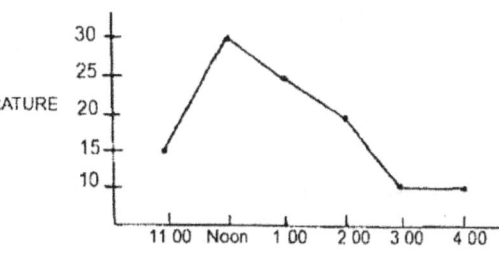

    18._____

19. If on a typical railroad track the distance from the center of one railroad tie to the next is 30 inches, approximately how many ties would be needed for one mile of track?
    A. 180   B. 2,110   C. 6,340   D. 63,360

    19._____

20. Which of the following is MOST likely to be the volume of a wine bottle?
    A. 750 milliliters   B. 7 kilograms
    C. 7 milligrams   D. 7 liters

    20._____

21. What is the reading on the gauge shown at the right?
    A. -7
    B. -3
    C. 1
    D. 3

    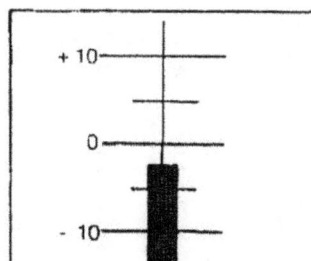

    21._____

22. Which statement below disproves the assertion, *All students in Mrs. Marino's 10th grade geometry class are planning to go to college?*
    A. Albert is in Mrs. Marino's class, but he is not planning to take mathematics next year.
    B. Jorge is not in Mrs. Marino's class, but he is still planning to go to college.
    C. Pierre is in Mrs. Marino's class but says he will not be attending school anymore after this year.
    D. Crystal is in Mrs. Marino's class and plans to attend Yale University when she graduates.

    22._____

23. A store advertisement reads, *Buy not while our prices are low. There will never be a better time to buy.*
    The customer reading this advertisement should assume that
    A. the prices at the store will probably never be lower
    B. right now, this store has the best prices in town
    C. prices are higher at other stores
    D. prices are always lowest at this store

24. *Given any positive integer, there is always a positive number B such that A × B is less than 1.*
    Which statement below supports this generalization?
    A. 8 × 1/16 = 1/2   B. 8 × 1/2 = 4
    C. 5/2 × 1/10 = 1/4   D. 1/2 × 1/2 = 1/2

25. Of the following expressions, which is equivalent to 4C + D = 12E?
    A. C = 4(12E-D)   B. 4 + D = 12E − C
    C. 4C + 12E = -D   D. $C = \frac{12E-D}{4}$

KEY (CORRECT ANSWERS)

1. D	11. A
2. C	12. A
3. B	13. D
4. B	14. C
5. B	15. D
6. D	16. C
7. C	17. B
8. B	18. D
9. A	19. B
10. C	20. A

21. B
22. C
23. A
24. A
25. D

SOLUTIONS TO PROBLEMS

1. Converting to decimals, we get $.\overline{6}$, .8, .714 (approx..), $.\overline{45}$. The smallest is $.\overline{45}$ corresponding to 5/11.

2. 40% = 40/100 = 2/5

3. 10,000 ÷ 100 = 100

4. $\frac{6}{7} + \frac{11}{12}$ = (72+77) ÷ 84 = $\frac{149}{84}$ ≈ 1.77 ≈ 2

5. Let x = required minutes. Then, 12/1 ½ = x². This reduces to 1 1/2x = 24. Solving, x = 16.

6. New cost is C + .25C = 1.25C

7. For PV = nRT, V = nRT/P

8. C = 5/9 (104-32) = 5/9(72) = 40

9. Since 40% is less than 50% (or half), we conclude that less than half of the class plans to go to work directly after graduation.

10. The probability of guessing right is 1/5 or 20%

11. Curve A is most accurate since as S increases, we see that T decreases. Note, however, that the relationship is NOT linear. Although S increases in equal amounts, the decrease in T is NOT in equal amounts.

12. 3(3+5y) = 24. This simplifies to 9 + 15y = 24. Solving, y = 1

13. The average salary is $395,421 ÷ 23

14. The price per pound is $50.80 ÷ 12.8 = $3,96875 or approximately $4.

15. Actual distance is (3 3/4)(150) = 562.5 miles.

16. The area of the back = (6)(5) = 30 sq. ft. The combined area of the two vertical sides is (2)(6)(3) = 36 sq. ft. The combined area of the horizontal sides is (2)(5)(3) = 30 sq. ft. Total area = 30 + 36 30 = 96 square feet.

17. Choice B is not relevant to solving the problem since the cost will be [(96)(75)/600][$20] = $240. So, the weight per bag is not needed.

18. For the graph, the largest temperature drop was from 2:00 P.M. to 3:00 P.M. The temperature dropped 20 – 10 = 10 degrees.

19. 1 mile = 5280 feet = 63,360 inches. Then, 63,360 ÷ 30 = 2112 or about 2110 ties are needed.

20. Since 1 liter = 1.06 quarts, 750 milliliters = (750/1000)(1.06) = .795 quarts. This is a reasonable volume for a wine bottle.

21. The reading is -3.

22. Statement C contradicts the given information, since Pierre is in Mrs. Marino's class. Then he should plan to go to college.

23. Since there will never be a better time to buy at this particular store, the customer can assume the current prices will probably never be lower.

24. Statement A illustrates this concept. Note that in general, if n is a positive integer. then $(n)(\frac{1}{n-1}) < 1$

25.

TEST 2

DIRECTIONS: Each question or incomplete statement is followed by several suggested answers or completions. Select the one that BEST answers the question or completes the statement. *PRINT THE LETTER OF THE CORRECT ANSWER IN THE SPACE AT THE RIGHT.*

1. Which of the following lists numbers in INCREASING order?
   A. 0.4, 0.04, 0.004
   B. 2.71, 3.15, 2.996
   C. 0.7, 0.77, 0.777
   D. 0.06, 0.5, 0.073

   1._____

2. $\frac{4}{10}+\frac{7}{100}+\frac{5}{1000} =$
   A. 4.75   B. 0.475   C. 0.0475   D. 0.00475

   2._____

3. 700 times what number equals 7?
   A. 10   B. 0.1   C. 0.01   D. 0.001

   3._____

4. 943-251 is approximately
   A. 600   B. 650   C. 700   D. 1200

   4._____

5. The time needed to set up a complicated piece of machinery is inversely proportional to the number of years' experience of the worker.
   If a worker with 10 years' experience needs 6 hours to do the job, how long will it take a worker with 15 years' experience?
   A. 4   B. 5   C. 9   D. 25

   5._____

6. Let W represent the number of waiters and D, the number of diners in a particular restaurant.
   Identify the expression which represents the statement: There are 10 times as many diners as waiters.
   A. 10W = D   B. 10D = W   C. 10D + 10W   D. 10 = D + W

   6._____

7. Which of the following is equivalent to the formula F = XC + Y?
   A. F − C = X + Y
   B. Y = F + XC
   C. $C = \frac{FY}{X}$
   D. $C = \frac{FX}{Y}$

   7._____

8. Given the formula A = BC/D, if A = 12, B = 6, and D = 3, what is the value of C?
   A. 2/3   B. 6   C. 18   D. 24

   8._____

9. 5 is to 7 as X is to 35. X =
   A. 7   B. 12   C. 24   D. 49

   9._____

10. Kramer Middle School has 5 seventh grade mathematics teachers: two of the math teachers are women and three are men.
    If you are assigned a teacher at random, what is the probability of getting a female teacher?
    A. 0.2   B. 0.4   C. 0.6   D. 0.8

    10._____

11. Which statement BEST describes the graph shown at the right?
    Temperature
    A. and time decrease at the same rate
    B. and time increase at the same rate
    C. increases over time
    D. decreases over time

11.____

12. If $3x + 4 = 22y$, find y when $x = 2$.
    A. 0   B. 3   C. 4 1/2   D. 5

12.____

13. A car goes 243 miles on 8.7 gallons of gas.
    Which numeric expression should be used to determine the car's miles per gallon?
    A. 243 × 87   B. 8.7 ÷ 243   C. 243 ÷ 8.7   D. 243 − 8.7

13.____

14. What is the average cost per book if you buy six books at $4.00 each and four books at $5.00 each?
    A. $4.40   B. $4.50   C. $4.60   D. $5.40

14.____

15. A publisher's sale offers a 15% discount to anyone buying more than 100 workbooks.
    What will be the discount on 200 workbooks selling at $2.25 each?
    A. $15.00   B. $30.00   C. $33.75   D. $67.50

15.____

16. A road crew erects 125 meters of fencing in one workday.
    How many workdays are required to erect a kilometer of fencing?
    A. 0.8   B. 8   C. 80   D. 800

16.____

17. Last month Kim made several telephone calls to New York City totaling 45 minutes in all.
    What does Kim need in order to calculate the average duration of her New York City calls?
    The
    A. total number of calls she made to New York City
    B. cost per minute of a call to New York City
    C. total cost of her telephone bill last month
    D. days of the week on which the calls are made

17.____

18.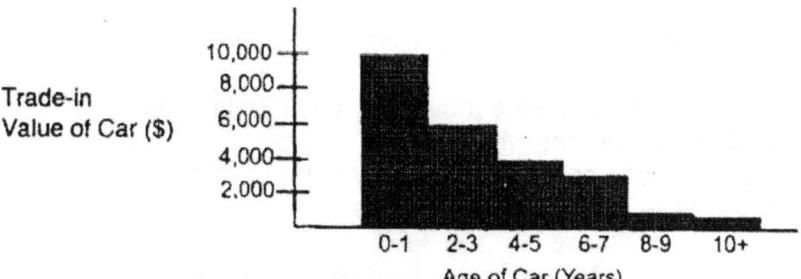

The above chart relates a car's age to its trade-in value.
Based on the chart, which of the following is TRUE?
A. A 4- to 5-year old car has a trade-in value of about $2,000
B. The trade-in vale of an 8- to 9-year old car is about 1/3 that of a 2- to 3-year old car.
C. A 6- to 7-year old car has no trade-in value.
D. A 4- to 5-year old car's trade-in value is about $2,000 less than that of a 2- to 3-year old car.

19. Which of the following expressions could be used to determine how many seconds are in a 24-hour day?
A. 60 × 60 × 24
B. 60 × 12 × 24
C. 60 × 2 × 24
D. 60 × 24

20. For measuring milk, we could use each of the following EXCEPT
A. liters
B. kilograms
C. millimeters
D. cubic centimeters

21. What is the reading on the gauge shown at the right?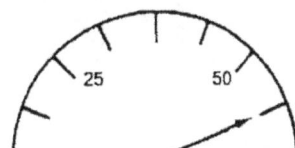
A. 51
B. 60
C. 62.5
D. 70

22. Bill is taller than Yvonne. Yvonne is shorter than Sue. Sue is 5' tall.
Which of the following conclusions must be TRUE?
A. Bill is taller than Sue.
B. Yvonne is taller than 5'4".
C. Sue is taller than Bill.
D. Yvonne is the shortest.

23. The Bass family traveled 268 miles during the first day of their vacation and another 300 miles on the next day. Maria Bass said they were 568 miles from home.
Which of the following facts did Maria assume?
A. They traveled faster on the first day and slower on the second.
B. If she plotted the vacation route on a map, it would be a straight line.
C. Their car used more gasoline on the second day.
D. They traveled faster on the second day than they did on the first day.

24. *The word LEFT in a mathematics problem indicate that it is a subtraction problem.*
    Which of the following mathematics problems prove this statement FALSE?
    A. I want to put 150 bottles into cartons which hold 8 bottles each. After I completely fill as many cartons as I can, how many bottles will be left?
    B. Sarah has 5 books but gave one to John. How many books did Sarah have left?
    C. Carlos had $4.25 but spent $3.75. How much did he have left?
    D. We had 38 models in stock but after yesterday's sale, only 12 are left. How many did we sell?

25. Let Q represent the number of miles Dave can jog in 15 minutes. Identify the expression which represents the number of miles Dave can jog between 3:00 P.M. and 4:45 P.M.
    A. 1 3/4 Q   B. 7Q   C. 15 × 1 3/4×Q   D. Q/7

KEY (CORRECT ANSWERS)

1.	C		11.	D
2.	B		12.	D
3.	C		13.	C
4.	C		14.	A
5.	A		15.	D
6.	A		16.	B
7.	C		17.	A
8.	B		18.	D
9.	C		19.	A
10.	B		20.	C

21.	C
22.	D
23.	B
24.	A
25.	B

SOLUTIONS TO PROBLEMS

1. Choice C is in ascending order since .y < .77 < .777

2. Rewrite in decimal form: .4 + .07 + .005 = .475

3. Let x = missing number. Then, 700x = 7. Solving, x = 7/700 = .01

4. 943 − 251 = 692 ≈ 700

5. Let x = hours needed. Then, 10/15 = x/6. Solving, x = 4

6. The number of diners (D) is 10 times as many waiters (10W). So, D = 10W, or 10W = D

7. Given F = XC + Y, subtract Y from each side to get F − Y = XC. Finally, dividing by X, we get (F-Y)/X = C

8. 12 = 6C/3. Then, 12 = 2C, so C = 6

9. 5/7 = x/35. Then, 7x = 175, so x = 25

10. Probability of a female teacher = 2/5 = .4

11. Statement D is best, since as time increases, the temperature decreases.

12. (3)(2) + 4 = 2y. Then, 10 = 2y, so y = 5.

13. Miles per gallon = 243/8.7

14. Total purchase is (6)($4) + (4)($5) = $44. The average cost per book is $44 ÷ 10 = $4.40

15. (220)($2.25) = $450. The discount is (.15))($450) = $67.50

16. The number of workdays is 1000 ÷ 125 = 8

17. Choice A is correct because the average duration of the phone calls = total time ÷ total number of calls.

18. Statement D is correct since a 4-5 year old car's value is $4,000, whereas a 2-3 year-old car's value is $6000.

19. 60 seconds = 1 minute and 60 minutes = 1 hour. Thus, 24 hours = (24)(60)(60) or (60)(60)(24) seconds.

20. We can't use millimeters in measuring milk since millimeters is a linear measurement.

21. The reading shows the average of 50 and 75 = 62.5

22. Since Yvonne is shorter than both Bill and Sue, Yvonne is the shortest.

23. Statement B is assumed correct since 568 = 269 + 300 could only be true if the mileage traveled represents a straight line.

24. To find the number of bottles left, we look only for the remainder when 150 is divided b 8 (which happens to be 6).

25. 3:00 P.M. to 4:45 P.M. = 1 hour and 45 minutes = 105 minutes
    Let Q = 15 minutes
    105 / 15 = 7
    7(15) = 105 = 7Q

EXAMINATION SECTION
TEST 1

DIRECTIONS: Each question or incomplete statement is followed by several suggested answers or completions. Select the one that BEST answers the question or completes the statement. *PRINT THE LETTER OF THE CORRECT ANSWER IN THE SPACE AT THE RIGHT.*

1. 2/3 × 12 equals
    A. 4
    B. 6
    C. 8
    D. 18
    E. None of the above

    1.____

2. 83.97
   1.78
   14.36
   9.03
   The sum of the above column is
    A. 99.13
    B. 99.24
    C. 109.14
    D. 109.23
    E. 109.24

    2.____

3. The value of x in the equation 5x = 75 is
    A. 13
    B. 15
    C. 70
    D. 80
    E. None of the above

    3.____

4. 65 ÷ .13 equals
    A. .501
    B. 5.01
    C. 50.1
    D. 501
    E. None of the above

    4.____

5. The sum of 6 feet 8 inches and 3 feet 4 inches is
    A. 2 ft. 2 in.
    B. 9 ft.
    C. 10 ft.
    D. 10 ft. 12 in.
    E. None of the above

    5.____

6. 3/4 − 1/2 + 1/8 equals
    A. 3/10
    B. 3/8
    C. 5/8
    D. 1 3/8
    E. None of the above

    6.____

7. 4 5/16 − 2 3/8 equals
    A. 1 15/16
    B. 2 1/16
    C. 2 ¼
    D. 2 15/16
    E. None of the above

    7.____

8. (−12)+(−3) equals
    A. −9
    B. +15
    C. +9
    D. −15
    E. None of the above

    8.____

9. The ratio of the lengths of two lines is 5 to 3. The length of the shorter line is 30 inches. The length of the longer line is _____ inches.
    A. 18
    B. 48
    C. 50
    D. 140
    E. None of the above

    9.____

2 (#1)

10. .025 written as a common fraction is
    A. 25/10
    B. 25/100
    C. 25/1000
    D. 25/10,000
    E. None of the above

    10.____

11. In the proportion 5/2 = 9/x the value of x is
    A. 1.8
    B. 3.6
    C. 22.5
    D. 36
    E. None of the above

    11.____

12. 33 1/3 percent of 3 equals
    A. 1
    B. 10
    C. 100/3
    D. 100
    E. None of the above

    12.____

13. $\sqrt{233}$ equals
    A. 15
    B. 20.5
    C. 25
    D. 112.5
    E. None of the above

    13.____

14. On the portion of the scale shown at the right, the reading to which the arrow points is _____ units.
    A. 6 3/16
    B. 6 3/5
    C. 6 3/4
    D. 7 5/8
    E. None of the above

    14.____

15. If 4x/5 – 6 = 10, then x equals
    A. 15 1/5
    B. 5
    C. 4
    D. 3 1/5
    E. None of the above

    15.____

16. The difference between 8 hours 0 minutes 6 seconds and 6 hours 4 minutes 15 seconds is _____ hr. _____ min. _____ seconds.
    A. 0; 54; 51
    B. 1; 54; 51
    C. 2; 4; 9
    D. 2; 54; 45
    E. None of the above

    16.____

17. The scores made by nine pupils on a science test are: 2, 4, 6, 6, 8, 10, 12, 14, 19.
    The MEAN score is
    A. 6
    B. 8
    C. 9
    D. 81
    E. None of the above

    17.____

18. A certain cost formula is represented graphically in the figure at the right. From the graph, when n = 7, the value of C is about
    A. 140
    B. 120
    C. 110
    D. 102
    E. None of the above

    18.____

19. A simplified form of the expression A = 1/2 bh + 1/2 ah is
    A. A = ½ h(b+a)
    B. bh + ah
    C. A = abh
    D. $\frac{A}{1/2bh}$ = 1/2 ah
    E. None of the above

20. The ratio of 6 inches to 3 feet is
    A. 6/1
    B. 2/1
    C. 1/2
    D. 1/18
    E. None of the above

21. The value of s in the equation 3s = 12 – s is
    A. 6
    B. 4
    C. 3 2/3
    D. 3
    E. None of the above

22. 16 2/3 percent of what number is 30?
    A. 5
    B. 18
    C. 160
    D. 180
    E. None of the above

23. The line graph shown at the right represents the temperature readings in Albany, New York, at two-hour intervals from 4 A.M. to 10 P.M. on a certain day in February. The APPROXIMATE change in temperature between 7 A.M. and 9 A.M. is _____ degrees.
    A. 3.5
    B. 3.0
    C. 2.5
    D. 2.0
    E. None of the above

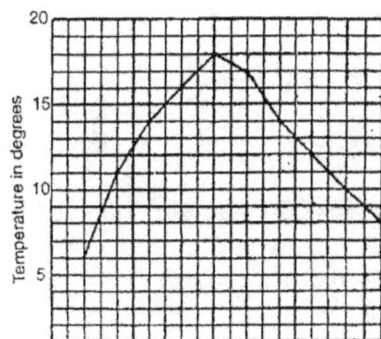

Questions 24-25.

DIRECTIONS: Questions 24 and 25 are to be answered on the basis of the following figure and information.

In the figure below, a square whose side is b is cut from a square whose side is a.

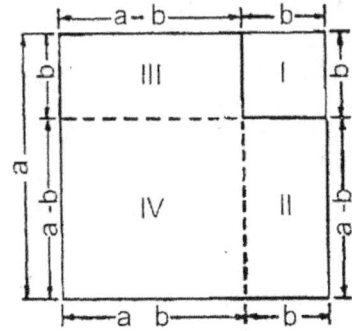

24. The sum of the perimeters of Section I and Section III can be represented by 24._____
    A. b² B. 4a – 2b C. 2a + 3b
    D. a(a-b) E. None of the above

25. The sum of the areas of Section II and Section IV can be represented by 25._____
    A. b² B. 4a – 2b C. 2a + 3b
    D. a(a-b) E. None of the above

26. The temperature reading (F) on the Fahrenheit scale equals 32 more than 26._____
    9/5 of the Centigrade reading (C).
    This rule when translated into symbols is expressed by
    A. F = 9/5C + 32 B. F = 9/5(C+32) C. F = 9/5 + 32C
    D. F + 32 = 9/5C E. None of the above

27. In the equation 6x – 114 = .3x, the value of x is 27._____
    A. 38 B. 20 C. 12 2/3
    D. 2 E. None of the above

28. What percent of 42 is 84? 28._____
    A. 4% B. 2% C. 50%
    D. 200% E. None of the above

29. The CORRECT name of the solid figure at the right is 29._____
    A. semicircle
    B. circle
    C. sphere
    D. cone
    E. cylinder

30. Which of these fractions has the LARGEST value? 30._____
    A. 1/2 B. 5/9 C. 7/12
    D. 2/3 E. 3/4

31. The formula for the area of a circle is A = 31._____
    A. π² B. 2/3 π² C. 2πr
    D. bh E. None of the above

32. The CORRECT name of the figure at the right is 32._____
    A. pentagon
    B. hexagon
    C. rectangle
    D. trapezoid
    E. square

33. The figure at the right is a
    A. rectangle
    B. square
    C. pentagon
    D. trapezoid
    E. parallelogram

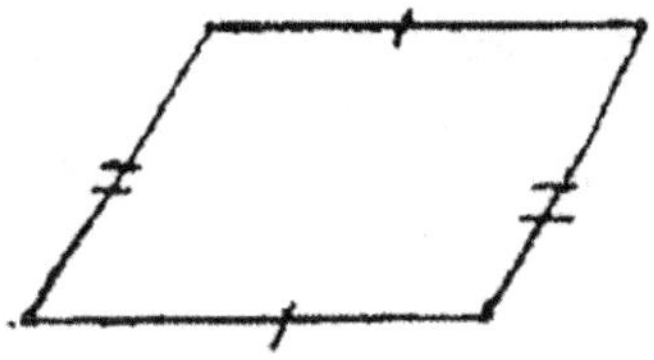

    33.____

34. If x = -18, y = 3, and z = -2, then x – y + z equals
    A. 3   B. -3   C. -23   D. -52   E. -56

    34.____

35. The number 335,560 rounded off to the nearest thousand is
    A. 335,000   B. 335,500   C. 336,000
    D. 340,000   E. None of the above

    35.____

36. In the triangle ABC at the right, the sum of the angles is _____ degrees.
    A. 360
    B. 180
    C. 90
    D. 35
    E. None of the above

    36.____

37. According to the map shown at the right, the APPROXIMATE distance between the southern point of New York City and Albany is _____ miles.
    A. 50
    B. 75
    C. 130
    D. 180
    E. 200

    37.____

38. If 6 is added to a certain number n, the result is 1. An equation which expresses this relationship is
    A. n + 6 = 1   B. n – 1 = 6   C. 6 – n = 1
    D. n + 1 = 6   E. None of the above

    38.____

39. In the expression $2n^3$, the 3 is called a(n)
    A. coefficient   B. factor   C. exponent
    D. multiplicand   E. None of the above

    39.____

40. The number of inches in n feet is represented by
    A. 12n   B. 3n   C. n/3
    D. n/12   E. None of the above

    40.____

41. The simple interest on $600 for 3 months at 4 percent per year is represented by 600 × .04x
    A. 1/4
    B. 1/3
    C. 3
    D. 4
    E. None of the above

42. The circle graph shown at the right indicates how a family's annual budget of $3,000 was planned.
    Food   40 percent
    Shelter   25 percent
    Clothes   15 percent
    Operating Expenses 10 percent
    Insurance & Savings 10 percent
    The part of the circle representing Shelter is _____ degrees.
    A. 25
    B. 45
    C. 90
    D. 250
    E. None of the above

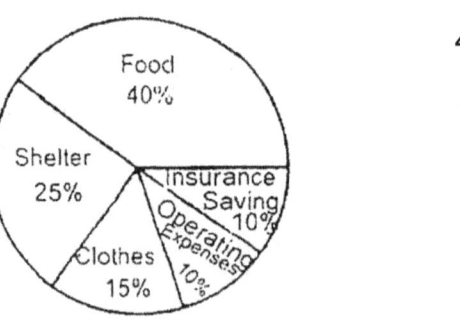

43. In the parallelogram ABCD shown at the right, each small square represents 4 square inches. The area of the right triangle AED represents _____ square inches.
    A. 3
    B. 12
    C. 24
    D. 48
    E. None of the above

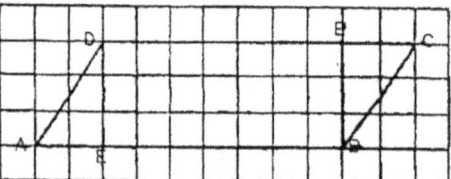

44. A surveyor measured angle x with a transit. (See figure at the right.) Angle x is called
    A. the angle of depression B from A
    B. an obtuse angle
    C. the supplement of angle
    D. the angle of elevation of B from A
    E. none of the above

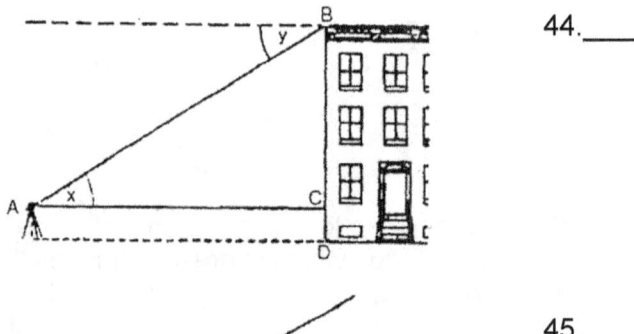

45. In the figure at the right, AOB is a straight line. An equation showing the relationship between u and v is
    A. u = 1/2v
    B. u = 180 − v
    C. u + v = 90
    D. v = 3u
    E. None of the above

46. If x = 4 when y = 6 and x varies directly as y, then when y = 15, x equals
   A. 20 B. 10 C. 1 3/5
   D. 1 1/3 E. None of the above

47. A discount of 15 percent from a marked price produces a net price which is _____ of the marked price.
   A. .15% B. .85% C. 15% D. 85% E. 115%

48. When the formula A = P + Prt is solved for t, t equals
   A. A – P – Pr B. $\frac{A-Pr}{P}$ C. $\frac{A-P}{1+r}$
   D. $\frac{A-P}{Pr}$ E. None of the above

49. The Greek letter π
   A. was assigned the value 3.1416 by the International Court of Law
   B. was given an arbitrary value of 22/7 by a famous mathematician
   C. was discovered to be exactly 3.142
   D. when multiplied by the radius of a circle equals the area
   E. is used as a symbol for the ratio of the circumference of a circle to its diameter

50. If the base and altitude of a triangle are doubled, the area
   A. remains constant B. is multiplied by 4 C. is doubled
   D. is divided by 4 E. is none of the above

51. Each side of the equilateral triangle in the figure at the right is s inches long. The length of an altitude of the triangle is represented as
   A. s in.
   B. S$\sqrt{2}$
   C. S$\sqrt{3}$
   D. $\frac{S\sqrt{3}}{2}$ in.
   E. None of the above

52. The length of a meter is about _____ inches.
   A. 1 B. 6 C. 12 D. 40 E. 100

53. A point which lies on the straight-line graph of the equation 2x – 3y = 12 is
   A. (3,-2) B. (2,-3) C. (-4,0)
   D. (0,6) E. None of the above

54. If the two parallel lines AB and CD in the figure at the right are cut by a third line, EF, then the FALSE statement is
    A. $\angle r + \angle s = \angle s + \angle y$
    B. $\angle y + \angle w = \angle t + \angle s$
    C. $\angle u + \angle w = \angle s + \angle x$
    D. $\angle r + \angle x = \angle t + \angle w$
    E. $\angle s + \angle u = \angle r + \angle t$

    54._____

55. The product of n^4 and n^2 equals
    A. $2n^8$ B. $2n^6$ C. n^8
    D. n^2 E. None of the above

    55._____

56. The volume of the rectangular solid shown at the right is
    A. 12 cu. in.
    B. 44 sq. in.
    C. 48 cu. in.
    D. 88 sq. in.
    E. None of the above

    56._____

57. Baseball bats listed at twenty-one dollars per dozen are sold to schools at a discount of 20 percent.
    How much do they cost the schools per dozen?
    A. $4.20   B. $16.80   C. $20.80
    D. $25.20   E. None of the above

    57._____

58. Last year a Chicago merchant's total business amounted to $30,000. For the goods sold, he paid $12,000, for rent he paid $2,500, for clerk services $4,742, and for other expenses $1,058.
    His average monthly net profit was
    A. $676.67   B. $891.67   C. $2,500.00
    D. $9,700.00 E. None of the above

    58._____

59. If the marked price of an article is $100 and the first discount is 10 percent and the second discount 2 percent, the sale price is
    A. $78.20   B. $88.00   C. $88.20
    D. $88.80   E. None of the above

    59._____

60. Mr. Smith agreed to pay an automobile agency a commission of 18 percent of the selling price of his car.
    If the selling price was $1,250, Mr. Smith would receive
    A. $225.00   B. $1,025.00   C. $1,227.50
    D. $1,475.00 E. None of the above

    60._____

61. Mr. Browne receives $30.45 per year on an investment of $870.
    At this rate, if his total investment was $1,500, his annual interest would be
    A. $52.50   B. $62.50   C. $625.00
    D. $655.45   E. None of the above

    61._____

62. The Ephrata National Bank discounted a 60-day note for $3,500 at 3½ percent per year.
    The proceeds of the note were
    A. $3,377.50
    B. $3,479.58
    C. $3,520.42
    D. $3,622.50
    E. None of the above

63. The normal weight of an adult can be found by using the formula w = 5.5(20+d), where w represents the weight in pounds and d the number of inches one's height exceeds 5 feet.
    By this formula, the normal weight of an adult who is 5'6" tall is _____ pounds.
    A. 134
    B. 140.25
    C. 140.8
    D. 143.0
    E. None of the above

64. In the figure at the right, triangles ACB and ADE are similar triangles. The length of side DE is _____ feet.
    A. 30
    B. 32
    C. 48
    D. 50
    E. None of the above

65. A square piece of tin shown in the figure at the right is used to make an open box. One-inch squares are cut from each corner of the piece of tin and the sides then turned up, to form a box containing 49 cubic inches.
    The length of a side of the original square piece of tin required to make this box is _____ inches.
    A. 5
    B. 7
    C. 8
    D. 9
    E. None of the above

KEY (CORRECT ANSWERS)

1.	C	11.	B	21.	D	31.	A	41.	A	51.	D	61.	A
2.	C	12.	A	22.	D	32.	A	42.	C	52.	D	62.	B
3.	B	13.	A	23.	C	33.	E	43.	B	53.	A	63.	D
4.	D	14.	E	24.	E	34.	C	44.	D	54.	E	64.	B
5.	C	15.	E	25.	D	35.	C	45.	B	55.	E	65.	D
6.	B	16.	E	26.	A	36.	B	46.	B	56.	C		
7.	A	17.	C	27.	B	37.	C	47.	D	57.	B		
8.	D	18.	A	28.	D	38.	A	48.	D	58.	E		
9.	C	19.	A	29.	E	39.	C	49.	E	59.	C		
10.	C	20.	E	30.	E	40.	A	50.	B	60.	B		

11 (#1)

SOLUTIONS TO PROBLEMS

1. $2/3 \times 12 = \frac{12}{1} = \frac{24}{3} = 8$

2. Adding, we get 109.14

3. If $5x = 75$, $x = 75/5 = 15$

4. $65.13 \div 13 = 501$

5. 6 ft. 8 in. + 3 ft. 4 in. = 9 ft. 12 in. = 10 ft.

6. $3/4 - 1/2 + 1/8 = 6/8 - 4/8 + 1/8 = 3/8$

7. 4 15/16 − 2 3/8 = 3 21/16 − 2 6/16 = 1 15/16

8. $(-12) + (-3) = -15$

9. Let x = length of longer line. Then, 5:3 = x:30. Solving, x = 50

10. .025 = 25/1000 (Can also be reduced to 1/40)

11. Cross-multiplying, $5x = 18$. Thus, 18/5 = 3.6

12. 33 1/3% of 3 = (1/3)(3) = 1

13. $\sqrt{225} = 15$, since $15^2 = 225$

14. The arrow points to 6 3/8

15. $4x/5 - 6 = 10$. Adding 6, $4x/5 = 16$. Then, $x = 16 \div 4/5 = 20$

16. 8 hrs. 0 min. 6 sec. − 6 hrs. 4 min. 15 sec. can be written as 7 hrs. 59 min. 66 sec. − 6 hrs. 4 min. 15 sec. to get 1 hr. 55 min. 51 sec.

17. Mean = (2+4+6+8+10+12+14+19) ÷ 9 = 9

18. When n = 0, c = 0. When n = 5, c = 100. Thus, c = 20n. Finally, for n = 7, c = (20)(7) = 140

19. A = 1/2 bh + 1/2 h(b+a)

20. 6 inches : 3 feet = 6 inches : 36 inches = 1/6

21. Add 5 to both sides to get $4s = 12$, so $s = 3$

22. 16 2/3% of x is 30. Then, 1/6 x = 30. Then, 1/6 x = 180

12 (#1)

23. At 7:00 A.M. the temperature was 12.5, while at 9:00 A.M. the temperature was 15. The change was 2.5 degrees.

24. Perimeter of Section I is 4b and the perimeter of Section III is $2b + 2a - 2b = 2a$. The sum of the perimeters is $4b + 2a$,

25. Area of Section II is $b(a-b) = ab - b^2$ and the area of Section IV is $(a-b)^2 = a^2 - 2ab + b^2$. The sum of the areas is $a^2 - ab = a(a-b)$.

26. Direct translation of words to symbols yields $F = 9/5C + 32$

27. Subtract 6x to get $-114 = 5.7x$. Solving, $x = 20$

28. $(84/42)(100)\% = 200\%$

29. The figure is a cylinder.

30. Converting each choice to a decimal, we get $.5, .\overline{5}, .58\overline{3}, .6, .75$. The largest is .75 corresponding to 3/4.

31. For a circle, $A = \pi r^2$

32. A five-sided enclosed figure with straight sides is called a pentagon.

33. A quadrilateral with opposite sides parallel is called a parallelogram. Rectangles and squares are parallelograms with 90° angles.

34. $x - y + z = 18 - 3 - 2 = 23$

35. Since the digit in the hundreds place is 5 or greater, the answer is 336,000.

36. The sum of the angles of any triangle is 180°.

37. The scale difference is about 2 inches, and since 50 miles corresponds to 3/4 inch, the actual distance is about $(50)(2 \div 3/4) = 133\ 1/3$ mi. Closest answer given s 130 mi.

38. 6 added to n means $6 + n$. Thus, $6 + n = 1$ or $n + 6 = 1$.

39. 3 is an exponent for $2n^3$.

40. 12 inches in 1 foot means 12n inches in n feet.

41. 3 months = 1/4 year

42. 25% of 360 degrees = 90 degrees.

43. Area of △AED = $(1/2)(2)(3) = 3$ square units = 12 sq. inches.

44. Angle X is the angle of elevation to B from A.

13 (#1)

45. Since u + v = 180, we can also write u = 180 − v

46. 4/x = 6/15 Cross-multiplying, 6x = 60. Solving, x = 10

47. 100% - 15% = 85%

48. A = P + Prt becomes A − P = Prt. Dividing by Pr, we get: t = (A−P)/Pr

49. π = ratio of circumference to diameter of a circle.

50. Let B = base, H = altitude. Original area of triangle = 1/2BH. If new base and altitude are 2B and 2H, new area = ½(2B)(2H) = 2BH, which is 4 times the value of 1/2BH.

51. Let x = altitude. Then, $x^2 + (s/2)^2 = s2$. This becomes $3/4s^2 = x^2$. Solving, x = s √3 /2

52. 1 meter ≈ 39.37 inches ≈ 40 inches.

53. Substituting (3,-2), 2(3) − 3(-2) = 12. The other points do not lie on 2x − 3y = 12.

54. The false statement is ∠2 + ∠u = ∠r + ∠t. It is only true that ∠x = ∠u and∠ r = ∠t).

55. $n^4 \bullet n^2 = n^6$, since exponents are added in multiplication.

56. Volume = (6)(4)(2) = 48 cu. in.

57. ($21)(.80) = $16.80

58. $30,000 - $12,000 - $2,500 - $4,742 - $1,058 = $9,700. The monthly amount is $9,700 ÷ 12 = $808.33

59. ($100)(.90) = $90. Then, ($90)(.98) = $88.20

60. 1,250 − (1,250)(.18) = $1,025

61. $30.45/$870 = 3.5%. Then, 3.5% of $1,500 = $52.50

62. (.035)(60/360) = .00583̄ = discount for 60 days.
The value of the note = (1 - .00583̄)($3500) = $3,479.58.

63. W = 5.5(20+6) = (5.5)(26) = 143

64. x/80 = 40/100. Solving, x = 32. Note that AD:AC = DE:BC

65. When folded, each new side is √49 = 7

EXAMINATION SECTION
TEST 1

DIRECTIONS: Each question or incomplete statement is followed by several suggested answers or completions. Select the one that BEST answers the question or completes the statement. *PRINT THE LETTER OF THE CORRECT ANSWER IN THE SPACE AT THE RIGHT.*

1. A solid which has a point at one end and a circle at the other end is a   1.____
   - A. cone
   - B. sphere
   - C. cylinder
   - D. prism

2. $(5 \times 10^2) + (3 \times 10^1) + (4 \times 1) =$ 2.____
   - A. 84
   - B. 534
   - C. 5034
   - D. (5+3-4)10

3. All members of R are members of T, but no members of T are members of V. Therefore, you know that   3.____
   - A. some members of R are members of V
   - B. no members of V are members of R
   - C. some members of V are members of T
   - D. no members of T are members of R

4. The multiplication of 6x48 can be distributed as   4.____
   - A. (6x40) + (8x8)
   - B. (6x20) + (20x8)
   - C. (6x20) + (6x20) + (6x8)
   - D. (6x6) + (6x8)

5. Which of these could be used as a divisor and NOT change a dividend?   5.____
   - A. 0
   - B. 1
   - C. The dividend itself
   - D. There is no such number

6. Through any one point, there can be   6.____
   - A. an unlimited number of lines
   - B. only one line
   - C. only one set of parallel lines
   - D. only two lines

7. Ten girls have an average of 25 points on a test. If 5 points are added to each girl's number, what will the average then be?   7.____
   - A. 3
   - B. 25.5
   - C. 27
   - D. 30

8. E + A =   8.____
   - A. 2EA
   - B. AE
   - C. A+E
   - D. A-E

9. A number that indicates how many times a base number is used as a factor is a(n)   9.____
   - A. prime number
   - B. rational number
   - C. reciprocal
   - D. exponent

10. Some of the multiples of a certain number are w, k, m, p, and z. Some of the multiples of another number are k, p, z, and r.
    A common multiple of the two numbers is

    A. r   B. w   C. m   D. k

11. Which is another way to multiply axbxc?

    A. (a+b)xc
    B. cxaxb
    C. bx(a+c)
    D. (axb) + (axc)

12. The set of any two points on a line and all points between them is a

    A. ray
    B. bisector of an angle
    C. half line
    D. line segment

13. What is the area of this rectangular region?
    A. 12 sq. ft.
    B. 20 sq. ft.
    C. 24 sq. ft.
    D. 36 sq. ft.

14. In the numeral (6568, the 6 that is underlined stands for how many times as many as the other 6?

    A. 10   B. 100   C. 1000   D. the same

15. According to the distributive principle, one third of 6 ft. 9 in. would be

    A. 23 in.
    B. 3 ft. 3 in.
    C. 2 ft. + 3 in.
    D. 1 yd. + 3 in.

16. Two names for the same thing are USUALLY indicated by which sign?

    A. ε B. =   C. ~   D. u

17. Mary has 60¢ saved to buy three hairbows which cost 250 each.
    Which sentence can be used to find out how many cents more (n) she needs?

    A. $60 \div n = 3 \times 25$
    B. $3 \times 25 = 60n$
    C. $60 \div 3 - n = 25$
    D. $3 \times 25 = 60 - n$

18. Which of these is a prime number?

    A. 43   B. 68   C. 87   D. 165

19. Which means 24 divided by a number equals twice the number?

    A. $\dfrac{24}{n} = \dfrac{2n}{24}$
    B. $24 \div n = \dfrac{n}{2}$
    C. $2 \times \dfrac{24}{n} = n$
    D. $\dfrac{24}{n} = 2n$

20. Which of these numerals can you be sure is NOT correctly written?   20._____

   A. 257 eight   B. 362 seven   C. 421 four   D. 453 six

21. What is 3754 rounded to the nearest 500?   21._____

   A. 3500   B. 3700   C. 3750   D. 4000

22. When a person measures, he ALWAYS   22._____

   A. tallies   B. compares   C. marks   D. weighs

23. Four is what percent of 37?   23._____
   To find the percent, a person may use the equation

   A. $\dfrac{4}{37} = \dfrac{n}{100}$ B. $\dfrac{4}{100} = \dfrac{37}{n}$

   C. $\dfrac{(100 \times 37)}{4} = n$ D. $\dfrac{37}{100} = \dfrac{n}{4}$

24. Angle a is a right angle.   24._____
    Therefore, the sum of the measurements of angles b and c is

    A. 45°
    B. 90°
    C. 180°
    D. 270°

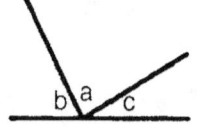

25. If 2 pencils cost 5¢, how many cents will 6 pencils cost at the same rate?   25._____
    The solution equation is

    A. $\dfrac{2}{6} = \dfrac{n}{5}$ B. $\dfrac{2}{5} = \dfrac{n}{6}$ C. $\dfrac{2}{5} = \dfrac{6}{n}$ D. $\dfrac{2}{n} = \dfrac{5}{6}$

26. a(b+c) = ab + ac illustrates the _____ principle.   26._____

    A. commutative   B. associative
    C. distributive   D. binary

27. If the measurement of angle a is 130°, the measurement of angle b   27._____
    is

    A. 30°
    B. 40°
    C. 50°
    D. 70°

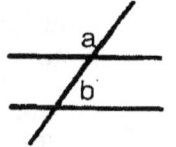

28. In which of these will the product be LESS than m when m is a positive number and not   28._____
    0?

    A. $m \times \dfrac{2}{3}$ B. $1\dfrac{1}{4} \times m$ C. $1.0 \times m$ D. $m \times \dfrac{5}{4}$

29. 15.94 x 0.5 is APPROXIMATELY

    A. 0.08   B. 0.8   C. 8   D. 80

30. If X = |2, 4, 6, 8| and Y = |3, 6, 9, 12|, then

    A. X ∩ Y = |2,3,4,6,8,9,12| B. X ∪ Y = |6|

    C. X ∪ Y = |2,3,4,6,8,9,12| D. X ∩ Y = |2,3|

31. If the measurement of angle b is 65 and of angle c is also 65, then the measurement of angle a is

    A. 60°
    B. 50°
    C. 40°
    D. 20°

32. What is the area within triangle JKL? _____ sq. ft.
    A. 48
    B. 50
    C. 95
    D. 100

33. The place holder, or the unknown, in an equation is called

    A. the empty set   B. a variable
    C. an equality   D. an inequality

34. If part of K is all of W, and all of K is part of M, you can be sure that

    A. all of W is part of M
    B. all of K is all of W
    C. K is less than M - W
    D. W + K is less than M

35.

On the number line above, all points to the right of zero, whether marked or not, represent numbers that are

    A. positive   B. whole
    C. fractions (rationals)   D. in base ten

36. $\sqrt{5^6}$

    A. 5^2 B. 5^3 C. 5^4 D. 5^{12}

37. Identify the rational number or numbers among the expressions 1/4, 3/4, 4/4, and 5/4.

    A. 1/4, 3/4   B. 1/4 *only*
    C. 5/4   D. all of them

38. The MOST precise of these measurements of length is

   A. 2 ft.   B. 3.25 ft.   C. 4 1/2 ft.   D. 29 in.

39. A circle graph showing that a person spends 25 percent of his budget for clothes will have an angle whose measurement is

   A. 22 1/2°   B. 25°   C. 45°   D. 90°

40. In Figure _____ , you do NOT see a vertex.

   A.   B.   C.   D.

41. The chart at the right demonstrates
   A. addition facts for the binary base
   B. addition facts for base three
   C. multiplication facts in a non-decimal base
   D. a magic square

	0	1	2
0	0	1	2
1	1	2	10
2	2	10	11

42. Which of these numerals indicates that 4 has been used as a factor twice?

   A. 4 + 4   B. 4/2   C. 4 x 2   D. 16

43. All the pupils in an elementary class who are each over 7 ft. 8 in. tall may be described as the

   A. odd numbers   B. solution set
   C. empty set   D. unique domain

44. 6784.65 is APPROXIMATELY 6.8 x

   A. 10^4 B. 10^2 C. 10^1 D. 10^3

45. If X is less than Y, and Z is greater than Y, then

   A. $\frac{z}{2} > \frac{y}{2}$ B. X+Y < Z

   C. Y > Z   D. $X = \frac{1}{2} y = \frac{1}{2} z$

46. If the length of each side of a square is doubled, the area of the square would be multiplied by

   A. 1   B. 2   C. 4   D. 8

47. -2 x -3 =

   A. 6   B. -1   C. -3   D. -6

48. Bob has laid out these right triangles to measure the distance across the river at AB. How wide is the river at AB?
    A. 60'
    B. 67 1/2'
    C. 75'
    D. 90'

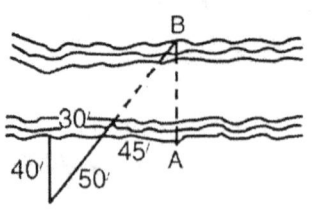

48.____

49. Which mathematical sentence below would you use to find the rate of interest earned on an investment of $1000 which earns $45 annually?

    A. $45 \div 1000 = \dfrac{100}{n}$
    B. $\dfrac{45}{100} = \dfrac{n}{1000}$
    C. $1000 \div 45 = \dfrac{100}{n}$
    D. $\dfrac{n}{100} = \dfrac{45}{1000}$

49.____

50. $5^6 \div 5^2 =$

    A. 1^3 B. 5^3 C. 5^4 D. 5^{12}

50.____

51. Suppose you were taking the 5 marbles from this box one at a time without looking until they are all gone. You draw one which is black. Now, what are the chances that you will draw a black marble the second time?

    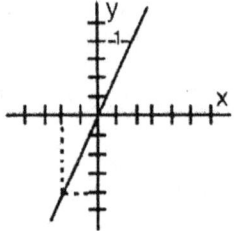

    A. 1/3   B. 1/4   C. 1/5   D. 2/5

51.____

52. This is a graph of the solution set for
    A. y = 2 + x
    B. x = 2 + y
    C. y = 2x
    D. x = 2y

52.____

53. A square, a rhombus, a rectangle, and a trapezoid are ALL

    A. pentagons   B. prisms
    C. parallelograms   D. quadrilaterals

53.____

54. A multiple of a number is

    A. a common denominator of that number and a greater number
    B. a multiplier
    C. one of two factors in a multiplication
    D. a product of that number and another factor

54.____

55. $\sqrt{13} \times \sqrt{13} =$

    A. 3.4   B. 13   C. $\sqrt{13}$ D. $\sqrt{26}$

55.____

56. ←—•—•—•—•—•—→
      P Q R S T

    $\overline{PR} \cap \overline{ST} =$

    A. ∅   B. $\overline{RS}$ C. $\overline{PT}$ D. $\overline{RT}$

57. In this group of symbols (⊥, =, +, ~, ≅, ≡), there is no symbol that means

    A. plus or minus   B. is equal to
    C. is similar to   D. is perpendicular to

58. The numeral in base ten for a certain number has four digits.
    The numeral in base four for the same number will have _____ digits.

    A. four
    B. more than four
    C. less than 4
    D. One can't tell without knowing what the number is

59. Some integers are positive numbers and some integers are negative numbers, but no positive numbers are negative numbers.
    Which diagram illustrates these facts?

    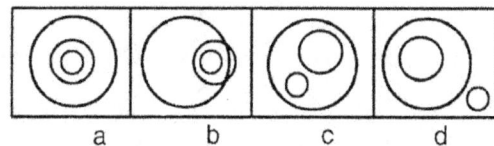

60. If A < B - C and all three are positive whole numbers greater than zero, then

    A. A < B   B. A + C > B
    C. $A < \frac{B+C}{2}$ D. B < C

61. If the sum of the digits of a numeral is 36, you can be sure that the number is divisible, without a remainder, by

    A. 2   B. 4   C. 6   D. 9

62. A car goes one mile in 75 seconds.
    To find the equivalent speed in miles per hour, which equation can be used?

    A. $\frac{60}{75} = \frac{60}{n}$ B. $\frac{n}{60} = \frac{75}{60}$
    C. $\frac{1}{75} = \frac{n}{60 \times 60}$ D. $75 \div 60 \times 60 = n$

63. The prime factors of three numbers are, respectively, |2,2,3,5|, |2,3,3|, and |3,3,2,5|.
    The GREATEST common factor of the three numbers is

    A. 6   B. 12   C. 30   D. 90

8 (#1)

64. Each square represents a digit in the numeral 3 □ □ □ 144. Even though you do NOT know what digits the squares represent, you can be sure that 3 □ □ □ 144 is divisible by

    A. 3   B. 6   C. 8   D. 9

64.____

65. Which fraction is the LARGEST?

    A. 9/8   B. 7/8   C. 6/7   D. 5/4

65.____

KEY (CORRECT ANSWERS)

1. A	16. B	31. B	46. C	61. D
2. B	17. A	32. A	47. A	62. C
3. B	18. A	33. B	48. A	63. A
4. C	19. D	34. A	49. D	64. C
5. B	20. C	35. A	50. C	65. D
6. A	21. D	36. B	51. B	
7. D	22. B	37. D	52. C	
8. C	23. A	38. B	53. D	
9. D	24. B	39. D	54. D	
10. D	25. C	40. C	55. B	
11. B	26. C	41. B	56. A	
12. D	27. C	42. D	57. A	
13. C	28. A	43. C	58. B	
14. B	29. C	44. D	59. C	
15. C	30. C	45. A	60. A	

SOLUTIONS TO PROBLEMS

1. A cone has a point at one end and a circle at the other end.

2. $5 \times 10^2 + 3 \times 10^1 + 4 \times 1 = 500 + 30 + 4 = 534$

3. The appropriate diagram would look like this:

   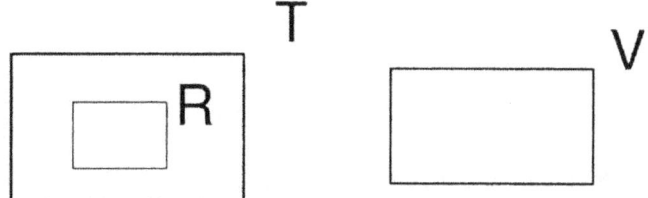

   Thus, no members of V are members of R.

4. Since $40 = 20 + 20 + 8$, $6 \times 48 = (6 \times 20) + (6 \times 20) + (6 \times 8)$

5. Any number divided by 1 remains unchanged.

6. An unlimited number of lines can pass through a given point.

7. Adding 5 points to each score will also raise the average 5 points to a new average of 30.

8. $E + A = A + E$ by the commutative law in algebra.

9. An exponent describes the number of times a base is used as a factor. Example, $n^3 = n \cdot n \cdot n$

10. A multiple in both lists is K (p,z were also in both lists)

11. $a \times b \times c = c \times a \times b$ always

12. A line segment is a portion of a line with endpoints.

13. Area = $(6)(4) = 24$ sq.ft.

14. The underlined 6 means thousands whereas the other 6 means tens. The first 6 is 100 times the other 6.

15. $\frac{1}{3}$ (6 ft. 9 in.) = 2 ft. 3 in. or 2 ft. + 3 in.

16. = means two things are the same.

17. Let n = additional cents needed. Then, $60 + n = (3)(25)$

18. 43 is a prime since it can only be divided evenly by itself and 1 (negative numbers excluded).

19. Let n = number. Then, $\frac{24}{n} = 2n$

20. 421_{four} has no meaning since only 0, 1, 2, 3 may be used in base four.

21. 3754 is closer to 4000 than to 3500, so rounded to the nearest 500, 3754 becomes 4000.

22. Measuring means comparing with some reference like a scale or a ruler, for example.

23. $\dfrac{4}{37} = \dfrac{n}{100}$ will yield what percent of 37 is 4.

24. $\angle a + \angle b + \angle c = 180°$. Since $\angle a = 90°$, $\angle b + \angle c = 90°$

25. Using a proportion, 2/5 = 6/n will yield the correct cost.

26. a(b+c) = ab + ac is the distributive property.

27. $\angle a + \angle b = 180°$. If $\angle a = 130°$, Then $\angle b = 50°$

28. $m \times \dfrac{2}{3} = \dfrac{2}{3}m$ which is less than m if m > 0.

29. (15.94)(.5) = 7.975 ≃ 8

30. X∪Y means the set of elements in X or Y or both = {2, 3, 4, 6, 8, 9, 12}.

31. $\angle a + 65° + 65° = 180°$. Thus, $\angle a = 50°$

32. Area = $(\dfrac{1}{2})(16)(6) = 48$ sq.ft.

33. A variable will represent the unknown in an equation.

34. The appropriate diagram appears as:

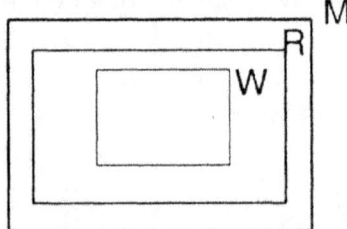

Thus, all of W is part of M.

35. All points to the right of zero represent positive numbers.

36. $\sqrt{5^6} = 5^3$ since $5^3 \cdot 5^3 = 5^6$

37. Any fraction with an integer in both numerator and denominator is a rational number.

38. 3.25 ft. is more precise than the other choices because the accuracy is in hundredths, and the others are whole numbers or contain accuracy only to one decimal place.

39. $(.25)(360°) = 90°$

40. A sphere does not contain a vertex, since there does not exist an intersection of line segments.

41. The given chart shows addition for base 3, where the only allowable digits are 0, 1, 2.

42. Since 16 = 4 x 4, the number 4 is a factor twice.

43. A set with no elements is called an empty set.

44. $6784.65 = 6.78465 \times 10^3$ or about 6.8×10^3

45. Since Z is greater than Y, then dividing by 2 yields Z/2 is greater than Y/2. Symbolically, Z/2 > Y/2.

46. Let x = original side of a square so that area = x^2.
    Doubling each side to 2x makes the area $(2x)^2 = 4x^2$.
    Now, $4x^2$ is 4 times as big as x^2.

47. (-2) x (-3) = 6. Two negatives multiplied yield a positive.

48. By similar triangles, 45'/AB = 30'/40'. Solving, AB = 60'

49. 45/1000 = n/100 will yield the annual rate of interest.

50. $5^6 5^2 = 5^4$. When dividing, subtract exponents.
    Note   Bases must be the same.

51. Since only 1 black marble exists out of 4 marbles, the probability is 1/4.

52. The line contains the points (0,0) and (2,4). The related equation is y = 2x.

53. A quadrilateral is any enclosed 4-sided figure.

54. A multiple of a number includes a product of that number and another factor. Example: 8 is a multiple of 4, since 8=4x2.

55. $\sqrt{13} \times \sqrt{13} = \sqrt{169} = 13$

56. $\overline{PR} \cap \overline{ST} = \emptyset$ since there are no points in common.

57. The missing symbol is $\pm$, which means plus or minus.

58. In base four, the placeholders are 1, 4, 16, 64, 256, 1024, 4096, etc. If the number is 1000 in base ten, it would correspond to a 5-digit number in base four. If the number is 9999 in base ten, it would correspond to a 7-digit number in base four. Thus, any 4-digit number in base ten would require more than 4 digits in base four.

59. Diagram C is correct, where the 2 smaller circles represent positive and negative numbers, respectively.

60. Since A < B - C, A + C < B. Now, A < A + C because A, B, C are all positive. Finally, A < A + C < B, so A < B.

61. The rule for divisibility of 9 is that the sum of the digits must divide (with no remainder) by 9. Of course, 36 is one such number.

62. 1 mile in 75 seconds = n miles in 3600 seconds.
This can also be written as 1/75 = n/60 X 60.

63. The factors in common are 2 and 3 and (2)(3) = 6

64. For a number to be divisible by 8, the portion of the number named by the last three digits (on the right) must be divisible by 8. Of course, 144 ÷ 8 = 18, which is a whole number.

65. Converting each fraction to a decimal, we get: 1.125, .875, .857 (approx.), 1.25. By inspection, 1.25 = 5/4 is the largest in this group.

EXAMINATION SECTION
TEST 1

DIRECTIONS: Each question or incomplete statement is followed by several suggested answers or completions. Select the one that BEST answers the question or completes the statement. *PRINT THE LETTER OF THE CORRECT ANSWER IN THE SPACE AT THE RIGHT.*

1. John is 1/6 of his father's age. In 20 years, he will be 1/2 of his father's age at that time. How old is the father?

   A. 24   B. 30   C. 36   D. 42   E. 48

   1._____

2. $(.7/.07)(49/100) = 4 + x$ $x =$

   A. 4.9   B. .09   C. .9   D. 3.1   E. 3.95

   2._____

3. Which is the largest?

   A. 23/25   B. 27/30   C. 15/16   D. 14/15   E. 7/8

   3._____

4. Clyde received a 10% raise in each of the last two years. His present salary is $43,560. What was his starting salary?

   A. $36,000   B. $38,000   C. $40,000   D. $42,700   E. $52,708

   4._____

5. At a convention of dentists, 1,000 dentists are from the east coast. One hundred dentists are women; 60 of the women are not from the east coast. How many male dentists are from the east coast?

   A. 900   B. 850   C. 800   D. 960   E. 940

   5._____

6. 1/3 of 1/4 is what percent of 5/12?

   A. .2   B. 5   C. 12   D. 20   E. 500

   6._____

7. Which line is parallel to the y axis?

   A. $x = 4y$ B. $x = 2/y^0$
   C. $x = y + 6$ D. $xy = 2$
   E. $xy = 2 + 4y^{-1}$

   7._____

8. The five tires that come with Mary's new car were rotated frequently so that each tire was used for exactly the same amount of time as the others. They were replaced when the odometer read 24,000 miles. How many miles had each been driven?

   A. 18,000 miles   B. 30,000 miles
   C. 20,000 miles   D. 24,000 miles
   E. 19,200 miles

   8._____

9. $\dfrac{-\binom{7646}{x}}{4---}$ What is the smallest number x could be?

   A. 2647   B. 4000   C. 3000   D. 646   E. 3646

   9._____

10. A bug sits at the edge of a 12 inch (diameter) phonograph record playing at 33 1/3 r.p.m. Approximately how fast (in feet/minute) is the bug moving?

    A. 3   B. 33   C. 50   D. 100   E. 396

11. An object floats if it weighs less than an equal volume of water. One cc of water weighs 1 gram. Each of the following objects weighs 2 kilograms. Which ones float? (All dimensions in cm.)

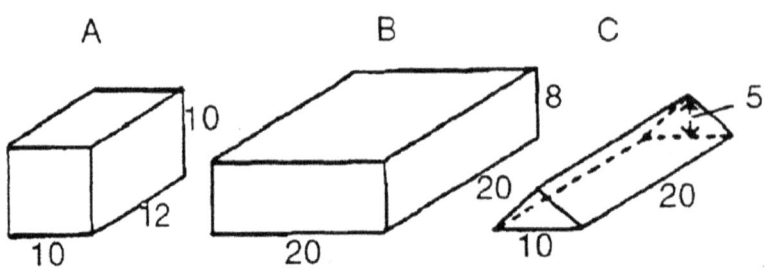

    A. A only   B. B only   C. C only   D. B & C   E. A & B

12. .04 is 25% of

    A. 0.01   B. 0.16   C. 0.1   D. 1.0   E. 1.6

13. $x^2 + 3x + 2 = 2$, $x < 0$.
    x.=

    A. $\dfrac{3-\sqrt{8}}{2}$ B. -1   C. -2   D. -3   E. -4

14. if 3x/4y = 1/8, then 4x/3y =

    A. 1/6   B. 1/3   C. 2/3   D. 24   E. 2/9

15. .3% of 25% equals

    A. 7.5   B. .75   C. .075   D. .0075   E. .00075

16. Arrange from least to greatest:

    I. .07   II. $\sqrt{.49}$ III. .075   IV. $(.835)^2$

    The CORRECT answer is:

    A. I, III, IV, II
    B. III, I, IV, II
    C. IV, I, II, III
    D. I, III, II, IV
    E. IV, II, III, I

17. A television set is priced at $490.00. The installment payment contract requires 20% of the price as a down-payment, plus installments of $47.75 per month over a period of 10 months to pay for the set, including interest charges.
    What is the total amount of interest charged?

    A. $83.00   B. $83.50   C. $85.50   D. $85.75   E. $125.50

18. A florist bought some plants for $150. He sold enough at 75 cents to meet the cost and had 100 plants left. How many were originally purchased by the florist?

   A. 150   B. 250   C. 300   D. 350   E. 400

   18.____

19. If $3x + y = 5$ and $5x + y = 6$, then $y =$

   A. 2/7   B. .5   C. 1   D. 2   E. 3.5

   19.____

20. A purse contains $3.20 in dimes and quarters. There are 3 less dimes than quarters. How many dimes are there?

   A. 7   B. 10   C. 13   D. 16   E. 20

   20.____

21. A lawn fertilizer is most effective if 25 pounds is spread over 10,000 square feet. A weed killer must be mixed with the fertilizer but only 3 pounds should be used on every 15,000 square feet. What should the ratio be between the fertilizer and the weed killer when mixed?

   A. 12.5 to 1   B. 3 to 2
   C. 8.33 to 1   D. 5.5 to 1
   E. 25 to 3

   21.____

22. If 1 yard = .9 meters, then 1.5 meters = how many yards?

   A. 1.65   B. 1.80   C. 1.60   D. 1.67   E. 1.35

   22.____

23. ( ) is to 40 as x/5 is to ( ).

   A. 4; x/50   B. 10; 40x   C. 8; x   D. 10; 8x   E. 5; x/40

   23.____

24. What is the approximate value of $\sqrt{360}$?

   A. 60   B. 18   C. 6   D. 16   E. 19

   24.____

25. An auto travels at an average of 45 mi/hr for 1 hour and then an average of 60 mi/hr for the next half hour. What is the average speed for the entire time period in miles/hr.?

   A. 47.5   B. 50   C. 52.5   D. 55   E. 62.5

   25.____

KEY (CORRECT ANSWERS)

1.	B	11.	B
2.	C	12.	B
3.	C	13.	D
4.	A	14.	E
5.	D	15.	E
6.	D	16.	A
7.	B	17.	C
8.	E	18.	C
9.	A	19.	E
10.	D	20.	A

21. A
22. D
23. C
24. E
25. B

SOLUTIONS TO PROBLEMS

1. Let the father's current age = x and John's current age = 1/6 x. In 20 years, their ages will be x + 20 and 1/6 x + 20. Then, 1/6 x + 20 = 1/2(x+20), which becomes 1/6 x + 20 = 1/2 x + 10. Solving, x = 30.

2. The left side of this equation becomes (10)(.49) = 4.9 Now, 4.9 = 4 + x. Solving, x = .9

3. Converting each fraction into a decimal equivalent, we get: .92, .9, .9375, .93, and .875, respectively. The largest is .9375 corresponding to 15/16.

4. Let x = initial salary. With the first 10% raise, his salary is 1.10x. The second 10% raise will bring his salary to (1.10x)(1.10) = 1.21x. Now, 1.21x = $43,560. Solving, x = $36,000

5. The number of female dentists from the east coast is 100 - 60 = 40. Thus, the number of male dentists from the east coast must be 1000 - 40 = 960.

6. 1/3 of 1/4 means (1/3)(1/4) = 1/12. Then, $\frac{1}{12} \div \frac{5}{12} = \frac{1}{5}$, and $\frac{1}{5}$ = 20%

7. Any line parallel to the y-axis has no slope, and so must be of the form x = c (c is a constant). x = 2/y° can be written as x = 2/1 or x = 2.

8. Since only 4 tires are used at the same time, each of the 5 tires will be used 4/5 or 80% of the elapsed time before replacement. (24,000)(.80) = 19,200.

9. To find the minimum x, we need to find the maximum for the answer (since this is a subtraction). The maximum answer upon subtracting is 4999. Solving, 7646 - x = 4999, we get x = 2647.

10. The circumference = (π)(1 foot) = 3.14 feet (approximately) 33 1/3 revolutions = (33 1/3)(3.14) = 104 2/3 feet, which is the rate per minute.

11. 2 kilograms = 2000 grams. The only object(s) which float must correspond to more than 2000 cc. Object A has a volume of only 1200 cc. Object B has a volume of 3200 cc. Object C has a volume of only (1/2)(10)(5)(20) = 500 cc. Object B will float since 3200 cc. of water weighs 3200 grams and 2000 < 3200. Objects A and C will not float.

12. Solve .04 = .25x to get x = .16.

13. Rewrite the equation as x^2 + 3x = 0. Then, x(x+3) = 0. The two answers are x = 0 and x = -3. With the restriction x < 0, we have x = -3.

14. 3x/4y = 1/8. Dividing both sides by 3/4, we get x/y =1/6. Now, multiply the entire equation x/y = 1/6 by 4/3 to get 4x/3y = (1/6)(4/3) = 2/9

15. .3% of 25% becomes (.003)(.25) = .00075

16. The equivalent decimals are .07, .7, .075, and .697225. Arranging from least to greatest: .07, .075, .697225, and .7, which correspond to I, III, IV, and II.

17. The actual payments are (.20)($490) + (10)($47.75) = $575.50 Interest amount = $575.50 - $490 = $85.50

18. The number of plants he sold = $150 ÷ $0.75 = 200.
    Since he had 100 plants left, he originally purchased 200 + 100 = 300 plants.

19. Subtract the first equation from the second to get 2x = 1. So, x = .5. Substitute this x value in either equation. Choosing the first equation, (3)(.5) + y = 5. Then, y = 3.5

20. Let x = number of dimes, x + 3 = number of quarters.
    Then, .10x + .25(x+3) = 3.20. Simplifying, .35x + .75 = 3.20. Finally, x = 7

21. For the weed killer, since 3 pounds should be used on 15,000 square feet, this translates into 2 pounds per 10,000 square feet. The ratio on the 10,000 square feet of lawn for fertilizer to weed killer is 25 to 2. This reduces to 12.5 to 1.

22. 1.5 meters = 1.5 ÷ .9 = 1.67 yards

23. Substituting choice C, 8 to 40 = 1/5 and x/5 to x = 1/5

24. $18^2 = 324$ and $19^2 = 361$. Thus, $\sqrt{360} \approx 19$

25. Total miles = 45 + (1/2)(60) = 75. Total time = 1 + 1/2 = 1 1/2 hours
    Average speed = 75 ÷ 1 1/2 = 50 mi/hr.

TEST 2

DIRECTIONS: Each question or incomplete statement is followed by several suggested answers or completions. Select the one that BEST answers the question or completes the statement. *PRINT THE LETTER OF THE CORRECT ANSWER IN THE SPACE AT THE RIGHT.*

1. 1/3 of 15 = 15% of

    A. 3/4 B. 45 C. 75 D. 5 E. 33 1/3

    1.____

2. A tree in an apartment building courtyard died, and the cost of cutting down the tree is $350.00. The city will share the cost with the landlord on a 2 to 3 ratio, the landlord paying the larger part. How much will the landlord have to pay?

    A. $233.00 B. $175.00
    C. $117.00 D. $150.00
    E. $210.00

    2.____

3. $\dfrac{1}{2} + \dfrac{4}{2x-1} = 6$. x =

    A. -1/2 B. 13/22 C. 19/22 D. -1/4 E. -15/22

    3.____

4. The capacity of a car's cooling system if 17 quarts. 1 3/4 gallons of antifreeze plus 1 pint of rust inhibitor are required to drop the freezing point to -18°. How much water is required to fill the system to capacity?

    A. 21 pints B. 9 pints
    C. 19 pints D. 10 quarts
    E. 18 pints

    4.____

5. If 1 inch = 2.54 cm., 3/4 cm. = how many inches?

    A. 1.9 B. 3.39 C. .75 D. .19 E. .3

    5.____

6. A box has the shape of a rectangular solid, with a base measuring 16 inches by 10 inches and a height of 8 inches. What is the approximate length of the sides of a cubic container having the same volume?

    A. 9.75 inches B. 10.00 inches
    C. 10.85 inches D. 12.65 inches
    E. 13.15 inches

    6.____

7. What is a valid formula for the line plotted on the graph?
    A. x = y
    B. x = 10/y
    C. x = 10 - y
    D. x = y/10
    E. x = y + 10

    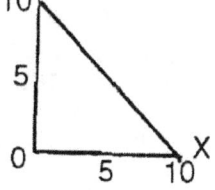

    7.____

8. In the fraction x/y, when 1 is added to the numerator, the fraction equals 1/3. When 3 is added to the denominator of x/y, the fraction equals 1/6. What is x/y?

    A. 2/6 B. 2/3 C. 2/9 D. 6/17 E. 2/12

    8.____

147

9. What is the *approximate* value of $\frac{(.03)^2(\sqrt{.25} + 3.5)}{.12}$?

   A. .03 B. .36 C. .003 D. 3.0 E. .0036

10. A woman is now three times as old as her son. In four years, the son will be one-half as old as the woman is now. How old is the woman now?

    A. 24 B. 28 C. 30 D. 21 E. 33

11. 1/5 of 27 = 25% of

    A. 21 3/5 B. 5.4 C. 1.35 D. 105/5 E. 21.5

12. A rancher had 70 head of cattle. A buyer made four purchases of cattle from the rancher. The rancher now has eighteen cattle remaining. On the average, how many cattle exchanged hands at EACH purchase?

    A. 10.5 B. 13 C. 15 D. 20 E. 52

13. $\sqrt{16 + x} = 4 + 2$ x =

    A. 36 B. 4 C. -10 D. 20 E. 2

14. If 10 cc of 20% acid is mixed with 20 cc of 40% acid, the percentage of acid in the resulting solution is

    A. 50 B. 30 C. 33 1/3 D. 35 E. 60

15. 5/6 + 5/9 - 2/3 + x = a whole number. Then x = ?

    A. 5/18 B. 13/16 C. 17/18 D. 18/13 E. 2/9

16. A piece of lumber is 63 inches long. It is to be cut in three pieces. Two pieces are to be of equal length, while the third piece is to be 9 inches longer than each of the other two pieces. How long will the longer piece of lumber be?

    A. 54 inches
    B. 36 inches
    C. 30 inches
    D. 27 inches
    E. 18 inches

17. The sun shining on a tree casts a shadow 45 feet long. A boy five feet tall standing near the tree has a 2 foot 10 inch shadow. How tall is the tree?

    A. 54 feet
    B. 22.5 feet
    C. 37.5 feet
    D. 79.4 feet
    E. 18 feet

18. x/95 = 7.5% x =

    A. 12.7 B. 7.1 C. 8.0 D. 1.26 E. 713

19. A street light shining on a signpost casts a shadow 6 feet long. A child 5 feet tall standing near the signpost casts a shadow 2 feet 3 inches long. How tall is the signpost?

    A. 13.3 feet
    B. 6.6 feet
    C. 12 feet
    D. 20 feet
    E. 15.3 feet

20. $\dfrac{(-2)^{15}}{(-2)^{12}} = ?$

   A. -4   B. +4   C. -8   D. +8   E. -16

21. Five consecutive whole numbers have a sum of 50. What is the second of the five numbers?

   A. 5   B. 7   C. 9   D. 10   E. 11

22. If z = 35% of w, and y = 15% of z, then y = _____% of w.

   A. 2.33   B. 42.9   C. 5.25   D. 2.25   E. 4.3

23. If (y + 2)x = 1/4, y =

   A. 1/4 - 2x
   B. 1/4x - 2
   C. 1/4x + 8
   D. x/4 - 2
   E. 1 - 8x/4

24. A set of drill bits are being sold for $200.00. The bits cost the dealer $160.00, plus a $20.00 shipping fee. What percent of the selling price will be profit for the dealer?

   A. 7%   B. 10%   C. 11%   D. 21%   E. 30%

25. Let A be the area of a circle whose diameter is 8. Which of the following numbers is closest to A?

   A. 50   B. 70   C. 100   D. 120   E. 200

KEY (CORRECT ANSWERS)

1.	E	11.	A
2.	E	12.	B
3.	C	13.	D
4.	C	14.	C
5.	E	15.	A
6.	C	16.	D
7.	C	17.	D
8.	C	18.	B
9.	A	19.	A
10.	A	20.	C

21. C
22. C
23. B
24. B
25. A

SOLUTIONS TO PROBLEMS

1. 1/3 of 15 = 5. Then, 5 ÷ .15 = 33 1/3

2. Let 2x = city's cost and 3x = landlord's cost. 2x + 3x = $350 Solving, x = $70. Then, landlord's cost is (3)($70) = $210

3. Multiplying the equation by (2)(2x-1), we get (1)(2x-1) + (4)(2) = (6)(2)(2x-1). Simplifying, 2x - 1 + 8 = 24x - 12.
This reduces further to 19 = 22x. So, x = 19/22

4. 1 3/4 gallons = (1 3/4)(4) = 7 quarts = 14 pints of antifreeze.
The capacity of the cooling system = 17 quarts = 34 pints. Since 1 pint of rust inhibitor is needed, the amount of water required is 34 - 14 - 1 = 19 pints.

5. 3/4 cm = 3/4 ÷ 2.54 = .295 or about .3 inches

6. The volume of the box = (16)(10)(8) = 1280 cubic inches. If a cubic container has a volume of 1280 cubic inches, each side must be $\sqrt[3]{1280} \approx 10.85$ inches.
(Actually, the answer is slightly closer to 10.86)

7. Since the coordinates of the two given points are (10,0) and (0,10), the slope of the line is (10-0) ÷ (0-10) = -1. Y = -1x + B, where B is the y-intercept. Now, B = 10 since (0,10) lies on this line. Y = -1x + 10 is the equation and this can be written as x = 10 - y.

8. From the given information, (x+1)/y = 1/3 and x/(y+3) = 1/6 Rewriting, we have y = 3x + 3 and y = 6x - 3. Adding these equations, 2y = 9x. Thus, x/y = 2/9.

9. $(.03)^2$ = .0009. ($\sqrt{.25}$ + 3.5) = 4.0. The answer becomes (.0009)(4)/.12 = .03. (Change the word *approximate* to *exact*.)

10. Let x = woman's age, 1/3x = son's age. Then, 1/3 x + 4 = 1/2 x.
This reduces to 1/6 x = 4, so x = 24.

11. 1/5 of 27 = (.2)(27) = 5.4. Then, 5.4 ÷ .25 = 21.6 = 21 3/5

12. 70 - 18 = 52. Then, 52 ÷ 4 = 13.

13. $\sqrt{16+x}$ = 6. Square both sides to get 16 + x = 36. Then, x = 20

14. The amount of acid in the resulting solution is (.20)(10) + (.40)(20) = 10 cc. The solution is 10 + 20 = 30 cc. Percentage of acid is (10/30)(100) = 33 1/3

15. 5/6 + 5/9 - 2/3 = (15 + 10 - 12)/18 = 13/18. Since choice A is 5/18, 13/18 + 5/18 = 18/18 = 1, which is a whole number.

16. Let x = length of each shorter piece and x + 9 = length of the longer piece. x + x + x + 9 = 63. Solving, x = 18. So, the longer piece must be 27 inches.

17. The ratio of the boy's height to his shadow is 60 inches to 34 inches = 30 to 17 (reduced). Let x = height of the tree. Then, x/45 = 30/17. Solving, x ≈ 79.4 feet

5 (#2)

18. x/95 = .075. x = (.075)(95) = 7.125 or about 7.1   18.____

19. The ratio of the child's height to his shadow is 60 inches to 27 inches = 20 to 9 (reduced). Let x = height of the signpost. Then, x/6 = 20/9. Solving, x - 13.33 or about 13.3 feet.   19.____

20. In division, we subtract exponents to get $(-2)^3$ = -8. Of course, the base must remain the same.   20.____

21. Let x, x+1, x+2, x+3, x+4 represent the numbers. Then, x + x+1 + x+2 + x+3 + x+4 = 50. Solving, x = 8. The second number must be 9.   21.____

22. y = .15z = (.15)(.35)w = .0525w. Thus, y is 5.25% of w.   22.____

23. (y+2)(x) = 1/4. Dividing both sides by x, we get y + 2 = 1/4x. Finally, y = 1/4x - 2   23.____

24. The dealer's total cost is $180 and his profit is $20. The percent profit on the selling price is (20/200)(100) = 10%.   24.____

25. A=$(\pi)(4)^2$ = 16 π = 50.265 or about 50. Note that the formula is Area = (π) (radius)^2.   25.____

MATHEMATICS PROBLEM SOLVING

EXAMINATION SECTION
TEST 1

DIRECTIONS: Each question or incomplete statement is followed by several sug-gested answers or completions. Select the one that BEST answers the question or completes the statement. *PRINT THE LETTER OF THE CORRECT ANSWER IN THE SPACE AT THE RIGHT.*

1. Mr. Marsh left an estate amounting to $24,000. By his will, 10% was to be given to a college, 15% to a church, and the remainder was to be divided equally among 3 nieces. How much money did *each* niece receive?

    A. $6120 B. $2000 C. $6333.33
    D. $6000 E. *None of these answers*

2. After selling one third of his apple crop, a farmer sold the remainder at the same price per bushel for $600. What was the *value* of the crop?

    A. $1000 B. $1200 C. $1800 D. $800
    E. *None of these answers*

3. A village has an assessed valuation of $2,400,000. The rate for school taxes is 80? per $100 valuation. If all but 2% of the taxes are collected, how many dollars remain *uncollected*?

    A. $18,816 B. $48,000 C. $384 D. $600
    E. *None of these answers*

4. When a = 2, c = 1, and d = 0, what is the value of the ex-pression $4a + 2c^2 - 3d^2$?

    A. 7 B. 9 C. 12 D. 15
    E. *None of these answers*

5. The difference between one half of a number and one fifth of it is 561. Find the number.

    A. 168 B. 2805 C. 1870 D. 5610
    E. *None of these answers*

6. Two triangles of the same shape are *always*

    A. similar B. equilateral C. congruent
    D. symmetrical E. equal

7. Which of the following is the BEST illustration of con-gruence?

    A. A pair of shoes
    B. Two dinner plates from the same set of dishes
    C. Any two tables
    D. A can of fruit and a cylinder
    E. A slide and its projection on a screen

8. On the average, 5 oranges will give 3 cupfuls of juice.
   If 2 cupfuls make a pint, how many oranges must be used to make 3 gallons of juice?
   A. 16 B. 20 C. 80
   D. 40 E. None of the above

   8.____

9. What is the difference in cost to a purchaser between an article listed at $500 less 10% and 20% and one listed at $490 less 20%?
   A. $18 B. $42 C. $58
   D. $48 E. None of the above

   9.____

10. A salesman receives a monthly salary of $80, a 2% commission on all monthly sales over $2,000 and an additional 1% commission on all sales over $11,000 a month.
    If his total sales for January came to $13,500, how much did he earn that month?
    A. 355 B. 365 C. 385
    D. 405 E. 415

    10.____

3 (#1)

KEY (CORRECT ANSWERS)

1. CORRECT ANSWER: D ($6,000)
   Since Mr. Marsh left 10% to a college and 15% to a church, 75% of his estate was to be equally divided among the three nieces, that is, 25% each. ¼ × $24,000 = $6,000.

2. CORRECT ANSWER: E (None of the above)
   Let x = the value of the crop. 2/3x = $600, x = $900.

3. CORRECT ANSWER: C ($384)
   Divide $2,400,000 by 100 to obtain the number of hundreds. The number is 24,000. 24,000 × .80 = $19,200 (total taxes to be collected) and $19,200 × .02 = $384 (taxes uncollected).

4. CORRECT ANSWER: E (None of the above)
   $4a + 2c^2 - 3d^2$ $4 \times 2 + 2 \times 1^2 - 30 \times 0^2 = 8 + 2 - 0 = 10$

5. CORRECT ANSWER: C (1,870)
   If x = the number, then the numbers are x/2 and x/5 (given).
   ∴ x/2 − x/5 = 561 or 3x = 5,610, x = 1,870

6. CORRECT ANSWER: A (Similar)
   By definition

7. CORRECT ANSWER: B (Two dinner plates from the same set of dishes)
   By definition, congruent figures agree in size and shape. Statement B appears to answer this requirement.

8. CORRECT ANSWER: C (80)
   Table: 2 pints = 1 quart and 4 quarts = 1 gallon. Since 8 pints = 1 gallon and 2 cupfuls = 1 pint, there are 48 cupfuls in 3 gallons. Let x − the number of oranges needed to make 3 gallons of juice. Then, 5(oranges)/3(cupfuls) = x(oranges)/48(cupfuls) or 3x = 240x = 80.

9. CORRECT ANSWER: E (None of the above)
   1. $550 × .10 = $50; $500 − $50 = $450
      $450 × .20 = $90; $450 − $90 = $360
   2. $490 × .20 = $98; $490 − $98 = $392
      $392 − $360 = $32.

10. CORRECT ANSWER: A ($355)
    Basic salary: $80 a month
    .02 × $11,500 ($13,500 − $2,000) = $230
    .01 × $2,500 ($13,500 − $11,000) = $25
    ∴ $80 + $230 + $25 = $335 (total monthly earnings)

TEST 2

DIRECTIONS: Each question or incomplete statement is followed by several suggested answers or completions. Select the one that BEST answers the question or completes the statement. *PRINT THE LETTER OF THE CORRECT ANSWER IN THE SPACE AT THE RIGHT.*

1. How much longer does it take an automobile to travel one mile at 20 miles per hour than at 30 miles per hour?
    A. 1 minute
    B. 10 minutes
    C. 20 minute
    D. 40 minutes
    E. None of the above

2. A man wishes to construct a poultry house 12 feet long in which to keep 20 hens.
   If each hen requires 4 square feet of floor space, how wide should he construct the poultry house?
    A. 28 feet
    B. 80 feet
    C. 5 feet
    D. 6 feet 8 inches
    E. None of the above

3. Aluminum bronze consists of copper and aluminum, usually in the ratio of 10:1 by weight.
   If a machine made of this alloy weighs 66 pounds, how many pounds of aluminum does it contain?
    A. 660
    B. 60
    C. 6.6
    D. 59.4
    E. None of the above

4. Mr. Brown owned a house, which he rented for $600 a month. The house was assessed at $90,000. In 2005 the rate of taxation was increased from $250 to $280 per $10,000 assessed valuation.
   By what amount should the monthly rent have been RAISED to absorb the increase in that year's taxes?
    A. $72.00
    B. $22.50
    C. $30.00
    D. $210
    E. None of the above

5. A dealer bought 3 gross of pencils at $3.80 a dozen. He sold the pencils at $.50 each.
   How much was his profit per gross?
    A. $79.20
    B. $26.40
    C. $2.20
    D. $6.60
    E. None of the above

6. How many cubic yards of earth had to be removed to make an excavation 30 feet long, 21 feet wide, and 6 feet deep?
    A. 1,260
    B. 3,780
    C. 140
    D. 420
    E. None of the above

7. By what number is the area of a circle MULTIPLIED if its radius is doubled?
    A. $2\pi r$
    B. 2
    C. 3.1416
    D. 4
    E. None of the above

2 (#2)

8. The State tax rate on 2003 incomes was 2% on the first $10,000 of income subject to tax and 3% on the next $20,000 or any part thereof. By special law, the State allowed a deduction of ¼ of the tax computed on the above schedule. In 2003, $18,000 of Mr. Brown's income was subject to tax.
What was the amount of his tax?
   A. $110
   B. $270
   C. $330
   D. $90
   E. None of the above

8._____

9. A baseball team won w games and lost 1 game. What fractional part of its games did it win?
   A. 1/W
   B. W/1
   C. W – 1/W
   D. W + 1/W
   E. None of the above

9._____

10. A pole is held upright by 3 guy wires, each fastened to the pole 12 feet above the ground. The other ends of these wires are fastened to stakes 16 feet from the foot of the pole.
Find the number of feet of wire required if 2 feet are added to each guy wire for making connections.
   A. 18 feet
   B. 66 feet
   C. 90 feet
   D. 54 feet
   E. None of the above

10._____

3 (#2)

KEY (CORRECT ANSWERS)

1. CORRECT ANSWER: A (1 minute)
   1. Since the automobile travels 1 mile at 20 miles per hour, it covers 20 miles in 1 hour or 1 mile in 3 minutes (60/20).
   2. Since the automobile travels 1 mile at 30 miles per hour, it covers 30 miles in 1 hour or 1 mile in 2 minutes (60/30)
   3. ∴ it takes automobile (1) 1 minute more than automobile (2) (3 minutes − 2 minutes = 1 minute)

2. CORRECT ANSWER: D (6 feet 8 inches)
   Total area of poultry house = 4 sq. ft. × 2 hens = 80 sq. ft.
   Formula: length × width = area
   Since the length, 12 ft., is given, we may represent the width by w.
   ∴ 12 × w = 80, w = 6 $^2/_3$ ft. = 6 feet 8 inches

3. CORRECT ANSWER: E (None of the above)
   In other words, 1 lb. of every 11 pounds of aluminum bronze is aluminum
   ∴ 1/11 × 66 lbs. = 6 lbs.

4. CORRECT ANSWER: B ($22.50)
   First rate of taxation: $90,000 (assessment) × .25 ($250 per $10,000)
   $\qquad$ = $2,250 (total taxes)
   Second rate of taxation (2005): $90,000 (assessment) × .28 ($280 per $10,000)
   $\qquad$ = $2,520 (total taxes)
   The increase in taxes = $270 per year ($2,520 - $2,250);
   ∴ the monthly rent should have been raised $22.50 ($270/12).

5. CORRECT ANSWER: B ($26.40)
   Since the selling price per dozen = $6.00 (.5 × 12) and the cost = $3.80 (given) per dozen, the profit per dozen = $2.20 ($6.00 - $3.80).
   ∴ the profit per gross (= 12 doz.) = $2.20 × 12 = $26.40

6. CORRECT ANSWER: C (140)
   Change the feet to yards since we are to deal with cubic yards.
   Formula: Volume = length × width × depth.
   By substitution, volume = 10 yds. × 7 yds. × 2 yds. = 140 cu. yds.

7. CORRECT ANSWER: D (4)
   Formula: Area of a circle = π^2
   If x = radius of original circle, then 2x = radius of new circle.
   Area of original circle $\pi \times 2$; area of new circle = $\pi(2x)^2 = 4\pi x^2$
   ∴ the area of the original circle has been multiplied by 4.

8. CORRECT ANSWER: C ($330)
   $10,000 × .02 = $200 (2% tax on the first $10,000)
   $8,000 × .03 = $240 (3% tax on the next $20,000, in this case $18,000, or $8,000).
   Total tax computed = $440; deduction = $110 (1/4 × $440).
   ∴ $440 - $110 = $330 (Mr. Brown's tax).

9. CORRECT ANSWER: E (None of the above)
   Formula: won/played = fractional part of games won.
   Games won = w; games played = w + 1
   ∴ w/w + 1 = fraction part of games won.

10. CORRECT ANSWER: B (66 feet)
    A right triangle is formed.
    Let x = the length of each guy wire.
    ∴ $x^2 = 12^2 + 16^2$ or $x^2 = 400$; x = 20 ft.; 20 ft. + 2 ft. = total length of each guy wire for making connections = 22 ft.
    ∴ 22 ft. × 3 = 66 ft. (total amount of wire needed for all 3 guy wires).

TEST 3

DIRECTIONS: Each question or incomplete statement is followed by several suggested answers or completions. Select the one that BEST answers the question or completes the statement. *PRINT THE LETTER OF THE CORRECT ANSWER IN THE SPACE AT THE RIGHT.*

1. What is the number of feet traversed in 1 second by an automobile that is traveling 30 miles an hour?
   A. 176
   B. 2
   C. 2,640
   D. 44
   E. None of the above

   1.____

2. The Jonesville Construction Company borrowed $225,000 for five years at 3 ½%.
   What was the ANNUAL charge for interest?
   A. $1,575
   B. $1,555
   C. $7,875
   D. $39,375
   E. None of the above

   2.____

3. The stock that Mr. Ames bought cost him $80 a share. The par value of the stock is $100.
   If the stock pays $6 a year in dividends, what rate of interest is Mr. Ames getting on his money?
   A. 16 ⅔%
   B. 7 ½%
   C. 3%
   D. 6%
   E. None of the above

   3.____

4. The figure shown at the right represents a rectangle whose dimensions are l and w, surmounted by a semicircle whose radius is r. Express the area of this figure in terms of l, w, r and π.
   A. wl + πr²/2
   B. lw + πr²
   C. lw + πr
   D. π/2 - r²lw
   E. None of the above

   4.____

5. If one machine can do a piece of work in 10 hours and a second machine can do the same work in 15 hours, how many hours will it take BOTH machines working simultaneously to do the work?
   A. 12 ½
   B. 25
   C. 5
   D. 6
   E. None of the above

   5.____

6. A baseball diamond is a square 90 feet on a side. Find, correct to the nearest foot, the distance from third base to first base.
   A. 180 feet
   B. 135 feet
   C. 127 feet
   D. 90 feet
   E. None of the above

   6.____

7. A painted wooden cube whose edge is 3 inches is cut into 27 one-inch cubes. How many of these small cubes have just two painted sides?
    A. 12   B. 18   C. 8
    D. 9   E. None of the above

8. A certain lending library charges a cents for the first week that a book is loaned and b cents for each day over one week.
    Write the formula for C, the cost in cents, of taking a book for d days from this library, (d > 7).
    A. C = a + bd   B. C = a + b(d-7)   C. C + ad
    D. C = 7a + b(d-7)   E. None of the above

9. How many gallons of water must be added to 20 gallons of a 10% solution of salt and water to REDUCE it to an 8% solution?
    A. 10   B. 2   C. 16
    D. 4   E. None of the above

10. The net profit of the ABC Company dropped from 34 million dollars in 2014 to 33 million in 2015.
    What percent of decrease does this represent? (Give answer correct to the nearest tenth of a percent)
    A. 97.0   B. 2.9   C. 3.0
    D. 97.1   E. None of the above

KEY (CORRECT ANSWERS)

1. CORRECT ANSWER: D (44)
   If the auto is traveling 30 miles an hour, this means that the auto covers 30 miles in one hour, or ½ mile in one minute (30 miles = 60 min.). To convert to seconds, as the answer calls for, divide ½ by 60 sec., viz, 1/2/60 = 1/120 mile in one second.
   Then, 120/x × 5,280 ft. (= 1 mile) = 44 ft. in one second.

2. CORRECT ANSWER: C ($7,875)
   Formula: Principal × rate × time = interest $225,000 × .035 × 1 yr. = $7,875.

3. CORRECT ANSWER: B (7 ½%)
   Formula: Principal × rate = interest (or dividend). Let x = rate of interest.
   By substitution, $80 × $6 or x = 6/80, x = .075 or 7 ½%

4. CORRECT ANSWER: A (wl + $\pi r^2/2$)
   This figure represents both a rectangle and a semicircle.
   Formulas: Area of rectangle = l (length) ×w (width) or lw or wl
   Area of semicircle: $\pi r^2 2$
   Area of this figure = wl + $\pi r^2/2$

5. CORRECT ANSWER: D (6)
   Formula: Time worked/Time required = Part of job completed
   Let x = number of hours it will take both machines together to do work.
   Then, x/10 = work of one machine and x/15 = work of second machine.
   We now form the equation: x/10 + x/15 = 1 (the entire job) or 15x + 10x = 150, or 25x = 150, x = 6.

6. CORRECT ANSWER: C (127 feet)
   A right triangle is formed when a line, x, is drawn from third base to first base.
   ∴ $x^2 = 90^2 + 90^2$ or $x^2 = 16,200x$,
   x = 127.2 ft. or 127 ft. (to the nearest foot).

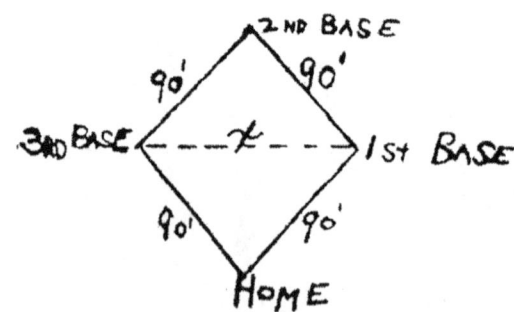

7. CORRECT ANSWER: A (12)
   By inspection

8. CORRECT ANSWER: B (C = a + b(d-7)
   a = cents charged for first week
   b = cents charged for each day over one week
   d-7 = extra days beyond the first week (given: d > 7)
   ∴ C = a + b(d-7)

4 (#3)

9. CORRECT ANSWER: E (None of the above)
Let x = number of gallons of water that must be added.
Then, 20 + x = quantity of solution after water is added.
10% × 20 gal. = 2 gal. salt in the first solution.
8% × (20+x) = amount of salt in second solution.
∴ 2 gal. (amount of salt in first solution) = .08(20+x) (amount of salt in the second solution)
or 2 = 1.60 + .08x or 8x = 40, x = 5 gal.

10. CORRECT ANSWER: B (2.9)
The drop in profit = one million dollars (34 million – 33 million)
∴ 1/34 = .0293 = 2.9% (to the nearest tenth of a percent).

TEST 4

DIRECTIONS: Each question or incomplete statement is followed by several suggested answers or completions. Select the one that BEST answers the question or completes the statement. *PRINT THE LETTER OF THE CORRECT ANSWER IN THE SPACE AT THE RIGHT.*

1. One manufacturing plant built 150 tanks in the last six months in 2005. This was an increase of 150% over the number built in the preceding six months. Find the number of tanks built in the preceding six months.
   A. 100
   B. 50
   C. 0
   D. 60
   E. None of the above

2. What is the difference between the area of a rectangle 10 feet by 6 feet and the area of a square having the same perimeter?
   A. 165 sq.ft.
   B. 8 sq.ft.
   C. No difference
   D. 4 sq.ft.
   E. None of the above

3. How many cubic yards of concrete are needed to make 1,200 square concrete posts 9 inches by 6 feet?
   A. 150
   B. 194,400
   C. 5,400
   D. 4,050
   E. None of the above

4. Find, correct to the nearest tenth of a foot, the diameter of the largest circular mirror that will pass through a doorway 7 feet high and 3 feet wide. (Neglect thickness of mirror.)
   A. 6.9 feet
   B. 7.0 feet
   C. 3.0 feet
   D. 7.6 feet
   E. None of the above

5. What is the GREATEST number of pictures, each 2½ inches by 3½ inches, that a photographer can print on an 8-inch by 10-inch piece of sensitized paper?
   A. 9
   B. 6
   C. 3
   D. 8
   E. None of the above

6. The net profits of the ABC Company dropped from 35 million dollars in 2004 to 28 million in 2005.
   What percent decrease does this represent?
   A. 7%
   B. 20%
   C. 25%
   D. 80%
   E. None of the above

7. If 12 gallons of gas drove one car a distance of 188.4 miles and the same amount of gas took another car a distance of 202.8 miles, how much BETTER mileage per gallon has the second car than the first?
   A. 1.7
   B. 5
   C. 12
   D. 14.4
   E. None of the above

1.____
2.____
3.____
4.____
5.____
6.____
7.____

8. The length of a rectangle is 12 inches and its width is 8 inches. Let the length of the rectangle be increased by 3 inches and the width be decreased by 3 inches.
   Which of the following statements is TRUE?
   A. The area of the rectangle remains the same.
   B. The area is increased by 9 square inches.
   C. The perimeter remains the same.
   D. The perimeter is increased by 6 inches.
   E. Both the perimeter and the area remain the same.

   8.____

9. Approximately how many tons of coal will a bin 10 feet by 6 feet by 5 feet hold if 1 ton fills 38 cubic feet of space? (Find the answer correct to the nearest ton.)
   A. 1
   B. 7
   C. 3
   D. 8
   E. None of the above

   9.____

10. The gauge on a 10-gallon oil tank indicates that exactly 3/8 of the oil remains in the tank.
    How many gallons will it require to fill the tank?
    A. 2¼
    B. 3¾
    C. 6½
    D. 7¼
    E. None of the above

    10.____

KEY (CORRECT ANSWERS)

1. CORRECT ANSWER: D (60)
   Let x = number of tanks built first half of 2005
   Let 1.5x (150%x) = increase in number of tanks built last half of 2005.
   x + 1.5x = number of tanks built last half of 2005.
   ∴ x + 1.5x = 150 or 25x = 1500, x = 60

2. CORRECT ANSWER: D (4 sq. ft.)
   Area of rectangle = length × width = 10 × 6 = 60 sq. ft.; perimeter of rectangle = 2.
   (length +width) = 2(10+6) = 32 ft.
   Perimeter of square = 32 ft. (given, same as that of rectangle)
   One side of square = 8 ft. (¼ of perimeter)
   Area of square = (side)2 = 82 = 64 sq. ft.
   ∴ 64 sq. ft. (area of square) – 60 sq. ft. (area of rectangle) = 4 sq. ft.

3. CORRECT ANSWER: A (150)
   First convert the inches and feet to yards since the answer calls for cubic yards, viz.,
   9 in. = ¼ yd. and 6 ft. = 2 yds.
   Formula: Volume (of a post) = length × width × height
   Volume (of 1200 posts) = 1200 × ¼ × ¼ × 2 = 150 cu. yds.

4. CORRECT ANSWER: D (7.6 feet)
   By drawing the diagonal (or diameter) AD, a right triangle
   is formed.
   Designate the diagonal by x.
   ∴ $x^2 = 3^2 + 7^2$ or $x^2 = 58$, x = 7.6 ft. (to the nearest
   tenth of a foot)

   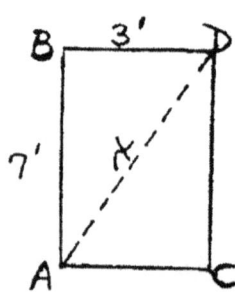

5. CORRECT ANSWER: D (8)
   This problem is solved by sketches of the only two possible ways of securing the greatest
   number of pictures, shown below.

   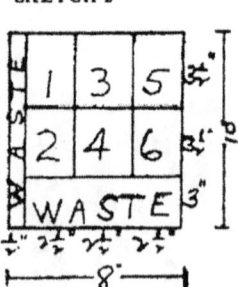

   8 pictures are secured when the 2½ in. side is cut along the 10 in. side of the sensitized
   paper and only 6 pictures are obtained when the 2½ in. side is cut along the 8i in. side of
   the sensitized paper.

4 (#4)

6. CORRECT ANSWER: B (20%)

$$\frac{7 \text{ (drop in net profits)(in millions of dollars)}}{35 \text{ (profit in 2004)(in millions of dollars)}} = \frac{1}{5} = 20\%$$

7. CORRECT ANSWER: E (None of the above)
The problem may be solved as follows:

Formula: $\frac{\text{distance}}{\text{gallons used}}$ = mileage

Mileage of car 1: by substitution, $\frac{188.4 \text{ miles}}{12 \text{ gal}}$ = 15.7 miles per gal.

Mileage of car 2: by substitution, $\frac{202.8 \text{ miles}}{12 \text{ gal}}$ = 16.9 miles per gal.

∴ car 2 exceeds car 1 in mileage by 1.2 miles per gal.

8. CORRECT ANSWER: C (The perimeter remains the same.)
Since the area of a rectangle = length × width, the area of the original triangle = 96 sq. in. (12" × 8") and the area of the newly-formed triangle = 75 sq. in. (15" × 5"). Using this information, we find that all of the statements, except C, are false. To prove statement C is true, we use the formula: perimeter = 2 (length+width).
By substitution, we find that the perimeter of the original rectangle = 40 in. (2(12+8)), and the perimeter of the newly-formed rectangle = 40 in. (2(15+5)).

9. CORRECT ANSWER: D (8)
Formula: volume = length × width × height
By substitution, the volume of the bin = 10 × 6 × 5 = 300 cu. ft.
Let x = no. of tons of coal that the above bin will hold.
We form the proportion: 1 ton : 38 cu. ft. = x : 300 cu. ft. or 38x = 300, x = 7.8 tons or 8 tons (to the nearest ton).

10. CORRECT ANSWER: E (None of the above)
Since 3/8 of the oil is left in the tank, 5/8 more is needed to fill it.
∴ 5/8 × 10 (capacity:given) = 6¼ gal.

TEST 5

DIRECTIONS: Each question or incomplete statement is followed by several suggested answers or completions. Select the one that BEST answers the question or completes the statement. *PRINT THE LETTER OF THE CORRECT ANSWER IN THE SPACE AT THE RIGHT.*

1. A pile of steel plates is 2.75 feet high. If the plates are .375 inch thick, how many are there in the pile? 1.____
   A. 7 B. 8 C. 14
   D. 88 E. None of the above

2. At the rate of $1.50 per 6-oz. bar of chocolate, how much would a pound of chocolate cost? 2.____
   A. $3.00 B. $3.40 C. $3.90
   D. $4.50 E. None of the above

3. A man walks diagonally from one corner of a rectangular lot to the opposite corner. 3.____
   If he walks at the rate of 5 feet a second, and the lot is 50 feet by 120 feet, how many seconds will he save by walking diagonally instead of walking along the perimeter of the lot?
   A. 8 B. 10 C. 17
   D. 34 E. None of the above

4. The afternoon classes in a school begin at 1 P.M. and end at 3:52 P.M. There are 4 class periods with 4 minutes between classes. 4.____
   How many minutes are there in each class period?
   A. 39 B. 40 C. 59
   D. 60 E. None of the above

5. A snapshot measures $1^7/_8$" × $2½$". It is to be enlarged so that the longer dimension will be 4". 5.____
   What will be the length of the SHORTER dimension?
   A. $2^3/_8$" B. $2½$" C. 3"
   D. $3^3/_8$" E. None of the above

6. The minimum temperatures at Jonesville for each day of one week were as follows: +7°, +13°, +5°, -4°, 0°, +3°. 6.____
   Find, to the nearest degree, the AVERAGE minimum temperature.
   A. 6° B. 2° C. 16°
   D. 4° E. None of the above

7. If the outer diameter of an iron pipe is 14.38 inches and the inner diameter is 12.50 inches, what is the thickness of the pipe? 7.____
   A. .94" B. 1.88" C. 16.88"
   D. 26.88" E. None of the above

168

8. In the fall of 2012, a store charged $4.40 a pound for chuck steak. In February 2013, the same store had increased by 50% the price of that grade of steak. Later, the government announced a ceiling of $5.50 a pound.
What percent reduction did the store have to make in its February 2013 price in order to comply with the government ruling?
   A. 11 1/9%
   B. 16 2/3%
   C. 20%
   D. 25%
   E. None of the above

   8._____

9. A certain whole number has 10 digits. If the square root of this number is taken, how many digits will there be in the integral part of the answer?
   A. 1
   B. 5
   C. 9
   D. 100
   E. None of the above

   9._____

10. Four tractors working together can plow a field in 12 hours.
How long will it take 6 tractors to plow a field of the same size if all tractors work at the same rate?
   A. 6 hr.
   B. 9 hr.
   C. 10 hr.
   D. 18 hr.
   E. None of the above

   10._____

KEY (CORRECT ANSWERS)

1. CORRECT ANSWER: D (88)
Convert 2.75 ft. to inches by multiplying by 12 = 33 in.
Then, 33/.375 = 88

2. CORRECT ANSWER: E (None of the above)
$1.50 is the price of a 6 oz. bar of chocolate.
Since 1 lb. = 16 oz., the cost of 1 lb. of chocolate = $4.00 (16 × 2½).

3. CORRECT ANSWER: A (8)
First, we must figure the number of feet that the man walks diagonally (AC in the diagram), and then we must find the number of feet that he will walk by going along the perimeter of the lot (from C to A by way of D, or CD + AD).
Since the diagonal represented by x forms a right triangle, we have the equation:
$x^2 = 50^2 + 120^2$ or $x^2 = 16{,}900$ x = 130 ft. (AC). CD + AD (walking along the perimeter) = 170 ft. (50+120).
∴ the man saves 4 ft. by walking diagonally (170-130); and since he walks at the rate of 5 ft. a second, he saves 8 sec. (40/5).

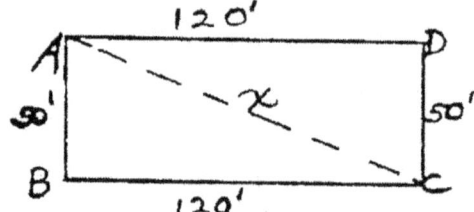

4. CORRECT ANSWER: B (40)
Total time = 2 hours 52 min. or 172 min. (3:52 P.M. – 1 P.M.). Since there are 4 class periods, there are 3 intervals of 4 min. each (12 min. in all) between these periods.
∴ 172 – 12 = 160 min. (total time for the class periods) and 160/4 = 40 min. (time in each class period).

5. CORRECT ANSWER: C (3")
Let x = length of the shorter dimension.
∴ $1^7/_8$: x = 2½ : 4 or
5/2x = 60/8 or 40x = 120, x = 3"

6. CORRECT ANSWER: B (2°)
The sum of the temperatures given = 16; the number of readings is 7.
∴ 16°/7 = $2^2/_7$° or 2° (to the nearest degree)

7. CORRECT ANSWER: A (.94")
Since the diameter of a circle is twice the radius, the outer radius is 7.19" (14.38"/2), and the inner radius is 6.25" (12.5÷2).
∴ the thickness of the pipe = .94" (7.19 – 6.25).

4 (#5)

8. CORRECT ANSWER: B ($16^2/_3\%$)
   $4.40 + .50($4.40) = $6.60 (price as of February 2013).
   Since the ceiling price was announced as $5.50, a reduction of $1.10 was necessary ($6.60 - $5.50).
   ∴ $1.10 ÷ $6.60 = $\frac{1}{6}$ = $16^2/_3\%$.

9. CORRECT ANSWER: B (5)
   In computing square root, we group the digits by two's, beginning with the decimal point and moving by two's to the left. Since there are 5 groups of two, each of which will have 1 digit in the answer, there will be 5 digits.

10. CORRECT ANSWER: E (None of the above)
    Let x = time required for 6 tractors
    ∴ 4:6 (tractors) = x:12 (time) or
    6x = 48, x = 8 hours

ARITHMETICAL CONCEPTS AND EXERCISES

1. DECIMAL FRACTIONS AND EQUIVALENT DECIMAL FORMS

A decimal fraction is one whose denominator is 1, 10, 100, 1000, etc. For instance, 7/1, 3/10, 46/100, 7/1000, and 512/100 are decimal fractions. Each decimal fraction may be written as a decimal number and vice versa.
Example: 3/10 = 0.3 (three tenths)
Example: 46/100 = 0.46 (forty-six hundredths)
Example: 7/1000 = 0.007 (seven thousandths)
Example: 512/100 = 5.12 (five and twelve hundredths)

2. DECIMAL PLACE VALUE

The chart below shows the place values of decimals. Note the decimal fractions to the right of the decimal point.

1,000,000's	100,000's	10,000's	1,000's	100's	10's	1's	.	1/10's	1/100's	1/1000's	1/10000's	1/100000's	1/1000000's
millions	hundred-thousands	ten-thousands	thousands	hundreds	tens	ones	decimal point	tenths	hundredths	thousandths	ten-thousandths	hundred-thousandths	millionths

Thus, 316,000 represents three hundred-thousands plus one ten-thousand plus six thousands. Similarly, 0.05 represents five hundredths. The numeral 0.055 represents five hundredths plus five thousandths.

Sometimes, numerals that look different represent the same number. For example,

.33 = 3/10 + 3/100

.3300 = 3/10 + 3/100 + 0/1000 + 0/10000

In general, adding zeros to the right of the decimal point at the end of a numeral won't change the value: 0.5 = 0.50, 0.612 = 0.612000, etc. (But don't try this if the decimal point is absent! For example, 5 ≠ 50 and 612 ≠ 612,000)

EXERCISES

1. Write each of the following as a sum of decimal fractions: Example: 0.31 = 3/10 + 1/100
   A. 0.713
   B. 0.0101
   C. 0.16724

2. Write each of the following as a single decimal fraction: Example: 0.41 = 41/100
   A. 0.3
   B. 0.03
   C. 0.005
   D. 0.13
   E. 1.65
   F. 7
   G. 37.126

3. ORDER OF DECIMAL NUMBERS

One of the great advantages of the decimal system is the ease with which two numbers can be compared; for example, which is larger: 37.39278 or 37.393841?

To answer a question like this, merely match the two numbers, decimal place by decimal place.

$$
\begin{array}{ccccccc}
3 & 7 & . & 3 & 9 & 2 & 7 & 8 \\
\updownarrow & \updownarrow & & \updownarrow & \updownarrow & \updownarrow & \updownarrow & \updownarrow \\
3 & 7 & . & 3 & 9 & 3 & 8 & 4 & 1
\end{array}
$$

Here the second value of the two is larger. Both numbers contain 3 tens, 7 ones, 3 tenths and 9 hundredths. The second number, however, contains 3 thousandths whereas the first number contains only 2 thousandths. (No matter what digits appear to the right of the thousandths place, the second number will now always be larger than the first.)

Hence, you need only compare two numbers, decimal place by decimal place, from left to right, until you reach a place where the digits differ. The larger digit will belong to the larger number; for example, which is larger: 0.33 or 0.3321? Match up the first digit 3 in both numbers. So far the values are equal. Match up the second digit 3. The values are still equal. What in the first gets matched with the digit 2 in the second number? Recall that 0.33 = 0.3300 so

$$
\begin{array}{cccccc}
0 & . & 3 & 3 & 0 & 0 \\
\updownarrow & & \updownarrow & \updownarrow & \updownarrow & \updownarrow \\
0 & . & 3 & 3 & 2 & 1
\end{array}
$$

the second number, 0.3321, is clearly larger than the first, 0.33.

EXERCISES

3. Identify the larger value.

   Example: 0.32 or 0.31. Answer: 0.32 because 0.32 contains 3 tenths and 2 hundredths, while 0.31 contains 3 tenths and only 1 hundredth. Note:

   ```
   0    3  2
   ↕    ↕  ↕
   0    3  1
   ```
   The value of 2 in the first number is larger than the value of 1 in the second number.

   Example: 0.32 or 0.317. Answer: 0.32 because, although both numbers contain 3 tenths, the first number contains more hundredths than the second. (Since the numbers differ at the second decimal place, we need not be concerned with the third or following decimal places.)

   Example: 0.31 or 0.317. Answer: 0.317 because 0.31 contains 3 tenths and 1 hudredth, but 0.317 contains 3 tenths, 1 hundredth, and 7 thousandths, or

   $0.31 = 3/10 + 1/100$ but $0.317 = 3/10 + 1/100 + 7/1000$

   A. 0.41689 or 0.4172*
   B. 3.716 or 3.7161
   C. 0.55 or 0.555
   D. .5 or .03
   E. 23.18 or 23.0971
   F. 14.386 or 14.00001
   G. 37.26 or 47.013

*NOTE: Some students feel that having many digits to the right of a decimal point makes a number small. This is an incorrect belief. It is the value of the digits that counts, not how many there are; for example:
    0.66666 is larger than 0.666,
    41.68888 is smaller than 41.7

4. Place in increasing order:

   A. 0.32, 0.3222, 0.370, 0.03
   B. 4.5, 4.05, 4.55, 4.3271
   C. 0.06, 0.31, 1.002, 0.56, 0.5

5. Identify three different numbers between 0.391 and 0.4

6. Which of the following lie between 0.6 and 0.41?
    0.06, 0.66, 0.5, 0.4444, 0.39, 0.599

7. An old document contains several six-digit decimal numbers. Unfortunately, some of the digits have faded and are indicated below by X's. Of the two values given, which number is the larger?

   A. 0.65X123 or 0.7XXXXXX
   B. 0.5X4000 or 0.6XX000
   C. 0.6X3124 or 0.6X4917
   D. 0.X5521X or 0.99131X

8. Which of the following lie between 1.003 and 1.2?
   1.125, 1.02, 1.00044, 1.111, 1.202

4. ADDING, SUBTRACTING, MULTIPLYING, AND DIVIDING DECIMALS

To add two or more decimal numerals, simply line up the decimal points and add. Thus, 3 + 4.68 + 7.1 becomes

$$\begin{array}{r} 3.0 \\ 4.68 \\ +7.1 \\ \hline 14.78 \end{array}$$

Subtraction is performed similarly.

Problem: Find 13.7 - 1.4

Solution:
$$\begin{array}{r} 13.7 \\ -1.4 \\ \hline 12.3 \end{array}$$

Problem: Find 1.2 - 0.687

Solution:
$$\begin{array}{r} 1.200 \\ -0.687 \\ \hline 0.513 \end{array}$$

To multiply two decimals, simply (a) multiply them as though they were whole numbers, (b) find the total number of digits to the right of the decimal point in the two numbers, (c) place the decimal point in your answer so that the number of digits to the decimal point's right is the number you found in (b).

Problem: Find 3.321 x 4.62

Solution:
```
    3.321      3 digits to right of decimal point
  × 4.62       2 digits to right of decimal point
  ------
    6642
   19926       Therefore, a total of 5 digit to right
   13284       of decimal point
  ------
  15.34302
```

Division of decimals is illustrated by the following two examples.

1. To see that 13.56 ÷ 12 = 1.13, simply proceed as though you are dividing whole numbers. However, note the placement of the decimal points.

Problem: Find $12\overline{)13.56}$

Solution:
```
      1.13
 12)13.56
    12
    ‾‾
    15
    12
    ‾‾
     36
     36
     ‾‾
      0
```

2. If the number you are dividing by is also a decimal, move the decimal points of both numerals before proceeding.

Problem: Find 56.58 ÷ 2.3

Solution: 56.58 ÷ 2.3   becomes

$2.3\overline{)56.58}$ and then

$2.3\overline{)56.58}$ or

$23\overline{)565.8}$ so

```
       24.6
  23) 565.8
       46
       ‾‾
       105
        92
       ‾‾‾
        138
        138
        ‾‾‾
          0
```

Thus, 56.58 ÷ 2.3 = 24.6

EXERCISES

9. Compute:

    A. 3.2 + 42.1
    B. 27.01 + 3.6
    C. 1.007 + 17 + 2.15
    D. 18.61 - 1.52
    E. 4 - 0.68
    F. 13.6 - 8.01

10. Find the product or quotient:

    A. 3.21 . 4.6*
    B. 18.6 . 1.021
    C. 68.64 ÷ 2.6

D. 174.512 ÷ 2.6
E. 14.5935 ÷ 4.7

NOTE: Like the symbol, x, the symbol, •, is sometimes used as the multiplicative symbol.

5. POWERS OF TEN, SCIENTIFIC NOTATION

The *powers of ten* are shown below:

...10^{-3} 10^{-2} 10^{-1} 10^{0} 10^{1} 10^{2} 10^{3}...
...0.001   0.01   0.1   1   10   100   1000...

Any decimal number may be multiplied by a power of ten. Simply look at the exponent of the power of ten; for example, the 3 of 10^3 or the -2 of 10^{-2}. That exponent tells you how many places to move the decimal point and the direction in which to move the decimal point in the number you are multiplying; thus, $324.213 \times 10^2 = 32421.3$. (The decimal moves two places to the right when multiplying by 102.) Also, $324.213 \times 10^{-2} = 3.24213$. (The decimal point moves two places to the left when multiplying by 10^{-2}.)

Scientific notation is the name given to a particularly succinct way of expressing unusually large or unusually small numbers; for example, 83,000,000 would be expressed as 8.3×10^7 in scientific notation.

A number expressed in scientific notation consists of one nonzero digit to the left of the decimal point and multiplication by some power of ten. For example:

Problem: Express in scientific notation: 461,000, 0.0018, 8,000,000 and 0.001001.

Solution:
$461,000 = 4.61 \times 10^5$
$0.0018 = 1.8 \times 10^{-3}$
$8,000,000 = 8.0 \times 10^6$
$0.001001 = 1.001 \times 10^{-3}$

EXERCISES

11. Express as a whole number or decimal:

    A. 10^2
    B. 10^4
    C. 10^{-5}
    D. 10^{-2}

12. Express as a power of ten:

    A. 1,000
    B. 0.001
    C. 100
    D. 0.000001

13. Express without using powers of ten:
    Example: $4.2 \times 10^3 = 4200$

    A. 3.608×10^7

B. 1.01×10^4
C. 3.0×10^2
D. 1.1721×10^{-6}

14. Express in scientific notation:

    A. 345,000,000
    B. 0.003
    C. 0.0001099
    D. 36

15. Express your answer as either an integer or a power of ten:

    A. 37 times what number equals 370,000?
    B. 10,000 is what number times 100?
    C. 10,000 is what number times 0.01?
    D. 13,000 times what number equals 13?
    E. 120 is what number times 1.2?

16. Fill in the blank with a power of ten:

    A. $3000 = 30 \times$ _____
    B. $30 = 3000 \times$ _____
    C. $3.45 = 3.45 \times$ _____
    D. $345 = 3.45 \times$ _____

6. FRACTIONS AS DECIMALS, ROUNDING DECIMALS

To write a fraction as a decimal, simply divide the numerator by the denominator.

Problem: Express as 1/4 as a decimal.

Solution:
```
      .25
   4)1.000
      8
      ‾‾
      20
      20
      ‾‾
       0
```

Since the division process may continue without end, it is sometimes necessary to approximate the answer by reporting only a few decimal places. This process is called *rounding*. Thus to convert 7/13 to a decimal, divide 13 into 7.0000 and obtain 0.5384.... If you round the answer to three decimal places, you will obtain 0.538. If the answer is rounded to the nearest hundredth (two decimal places), the answer would be 0.54. Rounding to the nearest tenth will give you 0.5.

To round to the nearest tenth, for example, look at the next digit to the right. If it is 4 or less, you simply drop all digits to the right of the tenths place. If it is 5 or more, you increase the tenths by one and then drop the digits to the right of that digit. Thus, rounded to the nearest tenth, 0.5321 becomes 0.5, whereas, 4.65182 becomes 4.7.

Rounding is not used solely for digits to the right of a decimal place. If 468,351 is rounded to, say, the nearest thousand, it becomes 468,000. Rounded to the nearest hundred, it becomes 468,400.*

*NOTE: Watch the wording when you are asked to round computations; for instance, *Round 4,168.3749 to the nearest hundredth* is not the same as *Round 4,168.3749 to the nearest hundred*. The answer to the first problem is 4,168.37, whereas the answer to the second problem is 4,200.

EXERCISES

17. Round to the nearest hundredth:

    A. 0.46802
    B. 0.5136
    C. 12.47491
    D. 1.725

18. Round to the nearest tenth:

    A. 317.64
    B. 34.550
    C. 1,435.0550
    D. 104.499

19. Round the numerals in item 18 above to the nearest ten.

20. Express as a decimal:

    A. 1/2
    B. 3/8
    C. 5/16

21. Express as a decimal rounded to the nearest thousandth:

    A. 1/7
    B. 9/16
    C. 3/17

7. ADDING, SUBTRACTING, MULTIPLYING, AND DIVIDING FRACTIONS

The easiest arithmetic operation to perform on fractions is multiplication. To multiply two fractions, simply multiply corresponding numerators and denominators.

Problem: Compute $\frac{3}{7} \times \frac{4}{11}$

Solution: $\frac{3}{7} \times \frac{4}{11} = \frac{12}{77}$

Problem: Compute 1/3 of 19

Solution: $\frac{1}{3}$ of $19 = \frac{1}{3} \times \frac{19}{1} = \frac{19}{3}$

Problem: Compute 1/2 of 18

Solution: $\frac{1}{2}$ of $18 = \frac{1}{2} \times \frac{18}{1} = \frac{18}{2} = 9$

To divide two fractions, use this rule: *invert and multiply.*

Problem: Compute $\dfrac{1}{3} \div \dfrac{3}{7}$

Solution: $\dfrac{1}{3} \div \dfrac{3}{7} = \dfrac{1}{3} \times \dfrac{7}{3} = \dfrac{7}{9}$

Problem: Compute $\dfrac{1}{7} \div 3$

Solution: $\dfrac{1}{7} \div 3 = \dfrac{1}{7} \div \dfrac{3}{1} = \dfrac{1}{7} \times \dfrac{1}{3} = \dfrac{1}{21}$

Adding and subtracting fractions is, in general, not as simple as multiplying and dividing fractions. However, fractions with equal denominators can be added or subtracted directly:

$\dfrac{1}{7} + \dfrac{3}{7} = \dfrac{4}{7}$** and $\dfrac{7}{8} - \dfrac{5}{8} = \dfrac{2}{8}$

**NOTE: To find the sum of two fractions, NEVER add denominators.

Thus, $\dfrac{1}{2} + \dfrac{1}{2} = \dfrac{2}{2} = 1, \dfrac{1}{2} + \dfrac{1}{2} \neq \dfrac{2}{4}$

Fractions with different denominators are more of a problem. In order to add or subtract, you must convert the fractions, so that the denominators are equal. This can be done by multiplying numerators and denoninators by the same whole number. In the first example below, the numerator and denominator of 1/2 are both multiplied by 3 in the first step.

Problem: $\dfrac{1}{6} + \dfrac{1}{2}$

Solution: $\dfrac{1}{6} + \dfrac{1}{2} = \dfrac{1}{6} + \dfrac{1}{2} \times \dfrac{3}{3}$ Therefore,

$= \dfrac{1}{6} + \dfrac{3}{6}$ and,

$= \dfrac{4}{6}$

Problem: $\dfrac{1}{15} + \dfrac{1}{5}$

Solution: $\dfrac{1}{15} + \dfrac{1}{5} = \dfrac{1}{15} + \dfrac{1}{5} \times \dfrac{3}{3}$ Therefore,

$= \dfrac{1}{15} + \dfrac{3}{15}$ and,

$= \dfrac{4}{15}$

Problem: $\frac{2}{7} + \frac{1}{3}$

Solution: $\frac{2}{7} + \frac{1}{3} = \frac{2}{7} \times \frac{3}{3} + \frac{1}{3} \times \frac{7}{7}$ yields

$= \frac{6}{21} + \frac{7}{21}$ and,

$= \frac{13}{21}$

Usually, fractions are reduced to lowest terms. Thus, 2/4 might be reduced to 1/2. To reduce 2/4 to lowest terms, divide both numerator and denominator by 2.

Here are three other examples.

Problem: Reduce these fractions: $\frac{21}{35}, \frac{10}{80}, \frac{63}{147}$

Solution: $\frac{21}{35} = \frac{3}{5}$ (numerator and denominator are divided by 7)

$\frac{10}{80} = \frac{1}{8}$ (numerator and denominator are divided by 10)

$\frac{63}{147} = \frac{3}{7}$ (numerator and denominator are divided by 21)

Finally, if you encounter fractions written in *mixed* form, you can easily convert them to pure fractional notation. For example, = 3/2. This is so because 1 = 2/2, so 1 1/2 = 1 +1/2 = 2/2 + 1/2 = 3/2. Likewise, 4 1/3 = 4 + 1/3 = 12/3 + 1/3 = 13/3*. You can also convert in the other direction. Start with 13/3 and, by dividing 3 into 13, you will see that it equals 4 1/3.

*NOTE: The general rule for such cases: $a\frac{b}{c} = \frac{a \times c + b}{c}$.

Thus, 4 1/3 = $\frac{4 \times 3 + 1}{3} = \frac{13}{3}$

EXERCISES

22. Perform the indicated operations:

A. $\frac{3}{7} \times \frac{5}{11} =$

B. $\frac{1}{2} \times \frac{1}{7} =$

C. $\frac{3}{5} \times 3 =$

D. $\dfrac{3}{7} \div \dfrac{4}{11} =$

E. $15 \div \dfrac{1}{3} =$

F. $\dfrac{1}{7} + \dfrac{5}{7} =$

G. $\dfrac{3}{11} - \dfrac{2}{11} =$

H. $\dfrac{1}{10} + \dfrac{1}{5} =$

I. $\dfrac{1}{8} + \dfrac{5}{16} =$

J. $\dfrac{3}{7} + \dfrac{7}{15} =$

K. $\dfrac{4}{9} + \dfrac{1}{7} =$

L. $\dfrac{13}{5} - \dfrac{3}{2} =$

23. Reduce to lowest terms:

   A. $\dfrac{5}{15}$

   B. $\dfrac{4}{32}$

   C. $\dfrac{48}{208}$

   D. $\dfrac{154}{231}$

24. Add.

Example: $3\dfrac{1}{3} + 4\dfrac{1}{4} = 7 + \dfrac{1}{3} + \dfrac{1}{4} = 7 + \dfrac{4}{12} + \dfrac{3}{12}$
$= 7 + \dfrac{7}{12} = 7\dfrac{7}{12}$

   A. $3\dfrac{1}{2} + 4\dfrac{1}{3}$

   B. $7\dfrac{2}{5} + 8\dfrac{1}{3}$

C. $5\dfrac{4}{5}+1\dfrac{1}{4}$

8. ORDER AMONG FRACTIONS

How can you tell which of two fractions is larger? Sometimes little work is required when you can compare both fractions to a third fraction. We know, for example, that 5/8 is larger than 3/10 because 5/8 is larger than 1/2, whereas 3/10 is smaller than 1/2.

For more difficult comparisons, we can convert both fractions to decimal form and then compare the decimals. Thus, to compare 5/8 and 3/5, we might divide numerators by denominators, converting both to decimals. We would find that 5/8 = 0.625 and 3/5 = 0.6. Since 0.625 is larger than 0.6, it follows that 5/8 is larger than 3/5.

Of course, if both fractions have the same denominator, you can see at once which is larger. Obviously, 4/7 is larger than 3/7.

EXERCISES

25. Which is larger? 8/21 or 3/8?

26. Which is larger?

A. $\dfrac{4}{7}$ or $\dfrac{3}{5}$?

B. $\dfrac{4}{17}$ or $\dfrac{5}{21}$?

C. $\dfrac{13}{15}$ or $\dfrac{8}{9}$?

27. Arrange in increasing order.

A. $0.5, \dfrac{4}{7}, \dfrac{1}{3}, \dfrac{7}{17}, \dfrac{9}{19}, \dfrac{13}{23}$

B. $\dfrac{9}{19}, 0.45, \dfrac{2}{5}, \dfrac{17}{40}, \dfrac{4}{9}$

28. Which values lie between 1/2 and 2/3 ?

$\dfrac{3}{5}, \dfrac{5}{8}, 0.72, 0.05, \dfrac{5}{11}$

9. MEANING OF *PERCENT*

The word *percent* and the symbol % mean *per hundred*. Thus, since 25/100 means 25 per hundred, we can write 25/100 = 25%. Likewise, 13/100 = 13% and 7/100 = 7%.

To say, *All items on display are marked down 25%* means that each item has its price reduced by 25/100 = 1/4.

You will get 50% better gas mileage with this model car indicates that your mileage will go up by 50/100 = 1/2 of what it might otherwise be.

A percent can be written in decimal form. Simply move the decimal point two places to the left.

$$50\% = 0.50$$
$$25\% = 0.25$$
$$133\% = 1.33$$

Percents may also be written as fractions:
$$50\% = 1/2$$
$$75\% = 3/4$$
$$125\% = 1\frac{1}{4}$$

EXERCISES

29. Write as a fraction.

    A. 20%
    B. 75%
    C. 9%

30. Write as a decimal.

    A. 15%
    B. 246%
    C. 30%
    D. 9%
    E. 100%
    F. 1%

31. Compute.
    Example: 45% of 200 = 0.45 x 200 = 90.00

    A. 35% of 300
    B. 8% of $81.50
    C. 17% of $63

32. Place in increasing order:

    $$\frac{1}{2}, \frac{3}{7}, 42\%, 56\%, \frac{3}{8}, 100\%$$

33. Change the percents to fractions and solve.

    A. What is 50% of 80?
    B. What is 25% of 80?
    C. What is 10% of 80?
    D. What is 42% of 100?

10. DECIMALS AND FRACTIONS AS PERCENTS

Since a percent can be expressed as a decimal by moving the decimal point two places to the left, one can reverse the process to express a decimal as percent. Move the decimal point two places to the right to convert a decimal to a percent.

Example:
- A. 0.50 = 50%
- B. 0.417 = 41.7%
- C. 3 = 300%

Convert fractions to percents by converting the fraction to a decimal, then changing the decimal to a percent. Thus, by dividing 7.000 by 13, we can convert 7/13 into 0.538461. Round off the answer to three decimal places, for example, then move the decimal point two places to the right: 0.538 = 53.8%. Hence, 7/13 is approximately 53.8%

Of course, if you have a fraction that has, or can easily be made to have, a denominator of 100, converting to a percent is easy.

Problem: Convert the following to percents:

- A. $\dfrac{20}{100}$
- B. $\dfrac{8}{100}$
- C. $\dfrac{1}{2}$
- D. $\dfrac{1}{5}$
- E. $2\dfrac{1}{4}$

Solution:
- A. $\dfrac{20}{100} = 20\%$
- B. $\dfrac{8}{100} = 8\%$
- C. $\dfrac{1}{2} = \dfrac{50}{100} = 50\%$
- D. $\dfrac{1}{5} = \dfrac{20}{100} = 20\%$
- E. $2\dfrac{1}{4} = 2 + \dfrac{25}{100} = \dfrac{200}{100} + \dfrac{25}{100} = \dfrac{225}{100} = 225\%$

EXERCISES

34. Express as percents

    A. 0.13
    B. 3.17
    C. 0.065

35. Express as percents.

    A. 1/10
    B. 3/4
    C. 51/100
    D. 2/5
    E. 1

36. Express as percents.

    A. 6/13
    B. 1/3
    C. 1/8
    D. 9/4

11. ESTIMATING THE OUTCOMES OF COMPUTATIONS

The art of estimating depends on rounding off numbers involved in computations so that you can calculate an approximate result mentally. Thus, $32.08 - $14.86 becomes $32 - $15 or approximately $17.

Estimation can involve not only decimal numerals, but fractions and percents as well. Thus, 3 5/8 + 2 1/4 could be rounded to 4 + 2 and estimated as 6. Round 3 5/8 up to 4; round to 2; and note that 4+2=6.

Suppose your dinner bill is $48.44 and you want to leave a 15% tip; approximately how much is 15% of $48.44? Do some mental estimation: 10% of $48.44 becomes 10% of $48. You know that 10% of anything can be found by simply moving the decimal point one digit to the left. So, 10% of $48.00 is $4.80; therefore, 5% of $48.00 must be 1/2 of $4.80 or $2.40. Since $4.80 (10% of 48)+ $2.40(5% of 48) is about $7, your tip is roughly $7.

EXERCISES

37. What whole number is closest to the following?

    A. 4.37
    B. 0.78
    C. 36.95

38. What multiple of 10 is closest to the following?

    A. 39.7
    B. 42.68
    C. 386.71

39. Estimate mentally:
    - A. $30 - $5.95
    - B. 1/2 of $29.65
    - C. 3 3/4 + 2 1/8 + 1 1/16
    - D. 5% of 86.21
    - E. 50% of $89.20
    - F. 6/7 + 10/11
    - G. 7 1/2 % of $19.86
    - H. 32.61 x 48
    - I. 4 1/3 x 91

40. John bought 3 textbooks that cost $14.95, $7.15, and $19.78. About how much will remain from the $50 that John brought with him?

41. You have a map of coastal Maine that reads *1 inch equals approximately 2.3 miles*. You estimate the distance from Wells to Saco as a little over 6 inches. Estimate the distance in miles.

42. A student has quiz grades of 86, 78, 52, 92. Estimate the student's average.

KEY (CORRECT ANSWERS)

1. A. $\dfrac{7}{10}+\dfrac{1}{100}+\dfrac{3}{1000}$

   B. $\dfrac{1}{100}+\dfrac{1}{10000}$ or $\dfrac{0}{10}+\dfrac{1}{100}+\dfrac{0}{1000}+\dfrac{1}{10000}$

   C. $\dfrac{1}{10}+\dfrac{6}{100}+\dfrac{7}{1000}+\dfrac{2}{10000}+\dfrac{4}{100000}$

2. A. $\dfrac{3}{10}$

   B. $\dfrac{3}{100}$

   C. $\dfrac{5}{1000}$

   D. $\dfrac{13}{100}$

   E. $\dfrac{165}{100}$

   F. $\dfrac{7}{1}$

   G. $\dfrac{37126}{1000}$

3. A. 0.4172 because 7/1000 is larger than 6/1000
   B. 3.7161 because 1/10000 is larger than 0/10000
   C. 0.555 because 5/1000 is larger than 0/1000
   D. 0.5 because 5/10 is larger than 0/10
   E. 23.18 because 1/10 is larger than 0/10
   F. 14.386 because 3/10 is larger than 0/10
   G. 47.013 because 4 tens is larger than 3 tens

4. A. 0.03, 0.32, 0.3222, 0.370
   B. 4.05, 4.3271, 4.5, 4.55
   C. 0.06, 0.31, 0.5, 0.56, 1.002

5. Any three decimals which start out 0.39...and where the digit to the right of the 9 is 1 or greater. (There may be any number of digits to the right of the decimal point, but it's only the first three which determine the correct answer.)

6. 0.5, 0.4444, and 0.599

7. A. 0.7XXXXX
    B. 0.6XX000
    C. You cannot tell. For example, the numbers might be 0.653124 and 0.654917, in which case the second is larger. But the numbers could be 0.653124 and 0.644917, in which case the first is larger.
    D. 0.99131X

8. 1.125, 1.02, 1.111

9. A. 45.3
    B. 30.61
    C. 20.157
    D. 17.09
    E. 4.00 - 0.68 = 3.32
    F. 13.60 - 8.01 = 5.59

10. A. 14.766
    B. 18.9906
    C. 26.4
    D. 67.12
    E. 3.105

11. A. $10^2 = 100$
    B. $10^4 = 10.000$
    C. $10^{-5} = 0.00001$
    D. $10^{-2} = 0.01$

12. A. $1000 = 10^3$
    B. $0.001 = 10^{-3}$
    C. $100 = 10^2$
    D. $0.000001 = 10^{-6}$

13. A. 36,080,000
    B. 10,100
    C. 300
    D. 0.0000011721

14. A. 3.45×10^8
    B. 3×10^{-3}
    C. 1.099×10^{-4}
    D. 3.6×10

15. A. 10,000 or 10^4
    B. 100 or 10^2
    C. 1,000,000 or 10^6
    D. 0.001 or 10^{-3}
    E. 100 or 10^2

16. A. 10²
    B. 10⁻²
    C. 10
    D. 10²

17. A. 0.47
    A. 0.51
    B. 12.47
    C. 1.73

18. A. 317.6
    B. 34.6
    C. 1435.1
    D. 104.5

19. A. 320
    B. 30
    C. 1440
    D. 100

20. A. 0.5
    B. 0.375
    C. 0.3125

21. A. 0.143
    A. 0.563
    B. 0.176

22. A. 15/77
    B. 1/14
    C. 9/5
    D. 33/28
    E. 45/1=45
    F. 6/7
    G. 1/11
    H. 3/10
    I. 7/16
    J. 94/105
    K. 37/63
    L. 11/10

23. A. 1/3
    B. 1/8
    C. 3/13
    D. 2/3

24. A. 7 5/6
    B. 15 11/15
    C. $5\frac{4}{5}+1\frac{1}{4}=6+\frac{4}{5}+\frac{1}{4}=6+\frac{16+5}{20}=6+\frac{21}{20}=6+1+\frac{1}{20}=7\frac{1}{20}$

25. We convert both to decimals by the long division process.
8/21 = 0.380...and 3/8 = 0.375.... Thus we can see by comparing the first two digits to the right of the decimal point that 8/21 is larger.

26. A. 3/5
B. 5/21
C. 8/9

27. A. $\dfrac{1}{3}(.33), \dfrac{7}{17}(.41), \dfrac{9}{19}(.47), 0.5, \dfrac{13}{23}(.56), \dfrac{4}{7}(.57)$

B. $\dfrac{2}{5}(.40), \dfrac{17}{40}(.43), \dfrac{4}{9}(.44), 0.45, \dfrac{9}{19}(.47)$

28. 3/5, 5/8

29. A. $\dfrac{20}{100} = \dfrac{1}{5}$

B. $\dfrac{75}{100} = \dfrac{3}{4}$

C. $\dfrac{9}{100}$

30. A. 0.15
B. 2.46
C. 0.30
D. 0.09
E. 1.00
F. 0.01

31. A. 0.35 x 300 = 105
B. 0.08 x $81.50 = $6.52
C. 0.17 x 63 = 10.71

32. $\dfrac{3}{8}(.38), 42\%(.42), \dfrac{3}{7}(.43), \dfrac{1}{2}(.50), 56\%(.56), 100\%(1.00)$

33. A. 40
B. 20
C. 8
D. 42

34. A. 13%
B. 317%
C. 6.5%

35. A. 1/10 = 10/100 = 10%
    B. 3/4 = 75/100 = 75%
    C. 51%
    D. 2/5 = 40/100 = 40%
    E. 1 = 100/100%

36. A. 6/13 = 0.4651... and is approximately 46.2%
    B. 1/3 = 0.3333... and is approximately 33.3%
       Some people prefer the exact answer 1/3 = 33 1/3%
    C. 1/8 = 0.125 = 12.5%
    D. 9/4 = 2.25 = 225%

37. A. 4
    B. 1
    C. 37

38. A. 40
    B. 40
    C. 390

39. A. $30 - $6 = $24
    B. 1/2 of $30 = $15
    C. 7
    D. 10% of 86 is 8.6, so 5% is 4.3. (You might call it 4.)
    E. 50% of $90 = $45
    F. 2
    G. 7% of $20 is $1.40 (0.07 × 20 = 1.40)
       8% of $20 is $1.60. So is about $1.50
    H. 30 × 50 = 1500
    I. $4\frac{1}{3} \times 90 = (4 \times 90) + (\frac{1}{3} \times 90) = 360 + 30 = 390$

40. $15 + $7 + $20 = $42. About $8 will be left.

41. 6 × 2.3 = (6×2) + (6×0.3) = 12+2 (since 6×0.3 = 1.8) = 14 miles

42. 86 + 92 + 78 + 52 roughly equal 90 + 90 + 80 + 50 = 310. The average would be approximately 320/4 = 80. The average should be slightly less than 80, perhaps 77 or 78.

MATHEMATICAL RELATIONSHIPS AND CONCEPTS

1. SOLVING LINEAR EQUATIONS

When solving simple linear equations, the goal is to rewrite the equation in the form *variable = constant* or *constant = variable*. To achieve the goal, you generally need to add the same quantity to both sides of the equation or to multiply both sides of the equation by the same quantity. Thus, to solve 3x - 6 = 14, we would add 6, the opposite of -6, to both sides, obtaining 3x = 20. We would then multiply both sides by 1/3, the *opposite* or *inverse* of 3, to obtain the final answer.

$$3x = 20$$
$$\frac{1}{3} \cdot 3x = \frac{1}{2} \cdot 20$$
$$x = \frac{20}{3} \text{ or } 6\frac{2}{3}$$

Notice that the equation has been reduced to the form *variable = constant*, that is $= 6\frac{2}{3}$. Here is another example. Solve for x:

Add -7 (the opposite of 7) to both sides
This reduces to

$$\frac{2}{3}x + 7 = 18$$
$$-7 \quad -7$$
$$\frac{2}{3}x = 11$$

Multiply both sides by $\frac{3}{2}$ because $\frac{3}{2}$ is the inverse of $\frac{2}{3}$

$$\frac{3}{2} \cdot \frac{2}{3}x = \frac{3}{2} \cdot \frac{11}{1}$$
$$x = \frac{33}{2} \text{ or } 16\frac{1}{2}$$

Some equations have variables on both sides of the equality symbol.

Problem: Solve for x: 3x + 7 = 5x - 11
Solution:

Add -3x to both sides
This reduces to:
Add 11 to both sides: This reduces to:
Multiply both sides by $\frac{1}{2}$:
The answer is:

$$3x + 7 = 5x - 11$$
$$-3x \quad\quad -3x$$
$$7 = 2x - 11$$
$$+11 \quad\quad +11$$
$$18 = 2x$$
$$\frac{1}{2} \cdot 18 = \frac{1}{2} \cdot 2x$$
$$9 = x$$

Problem: Solve for t: 4 + 3(t-2) = t + 1

Solution: When equations contain parentheses, always remove the parentheses first and then proceed as usual. Here, 3(t-2) is equivalent to 3t - 6. Thus,

4	+	3t	−	6	=	t + 1
3t	+	4	−	6	=	t + 1
		3t	−	2	=	t + 1

Reordered:
Reduced:
Add -t to both sides: $\quad -t \qquad\qquad = -t$
The result is: $\quad 2t - 2 = 1$
Add 2 to both sides: $\quad +2 \qquad\qquad +2$
The result is: $\quad 2t = 3$
Multiply both sides by 1/2: $\quad \frac{1}{2} \cdot 2t = \frac{1}{2} \cdot 3$

The answer is: $\quad t = \frac{3}{2}$

Problem: Solve for x: $0.17x + 1.2 = 6.3$

Solution: Sometimes you must multiply both sides by an appropriate power of ten in order to remove the decimals. Because the equation above has as many as two digits to the right of the decimal point, we multiply both sides by 10^2 or 100.

$$100(0.17x + 1.2) = 100(6.3)$$
$$17x + 120 = 630$$
$$17x = 510$$
$$x = 30$$

EXERCISES

1. Solve for x:
   A. $2x - 3 = 15$
   B. $5x + 8 = 20$
   C. $15 = 3x - 6$
   D. $\frac{2}{3}x - 7 = 4$
   E. $3/5x + 4 = 12$

2. Solve for x:
   A. $3x + 5 = 6x - 1$
   B. $4x - 5 = 12 - 9$
   C. $4 - 2x = 6x + 5$
   D. $12 - x = \frac{3}{2}x = 2$
   E. $300 - 140x = 3860x - 20$

3. Solve for the variable:
   A. $2x - 5 = 4(3x+1) - 2$
   B. $10t + 1 = 2(3t+5) - 1$
   C. $2(x+2) = 1 + 3(1-x)$
   D. $5 - (11 - 2x) = 7x + 7$

4. Solve for the variable:
    A. $0.42x - 1.2 = 7.2$
    B. $1.1a + 3 = 0.712$
    C. $-6.54 = 1.48t - 3.062$
    D. $\frac{1}{a} + 1 = 3$

2. EVALUATING ALGEBRAIC EXPRESSIONS

Evaluating algebraic expressions is mostly a matter of replacing variables with numbers. You may need to use your equation-solving knowledge to complete the process.

Problem: Find the value of y when x= 3 if $x = 3y - 6$.

Solution: $\quad x = 3y - 6$
Replace x by 3 $\quad 3 = 3y - 6$
$$+6 \qquad +6$$
$$9 = 3y$$
$$\frac{1}{3} \times 9 = \frac{1}{3} \times 3y$$

The answer is: $\quad 3 = y$

EXERCISES

5. Evaluate the following when a=2, b=3, c=2:
    A. $-3a + 5b$
    B. $a(b+c)$
    C. $3a + 2b + 4c$

6. Find the value of y when $x = 3$ if
    A. $y = 3x - 9$
    B. $x + y = 11$
    C. $2x + 3y = 7$
    D. $5 - (x+y) = 11$
    E. $3y = 2x$

7. Solve for y if $x = 20$:
    A. $y = \frac{2}{3}x - 4$
    B. $y = \frac{9}{5}x + 32$
    C. $\frac{1}{3}y + \frac{1}{4}x = \frac{1}{5}$

8. Interest (I) equals principal (P) multiplied by the interest rate per unit of time (r) multiplied by the number of the time periods (t) of the loan: I = Prt. What is the rate per year if an invested principal of $2000 earns $320 interest over a 2-year period?

9. What is the value of a if b = 0.2 and 3.2 + a + 0.3b = 0.25?

3. SOLVING LITERAL EQUATIONS

A literal equation is one involving more than one variable; for example, 3x + 2y = 6 or d = rt. Often literal equations need to be solved for one or another of the variables in the equation, Thus, d = rt is in a form where d is the solution. To *solve for* r, we may divide both sides of the equation by t to obtain $\frac{d}{t} = \frac{rt}{t}$ or $\frac{d}{t} = r$. We might also divide both sides by r to obtain $\frac{d}{r} = t$.

Thus, we have three *equivalent* equations: $d = rt;\ \frac{d}{t} = r;\ \frac{d}{r} = t$.

Solving literal equations involves our usual equation-solving techniques: We add (or subtract) the same quantity to both sides of the equation, and we multiply (or divide) both sides by the same quantity.

Problem: Rewrite 2x + 9y - 18 = 0 in terms of y:

Solution:
$$2x + 9y - 18 = 0$$
$$ +18\ \ +18$$
$$2x + 9y = 18$$
$$-2x\ \ \ \ -2x$$
$$9y = 18 - 2x$$

now divide both sides by 9:
$$\frac{9}{9}y = \frac{18 - 2x}{9}$$
$$y = \frac{18 - 2x}{9}$$

Problem: Solve the following for c: $F = \frac{9}{5}C + 32$

Solution:
$$F = \frac{9}{5}C + 32$$
$$-32 \qquad\qquad -32$$
$$F - 32 = \frac{9}{5}C$$

$$\frac{5}{9}(F - 32) = \frac{5}{9} \times \frac{9}{5}C$$

$$\frac{5}{9}(F - 32) = C$$

Problem: Solve for x: $y = 14 - 8x$

Solution:
$$y = 14 - 8x$$
$$\underline{-14 \qquad -14}$$
$$y - 14 = -8x$$
$$\frac{y - 14}{-8} = \frac{-8x}{-8}$$

Multiply numerator and denominator by -1 to eliminate the negative denominator

$$\frac{y - 14}{-8} = x$$

$$\frac{14 - y}{8} = x$$

EXERCISES

10. Solve the equations in terms of y
    A. $3x + y = 12$
    B. $xy = 8$
    C. $A = bry$
    D. $4x + 3y = 12$
    E. $4x - 13y = 17$
    F. $3x = 6y$

11. Rewrite $I = Prt$ in terms of P

12. Solve $s = a + (n - 1)d$ for d

13. Rewrite $L = a(l + ct)$ in terms of c

14. Suppose $xyz = 10$. Solve for x and then for y

15. Give two equivalent forms of the equation $7x - 2y = 14$ by solving for x and for y

4. DIRECT AND INVERSE VARIATION

If the numbers involved are simple, direct and inverse variation problems can be done mentally.

Consider this problem: Suppose y varies directly as x. If y is 8 when x is 2, what is y when x is 3?

To say, *y varies directly as x* means y is a multiple of x. Now, if y is 8 when x is 2, what multiple of x must y be? Clearly, 8 is 4 times 2 so y must be 4 times x: $y = 4x$. At this point, you can answer the question, *What is y when x is 3?* Since $y = 4x$, it follows that when x is 3, y is 12.

Consider this problem: Suppose y varies directly as x. When $y = 5$, then $x = 10$. What is the value of y when $x = 6$? The variable y varies directly as x. This means that y is a multiple of x. What do you multiply the x-value of 10 by to get the y-value 5? The multiplier is 1/2 because $1/2 \cdot 10 = 5$. Thus, if $x = 6$, then $y = 1/2 \cdot 6 = 3$.

EXERCISES

16. Solve these direct variation problems. In each case, y varies directly as x.
    A. If y is 3 when x is 1, then y = _____ when x = 6.
    B. If y is 10 when x is 2, then y = _____ when x = 4.
    C. If y is 2 when x is 4, then y = _____ when x = 9.
    D. If y is 5 when x is 15, then y = _____ when x = 9.
    E. If y is 3 when x is 2, then y = _____ when x = 10.
    F. If y is 12 when x is 4, then y = 15 when x = _____.
    G. If y is 3 when x is 9, then y = 4 when x = _____.
    H. If y is 3/2 when x is 1, then y = 6 when x = _____.
    I. If y is 5 when x is 2, then y = _____ when x = 6.

Although many variation problems can be solved or approximated mentally, there are mechanical, rote methods for solving such problems.

Consider problem 16I above: If y is 5 when x is 2, then y = _____ when x = 6. Some people might reason this way: *So y = 5 when x 2. That means that y equals two and a half times x. So if x = 6, then two and a half x's make 6 + 6 + 3 = 15, so when x = 6, then y = 15.*

Here is a mechanical way to do the same problem. Since y varies directly as x, y is a multiple of x: y = kx. By substituting the known values 5 and 2 for y and x respectively, you can solve for k. We know that y = kx, 5 = k.2. Therefore, 5/2 = k. If y = 5/2x and if x = 6, then y = 5/2.6 = 15. Thus, we have this procedure:

Use formula y = kx where $\frac{\text{Known y-value}}{\text{Known x-value}}$

EXERCISES

17. Solve these direct variation problems by using the formula y = kx. In each case, y varies directly as x. For each problem, identify the value of k you used and the value that goes in the blank.
    A. If y is 6 when x is 2, then y = _____ when x = 10.
    B. If y is 6 when x is 3, then y = _____ when x = 18.
    C. If y is 12 when x is 1/3, then y = _____ when x = 5.
    D. If y is 28 when x is -4, then y = _____ when x = 7.
    E. If y is 12 when x is 4, then y = 12.36 when x = _____.
    F. If y is 459 when x is 17, then y = 27 when x = _____.
    G. If y is 100 when x is -10, then y = -10 when x = _____.
    H. If y is 1.4 when x is 7, then y = 10 when x = _____.

18. The salary of an hourly worker varies directly with the number of hours she works per week. According to the records, she worked 24 hours last week and made $108. How many hours would she need to work this week to make $45?

19. The weight of a collection of machine screws varies directly as the number of screws in the collection. If 110 screws weigh 1.1 kg, how many screws are in a collection weighing 0.56 kg.?

By now you have noticed that y varies directly as x, when x increases so does y and when x decreases so does y. For instance, if x doubles then y also doubles. For inverse variations, however, if x doubles, then y decreases by half! Overall, for inverse variations one variable moves in the opposite direction from the other.

Direct Variation: If $y = 8$ when $x = 4$, then when $x = 8$, $y = 16$.
Inverse Variation: If $y = 8$ when $x = 4$, then when $x = 8$, $y = 4$.

Direct Variation: If $y = 15$ when $x = 3$, then when $x = 9$, $y = 45$.
Inverse Variation: If $y = 15$ when $x = 3$, then when $x = 9$, $y = 5$.

Suppose y is inversely related to x. Then if x doubles, y is 1/2 its former value. If the value of x is multiplied by 3, then the y-value is multiplied by 1/3, and so forth.

EXERCISES

20. Solve these inverse variation problems mentally. In each case, assume that y varies inversely as x.
    A. If $y = 6$ when $x = 8$, then $y =$ _____ when $x = 16$.
    B. If $y = 6$ when $x = 8$, then $y =$ _____ when $x = 24$.
    C. If $y = 6$ when $x = 8$, then $y =$ _____ when $x = 2$.
    D. If $y = 10$ when $x = 10$, then $y =$ _____ when $x = 5$.
    E. If $y = 10$ when $x = 10$, then $y =$ _____ when $x = 2$.
    F. If $y = 24$ when $x = 6$, then $y = 12$ when $x =$ _____.
    G. If $y = 24$ when $x = 12$, then $y = 2$ when $x =$ _____.
    H. If $y = 15$ when $x = 12$, then $y = 10$ when $x =$ _____.
    I. If $y = 1$ when $x = 1$, then $y = 1/3$ when $x =$ _____.

As is the case with direct variation, there is also a formula (if you need it) for solving inverse variation problems:

$$y = \frac{k}{x} \text{ where } k = \text{(known x-value)} \cdot \text{(known y-value)}$$

Let us solve problem 20C by means of the formula. In this problem, $k = 8 \cdot 6 = 48$. Thus, $y = \frac{48}{x}$. So, to find y when $x = 2$, we calculate $y = 48/x = 48/2 = 24$.

Let us use the formula to solve 20G. Here, $k = 12 \cdot 24 = 288$. So the formula is $y = \frac{288}{x}$. If $y = 2$, then to find x we proceed as follows:

$$y = \frac{288}{x}$$
$$2 = \frac{288}{x}$$
$$2x = 288$$
$$x = 144$$

21. Solve these inverse variation problems by using the formula $y = \dfrac{k}{x}$. In each case, y varies inversely as x. For each problem, identify the value of k you used and then the value that goes in the blank.
    A. If y is 12 when x = 2, then y = _____ when x = 1.
    B. If y is 6 when x = 2, then y = _____ when x = 3.
    C. If y is 2 when x = -3, then y = _____ when x = 1/2.
    D. If y is 6 when x = 4, then y = _____ when x = 3.
    E. If y is 3 when x = 2, then y = 1 when x = _____.
    F. If y is 10 when x = 9, then y = 45 when x = _____.

22. The pressure of a gas varies inversely as its volume. If the pressure is 21 pounds per square inch when the volume is 350 cubic inches, find the pressure when the volume is 70 cubic inches.

In place of phrases *varies directly as* or *varies inversely as,* you may encounter terms like *is directly proportional to* or *is inversely proportional to.* Problems 23-26 use this alternate wording.

23. The time required to heat water to a given temperature is directly proportional to the volume of water being heated. If 1 1/2 gallons of water take 12 minutes to heat, how many minutes will 2 gallons take to heat?

24. The scaled score on a particular test is directly proportional to the raw score. Lee had a scaled score of 500 and a raw score of 40. If Carlos had a scaled score of 375, what was his raw score?

25. The time required to travel one lap on a racetrack is inversely proportional to a car's average speed. A car averaging 90 mph takes 2 minutes to complete one lap. How long will it take to complete one lap at 120 mph?

26. A sociologist has developed a test for measuring *teaching anxiety* among junior high school teachers. She estimates that test scores are inversely related to years of teaching experience. If a teacher with 3 years experience scores 60, how many years experience has a teacher who scores 15?

5. RATIO AND PROPORTION

Ratio may be considered to be another word for *fraction.* The ratio of x to y is written x/y or x:y. Just as the fractions 2/4 and 1/2 are equal, we consider the ratio 2:4 to be the same as 1:2.

Thus, if an office employs 18 men and 15 women, we might report the ratio of men to women as 18:15, but more likely we would use 6:5 (dividing both terms by 3). On the other hand, the ratio of women to men would be 5:6. Watch out for the order of the numbers when writing ratios. The order of terms should match the order of groups or things to which they refer.

EXERCISES

27. Give the ratios required (using lowest terms).
    A. An office employs 10 female employees and 3 males. What is the ratio of males to females?
    B. A rectangle has length 20 and width 15. What is the ratio of length to width?
    C. John spends $200 a month for food and $300 a month for rent. What is the ratio of the amount he spends for food to the amount he spends for rent?
    D. A TV station airs 40 drama shows in a given week and 24 news/sports shows. What is the ratio of news/sports to drama for the TV station?

A proportion is a statement that two ratios are equal. Proportions are commonly used to solve ratio problems. Consider this problem: Bill needs to paint 3 identical bedrooms. He needs 5 gallons of paint for 2 of the rooms. How much paint will he need for all 3 rooms? We express the relationship this way

$$\frac{5}{2} = \frac{x}{3}$$ (Read 5 is to 2 as x is to 3) or this way

$$\frac{2}{5} = \frac{3}{x}$$ (Read 2 is to 5 as 3 is to x)

Note that both proportions will yield the same solution for x.

To solve a proportion, simply multiply as follows and solve the resulting equation:

Product: 15   Product: 2x

$$\frac{5}{2} = \frac{x}{3}$$

Thus,   15   =   2x
              7 1/2 =   x

So, 7 1/2 gallons are needed for 3 rooms.

Here is a second problem: 3 is to 7 as 8 is to what?

$$\frac{3}{7} = \frac{8}{x}$$

$$3x = 7 \times 8$$
$$3x = 56$$
$$x = \frac{56}{3}$$

28. A park ranger counts 16 trout out of 30 fish sampled in a given lake. If the lake contains 2000 fish in all, how many would you predict should be trout?

29. The ratio of a person's weight on Mars to the person's weight on Earth is 2:5. How much would a 120-pound Earth person weigh on Mars?

30. A map of your hometown has a scale that reads, *1 inch equals 6 miles.* If two locations on the map are 4 1⁄2 inches apart, what is the distance between them in miles?

31. Gerry's car burns 1 1/2 quarts of oil on a 700-mile trip. How much oil will be needed for a 3000-mile trip?

32. If a 6-foot person casts a 4-foot shadow, how tall is a tree that casts a 25-foot shadow?

33. The ratio of male to female faculty members in the Delendo School system is 2:5. If there are 36 male faculty, how many female faculty are there?

34. A collection of miniature dinosaur replicas are all constructed on the same scale. One dinosaur, whose length is estimated at 12 feet, measures 4 inches. Another measures 6 inches. Estimate its length in feet.

35. It is estimated that student scores on two different physical skills tests are proportional. John got 20 on the first test and 32 on the second. If Maria got 6 on the first test, estimate her score on the second.

6. PERCENT PROBLEMS

What is 10% of 60? Many percent problems, such as this one, can be done mentally:

10% of 60 becomes 1/10 of 60 or 6
10% of 90 is 9
10% of 463 is 46.3, etc.

More complicated problems involve changing percents to decimals and manipulating the resulting numbers

23% of 187 becomes 0.23 x 187 or 43.01
102% of 16 becomes 1.02 x 16 or 16.32

Proportions can be used to solve many percent problems. Consider this question: *50 is 25% of what number?* Since 25% = 1/4, you could determine the answer in this way: 50 is 1/4 of 200. But you could also set up a proportion: 50 is to x as 25 is to 100.

$$\frac{50}{x} = \frac{25}{100}$$

or 50 . 100 = 25x

200 = x

Problem: 10 is 30% of what number?

Solution:
$$\frac{10}{x} = \frac{30}{100}$$
1000 = 30x

$$\frac{1000}{30} = x$$

33.3 = x (rounding the answer)

So, 10 is 30% of 33.3 (rounded).

Problem: 25 is what percent of 60?

Solution: $\frac{25}{60} = \frac{x}{100}$

41.67 = x (rounding the answer)

So, 25 is approximately 41.67% of 60.

EXERCISES

36. What is:
    A. 10% of 50
    B. 1% of 50
    C. 20% of 50
    D. 21% of 50
    E. 25% of 40
    F. 50% of 160
    G. 100% of 86
    H. 150% of 50

37. What is:
    A. 17% of 80
    B. 12% of 116
    C. 8% of 21
    D. 7.5% of $15.60

38. Solve the following:
    A. 16 is 25% of what number?
    B. 13 is 86% of what number?
    C. 10 is what percent of 18?
    D. 17 is what percent of 51?

39. Solve the following:
    Example: A shirt that regularly sells for $15 is on sale for $12. What is the percent of the discount?
    The discount is $3 out of $15. 3 is what percent of 15?

    $3 = x \cdot 15$

    $$\frac{3}{15} = x$$

    $0.2 = x$

So, x = 20%. The discount is 20%.

Example: The sign says that all merchandise is marked down 12%, What should one pay for a dress normally priced $28? 12% of $28 becomes 0.12 m . $28 or $3.36. Thus, the sale price of the dress is $28 - $3.36 or $24.64.
- A. The price of a $32 shirt has just increased by 16%. What does it cost now?
- B. A used car is marked $6200, but the salesman claims that he can deduct another 15%. What would the new price be?
- C. A movie ticket that usually sells for $4 now costs $5. What is the percent of the mark-up?
- D. A tire selling for $60 has just been reduced to $56. What is the percent of the discount?

40. Three grapefruits weighing 14 oz. each were combined with seven oranges weighing 8 oz. each. What percent of the total weight was provided by
   - A. the grapefruits?
   - B. the oranges?

7. EXPRESSING RELATIONSHIPS SYMBOLICALLY

Consider this problem: In Academy School there are twenty times as many students as there are teachers. Express this fact symbolically, letting S represent the number of students and T, the number of teachers. Which of the following answers is correct?
- A. $T = S + 20$
- B. $S = T + 20$
- C. $T = 20S$
- D. $S = 20T$

The Academy School problem illustrates what is meant by *expressing relationships symbolically*. When you have taken a relationship expressed in words and have expressed it by means of an equation or formula, it is a good idea to create an example to test your answer to see if it is correct.

Consider the Academy School problem. There are twenty times as many students as teachers at the school. If Academy School had, for example, one teacher, how many students would there be? There would be 20. So, if $T = 1$, $S = 20$. If you take the number of teachers (T) and multiply it by 20, you will identify the number of students (S): $20T = S$. Therefore, choice D above is the correct answer.

Notice how choices A, B, C fail when you substitute $T = 1$, $S = 20$ in the equations. By testing your answer, you can avoid incorrect responses. A person who thought $T = 20S$ was the correct equation should discover the error by responding in this way: *I know that for 20 students I should have one teacher. If I let S = 20 in the equation T = 20S, I would get T = 20 . 20 = 400. Four hundred teachers for 20 students? Something is wrong!*

Problem: An item regularly sells for R dollars but is on sale for S dollars. Which expression gives the percent discount?

A. $\dfrac{(R-S)(100)}{R}$

B. $\dfrac{100S}{R}$

C. $\dfrac{R-S}{100}$

D. $(R-S)100$

Solution: How do we find percent discounts? Suppose something that normally sells for $10 is on sale for $8. This discount is $2 out of $10 or 2/10, 0.20, or 20%. The strategy used was this: The sale price (S) was subtracted from the regular price (R), then the answer was divided by the regular price (R) to get 2/10 or 0.20. We then moved the decimal point two places to the right to get the answer, 20%. This is the same as multiplying by 100. Thus, the formula is identified this way: R-S/R . 100. The answer is A.

Only practice and some familiarity with frequently encountered situations can help improve formula and equation-writing skills. Remember, if you have any difficulty at all with these problems, begin by creating an example to test your answer. We did this with both problems above.

EXERCISES

41. If 100 pounds of scrap metal cost p dollars, how much is 2 tons worth at the same rate? (Note: 2000 pounds = 1 ton)

    A. $2p$ B. $\dfrac{100-p}{2}$ C. $40p$ D. $\dfrac{2-p}{100}$

42. An item regularly sells for p dollars but is marked 25% *off*. Which of the following is not a correct expression for the sale price?

    A. $\dfrac{3}{4}p$ B. $(1-0.25)p$ C. $p - 1/4p$ D. $p - 25$

43. Given a car's odometer reading S at the start of a trip, the reading F at the trip's finish, and the elapsed time t, write an expression for the trip's average speed V.

44. The regular price p of an item has been increased by 20%. Write an expression for the new price.

45. If x is positive and increasing in value, then $y = 1/x$ is
    A. increasing and always positive
    B. increasing and always negative
    C. decreasing and always positive
    D. decreasing and always negative
    E. none of the above

46. If x is positive and increasing in value, then $y = \dfrac{1}{x}$ is

    A. increasing and always positive
    B. increasing and always negative
    C. decreasing and always positive
    D. decreasing and always negative
    E. none of the above

47. Write an expression that gives the total number of jars we need if each jar holds 0.5 liters and we need T liters in all. (Create an example to test your answer.)

48. Louise is trying to write an equation involving P, Q, and R. She has created an example showing that when P and Q are both 1, R must be 4. Which one or more of the following equations indicates this relationship?

    A. R = 5P - Q
    B. $1 = \dfrac{P+Q+R}{6}$
    C. R = 5(P-Q)
    D. 4Q = PR

49. Which of the following have the property that when x is positive and decreasing, y is positive and increasing?

    A. y = 4 - 1/x
    B. y = (4+x) 100
    C. xy = 1
    D. 1/x + 1/y = 3

50. Textbooks you plan to order cost $P. However, you receive a 20% discount on each book after the first 100 ordered. Which of the following will express your dollar cost if you order T textbooks, where T is larger than 100?

    A. 100P + 0.8(T-100)
    B. (100-0.20)PT
    C. 20P + 0.8PT
    D. 100P + 0.8PT

51. Suppose that personal income is taxed at a 15% rate for the first $20,000 and 28% for all income over that amount. Write an expression for the total tax paid on an income of D dollars, where D is larger than $20,000.

8. GRAPHS AND TABLES

For most people, reading graphs and tables is a matter of attention to detail and common sense. Carelessness is the most frequent cause of error. The exercises below will give you some idea of the most frequently encountered ways of displaying data and relationships pictorially.

52.

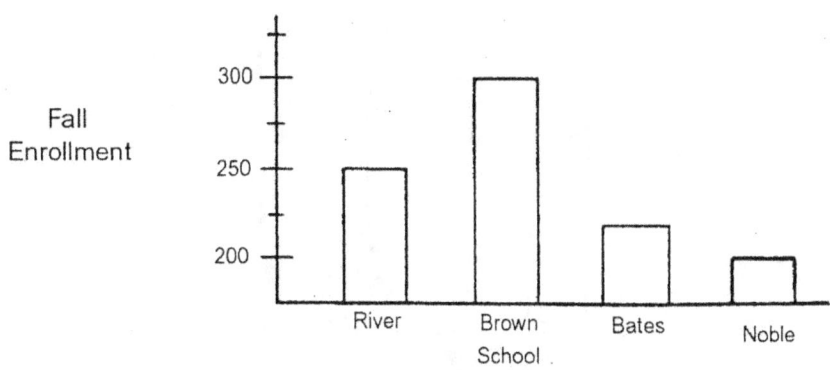

A. What is the total enrollment at the four schools?
B. What, approximately, is the ratio of the enrollment at Noble School to that at River School?
C. How many times greater is enrollment at Brown School than at Noble School?

53. This graph shows spending for the town of Amsden last year. What percentage went for police and fire protection?

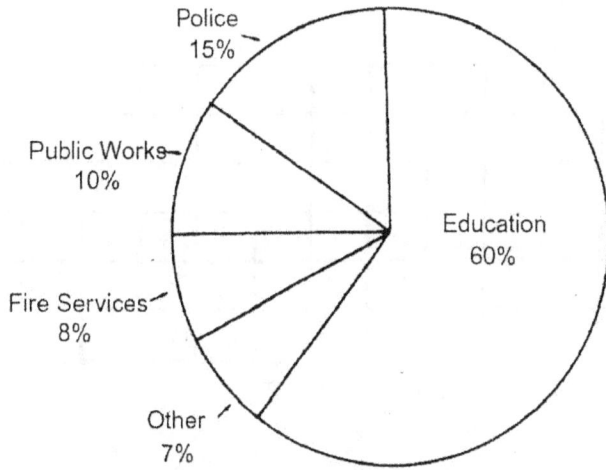

54. The graph below represents milk production for three counties last year. (Each symbol represents 10,000 gallons.) What was the approximate milk production in Balch County last year?

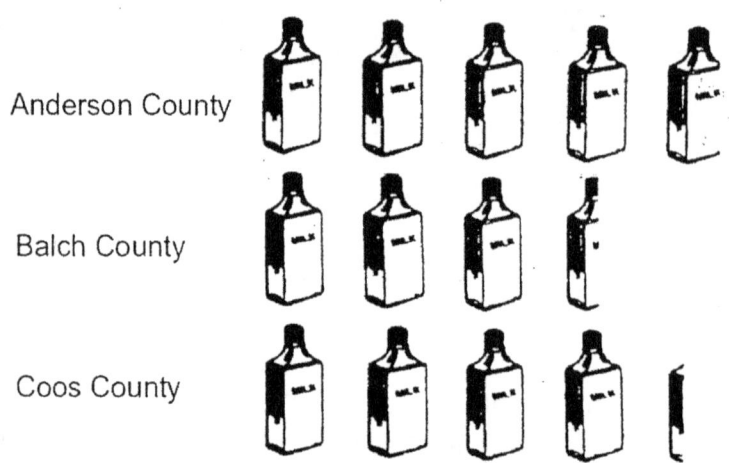

Anderson County

Balch County

Coos County

55. Mrs. Menon's mathematics group has been working independently on some lesson units. Mrs. Menon's record book is shown below. She enters S on the day a student starts Unit 1. On the day a student completes a unit, she enters that unit's number in her book.

DAY

	1	2	3	4	5	6	7	8	9	10	11	12	13
Andrew	S	1		2			3		4		5		6
Susan		S	1		2			3			4	5	
Louts				S		1	2		3		4		5
Tomas			S	1		2		3	4		5		6
Fran					S	1	2		4		5		6

UNITS COMPLETED

A. Susan took 11 days to complete units 1-5. How many days did Louis take to complete the same units?
B. At the end of the 11th day, which student had been working at the most rapid pace?

56. The distance (d) a person walks varies directly with time (t). Which graph best represents this situation?

A.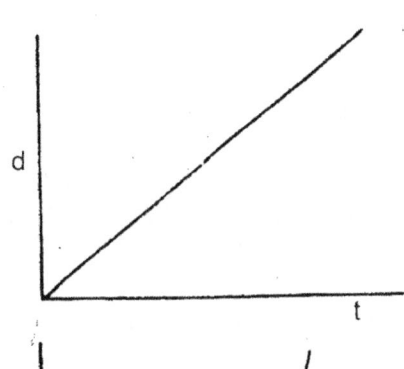

B.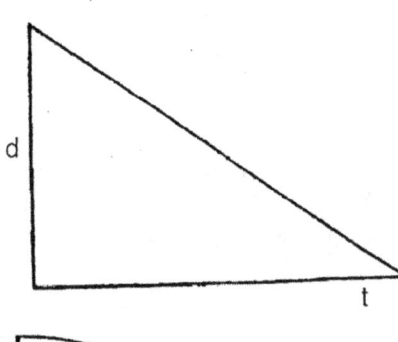

C.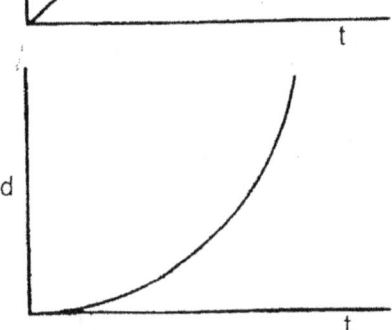

D.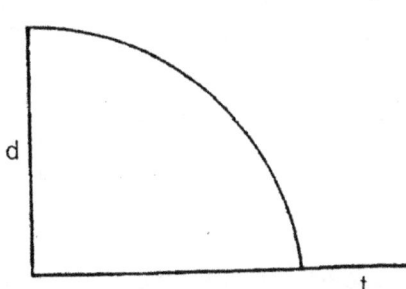

57. Which graph best represents the number of hours (T) from sunrise to sunset in Hartford, Connecticut, from January of one year to January of the next?

A.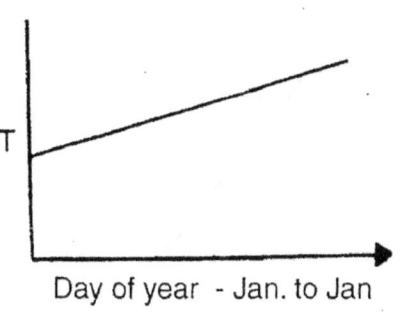

B.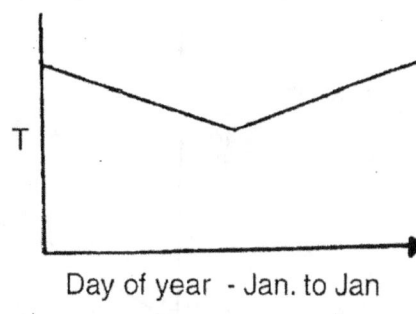

C.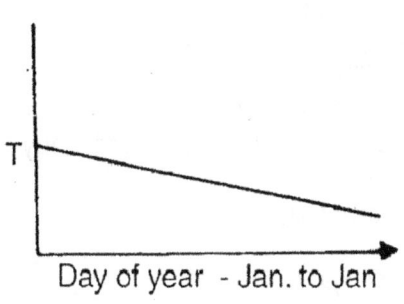

D.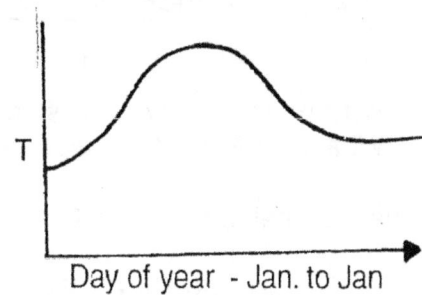

58.

City	TEMPERATURE Noon	6 PM
A	72°	54°
B	80°	70°
C	62°	50°
D	90°	66°

A. In which city did the temperature drop the most rapidly between noon and 6 M.?
B. Assuming an equivalent decrease in temperature per hour, what was the rate of temperature decrease in city A between noon and 6 P.M.?

59. Lee has been studying designs for picnic tables as shown below. Which design gives Lee the greatest surface area per dollar?

Design	Surface Area of Table	Cost of Materials
#1	20 square feet	$48.00
#2	18 square feet	$44.00
#3	24 square feet	$60.00

60. Ms. Haddad's 30 students took a standardized examination. The data below indicate the quartile in which each of her students' scores lie.

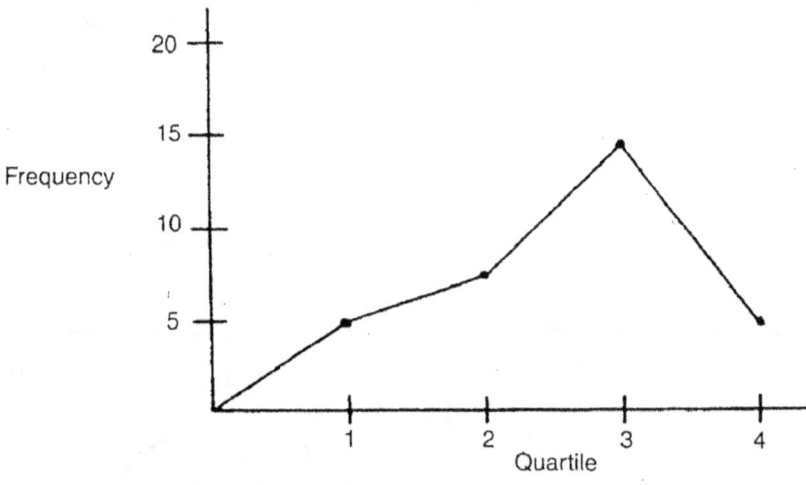

A. Approximately how many students have scores in the 4th quartile?
B. What quartile contains more of Ms. Haddad's students' scores than any other?

61. Use the table below to respond to the statements that follow.

SMOKERS BY FAMILY INCOME AND SEX

Family Income	Male	Female
Under $5,000	40%	32%
$5,000 - $14,999	36%	32%
$15,000 - $24,999	36%	30%
$25,000 or more	32%	26%

		Yes	No	Cannot Tell From Table Data
A.	60% of males with family incomes of under $5,000 are non-smokers	___		___
B.	58% of the people with family incomes of $25,000 or more are smokers	___	___	___
C.	Among those with family incomes of $25,000 or more, more males than females smoke.	___	___	___
D.	36% of those with family incomes of under $5,000 smoke.	___	___	___
E.	Among 600 females with family incomes in the $15,000-$24,999 range, there are about 180 smokers.	___	___	___

9. BASIC PROBABILITY CONCEPTS

When a student says, *The probability that I will pass the examination tomorrow is 2/3,* what does that student mean? She means that, were she to find herself in that situation many times, on about 2/3 of those occasions she would pass the exam. On about 1/3 of the occasions she would not pass.

Imagine a person playing a game which involves rolling a die. When he says, *The probability that I will roll a three is 1/6,* what does he mean? In this case, he means that of the six possible out-comes when rolling a die (1, 2, 3, 4, 5, 6), one possible outcome out of six is three. It is also true that, were he to roll that die a large number of times, about 1/6 of the times he would roll a three. (Thus, in 600 rolls, he would expect to get approximately 100 three's.)

Problem: The names of 5 students - Deborah, Andrew, Thomas, Jose, and Maria - are placed in a hat. One name is withdrawn at random. What is the probability that
    A. Deborah's name is chosen?
    B. The name chosen is either Deborah's or Andrew's?
    C. A boy's name is chosen?

Solution:
    A. Deborah's name is 1 of 5. Thus, the answer to A is 1/5.
    B. 2/5
    C. 3/5

Problem: Consider the data below on 100 different students.
If we choose one student at random from the 100 students shown on the chart, what is the probability of choosing
    A. a boy?
    B. a girl?
    C. a student with glasses?
    D. a girl with glasses?

	Glasses	No Glasses
Boys	15	45
Girls	10	30

Solution:
A. Of the 100 students, 15 + 45 = 60 are boys. Thus, the probability of choosing a boy is 60/100 = 6/10 = 3/5.
B. There are 10 + 30 = 40 girls. Thus, 40/100 = 2/5 is the probability of choosing a girl. You could also reason this way: The probability of choosing a boy is 3/5. The probability of not choosing a boy is, therefore, 1 - 3/5 = 2/5.
C. 15 + 10 = 25 out of 100 students. Thus, the answer is 25/100 = 1/4.
D. 10/100 or 1/10.

EXERCISES

62. A hat contains six tickets numbered 1, 1, 2, 2, 3, 3, respectively. One ticket is withdrawn at random. What is the probability that the ticket drawn
    A. is a 1?
    B. has an even number on it?
    C. is either a 2 or 3?
    D. has a 5 on it?
    E. has a number less than 3 on it?

63. Kim keeps records of his hens' daily egg production for 3 weeks and identifies the results listed in the table below. Based on these data, answer the questions that follow.

Eggs Laid Per Day	Number of Days
1	//
2	////
3	//// //
4	/
5	///
6	//
7	//

    A. What is the probability of getting 5 or more eggs on a given day?
    B. What is the probability of not getting exactly 4 eggs on a given day?

64. Here are some data on student test performance at a particular school. Based on the data, answer the questions that follow.

	Above Mean	Below Mean
Boys	246	54
Girls	280	20

    A. What is the probability that a randomly chosen student scored above the mean?
    B. What is the probability that a randomly chosen female student scored below the mean?

65. The science students at our school have kept records indicating that the probability of rain at noon on a given day is 1/3 during the month of October.
   A. We have 21 school days this October. How many of rainy-days-at-noon do we anticipate?
   B. What is the probability of no rain at noon during October?
   C. Suppose that the probability of the sun shining at noon is 1/6 during October. What is the probability of neither rain nor sun at noon during October?

66. Here is a summary of student performance on a statewide test. Based on the data, answer the questions that follow.

Class	Number Passed	Number Failed
Ms. Adams	20	5
Ms. Blake	18	6
Ms. Gomez	22	2

   A. What is the probability that a randomly chosen student has passed the exam?
   B. What is the probability that a student who has failed belongs to Ms. Adams' class?

67. Based on statewide test data, here are probabilities of scoring in certain categories:

Score	Probability
0-50	0.16
51-60	0.24
61-70	0.30
71-80	0.20

   A. If 5,000 students took the test, how many would you predict had scores below 51?
   B. Eighty students at School A took the test. Fifteen students scored 50 or below. Is this better or worse than the state as a whole?
   C. Overall, what was the probability of scoring above 80 on the statewide test?

10. NEEDED AND EXTRANEOUS INFORMATION IN PROBLEM SOLVING

Problems with missing or with extra information are very common in real-life situations, but relatively rare in textbooks. These problems may not be necessarily difficult, but they often trap unwary readers whose schooling has led them to expect that all school problems and test problems contain precisely the information needed for a solution. But that is not always so. It is important to read problems carefully and use your common sense; imagine you are not faced with a *mathematics* problem on a test, but have encountered the problem in your daily life. Ask yourself, what information would you need to solve it?

EXERCISES

68. Pedro wants to tile a rectangular floor measuring 7.2 m by 5.4 m. Tiles cost 35¢ each at a store. What additional information will Pedro need before he can tell how much he needs to spend on tiles at a store?

69. Consider this situation: A manager bought 100 identical video cameras for $2,568. He sold them for $5,042. This situation includes three numerical pieces of information, not all of which may be needed to answer the questions below. What are the answers? What information is extraneous in each case?

	Answer	Extraneous Data
A. What was the total profit?	_____	_____
B. What was the selling price of each camera?	_____	_____
C. What did the manager pay for the cameras?	_____	_____
D. What was the manager's profit per camera?	_____	_____

70. Identify the additional information, if any, needed for each of the following problems.
    A. When mixing concrete for a patio, a contractor uses sand and gravel in a ratio of 3 to 4. How many cubic yards of gravel did the contractor use?
    B. The distance from Ampex to Bodwick is 38 miles. The distance from Bodwick to Cranmore is 20 miles. How far is it from Ampex to Cranmore?
    C. Ten percent of Ms. Mora's fourth graders failed the state's mastery test in reading. Four percent of Mr. Gomez's class failed. What was the total number of failing students in the two classes?
    D. All the rooms in Lauren's house are the same size. To paint two of those rooms she needs three gallons of paint. How many gallons does she need to paint all her rooms?
    E. A team wins 105 games. This is 70% of the games they played. How many games did they lose?

71. Identify any extraneous data.
    A. Of 180 class days last year, Lisa missed 9. If the probability of her missing school that year was 1/20, what was the probability of her being in school on a given day?
    B. The 30 students in Ms. Gate's class paid an average of $12.50 each during the year for special class materials, fees, etc. How much more, on the average, would each student need to pay for the class average to be $14 per student?
    C. A car averaged 20 miles per hour traveling from point A to point B. On the return trip, it averaged 40 miles per hour and took 2 1/2 hours. How far did the car travel for the entire trip?
    D. Tickets to the student production of OUR TOWN sell for $3 each. Yesterday, 30 students and 7 teachers bought tickets. Today $123 worth of tickets were sold, including another 30 student tickets. How many nonstudents bought tickets these two days?

KEY (CORRECT ANSWERS)

1. A. $x = 9$
   B. $x = \dfrac{12}{5}$
   C. $x = 7$
   D. $\dfrac{2}{3}x = 11$, so $x = \dfrac{3}{2} \cdot \dfrac{11}{1} = \dfrac{33}{2}$
   E. $\dfrac{3}{5}x = 8$, so $x = \dfrac{5}{3} \cdot \dfrac{8}{1} = \dfrac{40}{3}$

2. A. $x = 2$
   B. $x = 2$
   C. $x = x = -\dfrac{1}{8}$
   D. $x = 4$
   E. $x = \dfrac{320}{4000} = \dfrac{2}{25}$

3. A. $x = -\dfrac{7}{10}$
   B. $t = 2$
   C. $x = 0$
   D. $x = -\dfrac{13}{5}$

4. A. $x = 20$
   B. $a = -\dfrac{52}{25}$ or -2.08
   C. $t = -\dfrac{3478}{1480} = -\dfrac{47}{20}$
   D. $\dfrac{1}{a} = 2$, so $a = \dfrac{1}{2}$

5. A. 9
   B. 10
   C. 20

6. A. 0
   B. 8
   C. 1/3
   D. -9
   E. 2

24

7. A. $\dfrac{28}{3}$

    B. 68

    C. $-\dfrac{72}{5}$

8. $320 = \$2000 \times r \times 2$, so $r = \dfrac{320}{4000} = \dfrac{32}{400} = \dfrac{8}{100} = 8\%$

9. $a = -\dfrac{301}{100} = -3.01$

10. A. $Y = 12 - 3X$

    B. $y = \dfrac{8}{x}$

    C. $y = \dfrac{A}{br}$

    D. $y = \dfrac{12-4x}{3} = 4 - \dfrac{4}{3}x$

    E. $y = \dfrac{17-4x}{-13} = \dfrac{4x-17}{13}$

    F. $y = \dfrac{3x}{6} = \dfrac{1}{2}x$

11. $P = \dfrac{I}{rt}$

12. $\dfrac{s-a}{n\,1} = d$

13. $L = a + act;\ L - a = act;\ \dfrac{L-a}{at} = C$

14. $x = \dfrac{10}{yz};\ y = \dfrac{10}{xz}$

15. $x = \dfrac{14+2y}{7};\ y = \dfrac{14-7x}{-2}$ or $y = \dfrac{7x-14}{2}$

16. A. 18   D. 3   G. 12
    B. 20   E. 15   H. 4
    C. 4 1/2   F. 5   I. 15

17. A. $k = \frac{6}{2} = 3$, so y = 3x and y = 30

B. $k = \frac{6}{3} = 2$, so y = 2x and y = 36

C. $k = 12 \div \frac{1}{3} = 12 \times \frac{3}{1} = 36$, so y = 36x and y = 180

D. $k = \frac{28}{4} = -7$, so y = -7x and y = -49

E. $k = \frac{12}{4} = 3$ so y = 3x and 12.36 = 3x. Therefore, x - 4.12

F. $k = \frac{459}{17} = 27$, so y = 27x and 27 = 27x. Therefore, x = 1

G. $k = \frac{100}{10} = -10$, so y = -10x and -10 = -10x. Therefore, x = 1

H. $k = \frac{14}{7} = 0.2$, so y = .2x and 10 = .2x. Thus, 100 = 2x and x = 50

18. $k = \frac{\text{known y-value}}{\text{known x-value}} = \frac{24}{108} = \frac{2}{9}$, so $y = \frac{2}{9}x$. If x = 45, then $y = \frac{2}{9} \cdot \frac{45}{1} = \frac{90}{9} = 10$.

She needs to work 10 hours this week. If you reversed the x's and y's, you should have obtained $k = \frac{108}{24} = \frac{9}{2}$, so $y = \frac{9}{2}x$. When y = 45, we have $45 = \frac{9}{2}x$ and, multiplying both sides by $\frac{2}{9}$, we get $\frac{2}{9} \cdot \frac{45}{1} = x$, so x = 10.

19. If y = 110 when x = 1.1, then what is y when x = .56?

$K = \frac{110}{1.1} = \frac{1100}{11} = 100$ and y = 100x. So, when x = .56, then y = 100 × .56 = 56.

20. A. 3
B. 2
C. 24
D. 20
E. 50
F. 12
G. 144
H. The value of y has been multiplied by 2/3. The value of x will therefore be multiplied by 3/2 (or 1 1/2). Since x = 12 and 1 1/2 twelves are 18, the answer is x = 18.
I. 3

21. A. $k = 12 \times 2 = 24$, so $y = y = \dfrac{24}{x}$. Thus when $x = 1$, $y = 24$.

   B. $k = 6 \times 2 = 12$, so $y = \dfrac{12}{x}$. Thus when $x = 3$, $y = 4$.

   C. $k = 2(-3) = -6$, so $y = -\dfrac{6}{x}$. Thus when $x = \dfrac{1}{2}$, $y = -6 \div \dfrac{1}{2} = -\dfrac{6}{1} \times \dfrac{2}{1} = -12$

   D. $k = 6 \cdot 4 = 24$, so $y = y = \dfrac{24}{x}$. Thus when $x = 3$, $y = 8$.

   E. $k = 3 \cdot 2 = 6$, so $y = y = \dfrac{6}{x}$. Thus if $y = 1$, we have $1 = \dfrac{6}{x}$ and $x = 6$.

   F. $k = 10 \cdot 9 = 90$, so $y = \dfrac{90}{x}$. Thus if $y = 45$, we have $45 = \dfrac{90}{x}$ and $x = 2$.

22. If y is 21 when x = 350, then what is y when x = 70?

    $k = 21 \cdot 350$, so $y = \dfrac{21 \cdot 350}{x}$. If $x = 70$, then $y = \dfrac{21 \cdot 350}{70}$ $21 \cdot 5 = 105$ pounds per square inch.

23. If y = 1 1/2 when x = 12, then when y = 2, what is x?
    Here, $1\,1/2 \cdot 8 = 12$, so $2 \cdot 8 = 16$. Therefore, $x = 16$ when $y = 2$.

24. Let y represent the scaled score and x represent the raw score. Then,

    $k = \dfrac{500}{40} = \dfrac{25}{2}$, so $y = \dfrac{25}{2}x$. Thus, if $y = 375$, we have $375 = \dfrac{25}{2}x$. Therefore,

    $x = \dfrac{2}{25} \cdot 375 = 30$.

25. Let y represent the speed and x the number of minutes. Notice that 90 plus one-third of 90 is 120. So, since y has increased by $1\dfrac{1}{3}$ (or $\dfrac{4}{3}$), x will decrease by $\dfrac{3}{4} \cdot \dfrac{3}{4} \cdot 2 = \dfrac{6}{4} = \dfrac{3}{2}$ so the answer is 3/2 minutes, or 1 1/2 minutes.

26. Going from 60 to 15 represents a decrease by a factor of 1/4. Thus, the years of experience will increase by a factor of 4, and the answer is 12.

27. A. three to ten or $\dfrac{3}{10}$ or 3:10

    B. $\dfrac{20}{15} = \dfrac{4}{3}$ or 4:3 or four to three

    C. $\dfrac{200}{300} = \dfrac{2}{3}$ or 2:3 or two to three

    D. $\dfrac{24}{40} = \dfrac{3}{5}$ or 3:5 or three to five

28. 16 trout out of 30 fish. How many trout out of 2000 fish?
    $\dfrac{16}{30} = \dfrac{x}{2000}$, so $16 \times 2000 = 30x$ and $x = \dfrac{32000}{30}$ trout. Since $\dfrac{32000}{30} = 1066.7$, the ranger would estimate that roughly 1067 trout are in the lake.

29. $\dfrac{\text{Mars}}{\text{Earth}} = \dfrac{2}{5} = \dfrac{x}{120}$ so $240 = 5x$, and $x = 48$ pounds.

30. $\dfrac{1}{6} = \dfrac{4\frac{1}{2}}{x}$, so $x = 6 \times 4\frac{1}{2} = 27$ miles.

31. $\dfrac{1\frac{1}{2}}{700} = \dfrac{x}{3000}$, so $1\frac{1}{2} \times 3000 = 700x$ or $4500 = 700x$ and $x = \dfrac{45}{7} = 6\dfrac{3}{7}$ quarts.

32. $\dfrac{6}{4} = \dfrac{x}{25}$ and $6 \cdot 25 = 4x$. Therefore, $x = \dfrac{150}{4} = 37\dfrac{1}{2}$ feet

33. $\dfrac{2}{5} = \dfrac{36}{x}$, so $2x = 180$ and $x = 90$ females.

34. $\dfrac{12 \text{ feet}}{4 \text{ inches}} = \dfrac{x \text{ feet}}{6 \text{ inches}}$, so $12 \cdot 6 = 4x$, and $x = 18$ feet.

35. $\dfrac{20}{32} = \dfrac{6}{x}$, so $20x = 192$ and $x = \dfrac{192}{20} = 9.6$.

36. A. 5   D. 10.5   G. 86
    B. 0.5   E. 10   H. 75
    C. 10   F. 80

37. A. 13.6   C. 1.68
    B. 13.92   D. $1.17

38. A. Mental solution: 16 is 1/4 of what? Answer: 4 x 16 or 64 Algebraic solution:
$\frac{16}{x} = \frac{25}{100}$; 1600 = 25x, therefore $x = \frac{1600}{25} = 64$

B. $\frac{13}{x} = \frac{86}{100}$; 1300 = 86x, so $x = \frac{1300}{86}$ or approximately 15.1

C. $\frac{10}{18} = \frac{x}{100}$, so $x = \frac{1000}{18} = 55.55...$ Thus, x is approximately 55.6%

D. $\frac{17}{51} = \frac{x}{100}$, so $x = \frac{1700}{51}$ 33.33.... Thus, x is approximately 33.3% (or exactly 33 1/3%).

39. A. 16% of $32 = 0.16 x 32 = $5.12. The shirt now costs $32 + $5.12 or $37.12
B. 15% of $6200 = 0.15 x 6200 = $930. The new price would be $6200 - $930 = $5270
C. The mark-up is $1. The percent mark-up is $1 out of a price of $4 or 1/4 = 0.25 = 25%
D. The discount is $4 out of a price of $60 or 4/60 = 0.0666... or approximately 6.7%

40. A. The total weight is 3 x 14 + 7 x 8 = 98 oz. Of the total, the grapefruits provide 42/98 = 0.4285...or approximately 43%
B. If the grapefruits provide 43% of the total weight, then the oranges must provide the rest: 57% because 43% + 57% = 100%

41. C

42. D

43. We use the formula d = rt, except that we are interested in the rate of travel r. Thus, r = d/t. In terms of this problem, r is denoted by V and we have V = F-S/t

44. p + 0.2p or 1.2p

45. C

46. e. Let x be 1/2, 1, 2. The corresponding y values are -1 1/2, 0, 1 1/2. The expression x - 1/x is always increasing but it is negative when x is less than 1 and positive when x is larger than 1.

47. T/0.5 or 2T

48. If you let P = 1 and Q = 1, then R = 4 for equations a, c, d

49. b, d (Try substituting some positive, decreasing values for x; for example, x = 10, 2, 1. What happens to y?)

50. Total Cost

$$100 \times P$$
$$+ (T - 100) \cdot .8P$$
$$\overline{100P + (T - 100) \cdot .8P}$$

$p each for 100 books 80% of P (.8P) for each book over 100 (T-100)

$$100P + (T-100).8P = 100P + T \times .8P - 100 \times .8P$$
$$= 100P + .8TP - 80P$$
$$= 20P + .8TP$$

Therefore, c is the correct response.

51. $.15 \times 20{,}000 + .28 \times (D-20{,}000)$
   $= 3000 + .28D - .28 \times 20{,}000$
   $= 3000 + .28D - 5600$
   $= .28D - 2600$

52. A. approximately 975 students
    B. 200 to 250 or 4:5
    C. 1 1/2

53. 23%

54. 35,000 gallons

55. A. 10 days
    B. Fran

56. Choice A is correct: If t doubles, d doubles, etc.

57. Choice D

58. A. City D
    B. 18 degrees/6 hours = 3 degrees per hour
       (The rate of decrease for city D was 4 degrees per hour.)

59. #1 gives 20/48 square feet per dollar (20/48 = 5/12)
    #2 gives 18/44 square feet per dollar (18/44 = 9/22)
    #3 gives 24/60 square feet per dollar (24/60 = 2/5)
    Comparing the order of these fractions, 2/5 is less than 9/22, which is less than 5/12.
    Thus, 5/12 square feet per dollar is the best Lee can do. Choice #1 is best.

60. A. 5
    B. The third quartile

61. A. Yes
    B. No. The correct figure will lie somewhere between 26% and 32%, depending on the ratio of men to women. Suppose, for example, that there are 200 males and 100 females in the $25,000 plus category. Of the males, 32% or 64 smoke. Of the females, 26% or 26 smoke. Altogether 90 out of 300 smoke, that is, 90/300 = 30/100 = 30%. Thus, 26% of the females are smokers, 32% of the males are smokers,

and 30% of the entire group smokes. (Note that 30% is closer to the male percentage of 32% than it is to the female percentage of 26%. This is because there are more males than females in the entire population.)

C. You cannot tell. A higher percentage of males are smokers, but the absolute number of males who smoke could be smaller. Perhaps there are 300 people in this category; for example, 100 males and 200 females. 32% of 100 means 32 males smoke. 26% of 200 means 52 females smoke.

D. You cannot tell. The correct figure will lie somewhere between 32% and 40%, but will not be 36% unless the number of males equals the number of females in the under $5,000 category. (See the answer to B above)

E. Yes.

62. A. 2/6 or 1/3
     B. 2/6 or 1/3
     C. 4/6 or 2/3
     D. 0/6 or 0
     E. 4/6 or 2/3

63. A. On 7 of the 21 days, egg production was 5 or more dozen. Thus, the probability is 7/21 or 1/3.
     B. The probability of getting exactly 4 dozen eggs is 1/21. The probability of not getting 4 dozen is 20/21.

64. A. There are 600 students in all (246 + 54 + 280 + 20 = 600). Of these, 246 + 280 = 526 scored above the mean. The probability would be 526/600 (or 263/300).
     B. 20/300 or 1/15

65. A. 7
     B. 2/3
     C. The probability of either rain or sun is 1/3 + 1/6 = 1/2. The other half of the time you get neither rain nor sun. The probability of neither rain nor sun is 1/2.

66. A. 60 out of 73 students passed: 60/73
     B. 5/13

67. A. 0.16 × 5000 = 800
     B. 15/80 = .1875, which is larger than the statewide figure of .16. Since a score below 51 is presumably not good, your students did worse than the state as a whole.
     C. The probability of scoring in the 0-80 range is .16 + .24 + .30 + .20 = .90. The missing .10, therefore, must have scores above 80.

68. He needs to know the size of a tile so that he can decide how many tiles he needs.

69. A. $2474; 100 cameras
     B. $50.42; $2568
     C. $2568; 100 and $5042
     D. $24.74; no extraneous data

70. A. How many cubic yards of sand did the contractor use or how many cubic yards of both sand and gravel did the contractor use?
    B. We need to know where Ampex and Cranmore are in relation to Bodwick. Do the three towns lie on a line with Bodwick in the middle (Figure 1) or with Cranmore in the middle (Figure 2)?

    ```
    <----38----><--20-->           <-----38----->
    A        B       C             A      C<-20->B
         Figure 1                       Figure 2
    ```

    Do the three towns form the vertices of a right triangle, etc.?
    C. What is the number of students in each class?
    D. How many rooms are in that house?
    E. No information is needed. 105 = .70x so 1050 = 7x and x = 150. The team played 150 games and won 105. They lost 45 games.

71. A. The information in the first sentence is extraneous. Alternately, if you use the information in the first sentence, then 1/20 is extraneous.
    B. The 30 is not needed.
    C. The first sentence is irrelevant.
    D. We don't need to know that yesterday 30 students bought tickets; only the non-student data are relevant.

ESSAY WRITING

THE WRITING PROCESS

Under ideal conditions, writing involves a series of steps:

1. Pre-writing activities which facilitate understanding the purpose and the audience for a particular piece of writing and which might include generating ideas through brainstorming, notes, reflection, research, or discussion;

2. Focusing the material generated in step one by framing a thesis (controlling idea) and a direction (organization);

3. Getting the first draft on paper, using standard grammar, correct mechanics, and accurate spelling;

4. Assessing the success of the first draft by yourself or in consultation with a reliable reader;

5. Revising the draft by clarifying the thesis, topic sentences, supporting detail, and word choice; and

6. Proofreading for mistakes in grammar and spelling.

Ideal conditions do not always exist in the real world. Often you have to write under pressure and produce a clear statement. This is the case in a test situation. You must streamline the writing process to compose an acceptable essay in approximately one hour. This section will help you to practice necessary strategies by describing how you might do the following:

1. Turn the directions into a purpose statement.
2. Brainstorm for material to put in the essay.
3. Group and focus your ideas.
4. Compose your essay with clear signals for the reader.
5. Proofread for word choice, grammar, and mechanics.

TURN DIRECTIONS INTO PURPOSE STATEMENTS

For each of the following sets of essays, the directions specify a topic, an audience, and some possible ways to develop the essay. You have some choice about how to develop the essay, but you must stick to the topic given and a style appropriate to the audience. The directions consist of four sentences which give

1. an indication of audience,
2. a description of audience,
3. suggestions for development, and
4. a restatement of the topic.

You can distinguish the sentences that suggest development because they contain words which give options rather than commands; for example, the sentences that give you commands about the topic will look like this:

In writing, tell the panel why you are considering teaching as a career.

On the other hand, sentences that suggest development will look like this:
The reasons may include…
You might want to consider…
The experiences could be…

Your first step, then, is to sort out the essential commands in the directions and convert them into a clear purpose statement such as *I will explain my reasons for choosing teaching as a career.* The purpose statement must cover all the essential parts of the assignment.

EXERCISE B

For each of the following sets of directions, underline the sentences that give you commands about the topic and write a purpose statement, using your own words if possible.

Prompt 1
A committee of teachers and administrators is reviewing your qualifications for a scholarship. In writing, tell the committee about a special activity you engage in, either in school or outside of school. It could be a job, an organization you belong to, a hobby or sport you participate in, or something you do with your family. Tell the committee what your special activity is and explain why this activity is important to you.

Prompt 2
A superintendent of schools has reviewed your application for a teaching position. Before holding a formal interview with you, the superintendent wants you to provide a writing sample that tells what motivated you to choose teaching as a profession. You might want to discuss a special learning experience you had or your interest in a chosen field or subject. Tell the superintendent what your motivation is and explain why your learning experience or your interest in a special field or subject is important to you.

Prompt 3
Your college advisor has just notified you that the college has instituted an open curriculum. As a result, you may choose any three courses or activities you wish to take next semester. You will be given equal course credit for academic subjects and activities such as sports, cultural

activities (music, theater, art), school newspaper or literary magazine activities, fraternities, sororities, community projects, or any other activity whose importance you can justify. In writing, indicate what three courses you would select and how each one would make you a better person.

Prompt 4
You have just been given the opportunity to write a letter of application to the Director of Admissions at the college of your choice. Imagine that cost is not a concern to you; you may choose a college that offers a traditional liberal arts curriculum or one that allows you to study only those courses that relate to your field of interest. In your essay, tell the Director of Admissions the type of college you are choosing and identify the reasons for your choice.

Prompt 5
A committee of teachers is reviewing your application for admission into the teacher education program of your choice. The committee has asked you to write an essay that describes a book that made the most lasting impression on you or from which you believe you learned some valuable lesson. The book may be on any subject, fiction or nonfiction, that is meaningful to you. The book need not be something you read for a course. Explain to the committee what your impression or lesson is and why it is important to you.

BRAINSTORM FOR MATERIAL TO PUT IN THE ESSAY

The directions on the subtest often contains suggestions for areas to explore. The sample directions which ask for an essay on your reasons for choosing a teaching career suggest that you consider *examples set by other people, benefits you expect from a teaching career, or the challenges you think teaching offers.* Remember that these suggestions are only suggestions. Before you respond to them, you should think about how you would accomplish the writing task if the suggestions had not been made. To be convincing, the material in your essay must come from your own experiences and knowledge. Brainstorming can help you accomplish this.

There are different ways to brainstorm. Some people prefer to write freely for 5-10 minutes. Others like to make lists or sketches. Others mull over ideas and ask themselves questions before jotting down a few key words. If you have a method that works for you, stick with it. If you don't, try one of the three approaches just mentioned.

EXERCISE C

1. Think about your reasons for wanting to teach and jot down a list of those reasons.

2. Compare your list with the suggestions given for considering teaching as a career: (examples, benefits, and challenges).

3. Which reasons fit the category of the rewards of teaching?

4. Which reasons could be labeled challenges of teaching?

5. Which reasons are related to examples set by other people?

6. What labels or categories do your other reasons fall under?

7. Are some of your reasons related to experiences that you have had as a learner or teacher (e.g., sports, scouting, 4-H, religious classes)?

8. Are some of your reasons related to your interest in a particular subject such as mathematics or art?

9. Are some of your reasons related to particular qualities you possess such as patience, enthusiasm, or tolerance?

LISTEN TO YOUR INNER VOICE

The purpose of brainstorming is to come up with enough detail or elaboration to satisfy the evaluation requirements. You should aim to produce enough material for an introduction and at least three additional paragraphs. Once you list a few initial ideas, the best way to generate more detail is to imagine a voice saying, *Tell me more about that.* Let's suppose that your initial list of reasons for wanting to teach looked like this.

- I like kids.
- Summers off.
- Make a contribution to society.
- Encouragement from teachers.

Responding to that imaginary voice saying, *Tell me more*, might help you elaborate the first reason as follows:

I like kids...
    because they all have some undeveloped potential.
    because their responses aren't always predictable.
    because they get so excited when they learn something new.

Another way to elaborate on the first reason is through examples:

- The two boys I used to babysit.
- The girl I helped to get over her fear of water.
- The special education student who was my *little brother*.

Imagine the voice asking for more information until you believe you have enough for a satisfactory essay. Not every statement will give you as much room for development as others, but you can expand upon all of the statements. Each time you elaborate, your writing becomes more specific. Including specific detail makes your ideas concrete and your writing more convincing. Specific detail is one of the criteria for evaluating your essay.

EXERCISE D

1. Go back to the list of purpose statements that you developed in Exercise C, and brainstorm for material you might include in an essay.

2. Go back to your list of reasons for wanting to teach and elaborate as much as you can on each one.

GROUP AND FOCUS YOUR IDEAS

A good essay is unified by a controlling idea or thesis which dictates a pattern of organization. The thesis should be stated in one or two sentences. The words you choose to write the thesis statement should repeat or echo the directions for the essay. This strategy will ensure that you state the topic clearly. One way to write a thesis is to do one of the following:

1. Look at your purpose statement.
   Example 1: I must explain my reasons for choosing teaching as a career.
   Example 2: I must explain how a learning experience motivated me to go into teaching.

2. Look at the list of ideas you generated by brainstorming and try to sum up the ideas in a sentence or two:
   Sample Thesis 1: I have chosen teaching as a career because I enjoy young children, particularly those who have a learning disability. Teaching is a career that will enable me to make a contribution to society.
   Sample Thesis 2: The experience that I had as a *big brother* to a special education student helped me to realize that everyone has the potential to learn. This experience strengthened my interest in teaching as a career.

The thesis prepares the reader for what is to follow. It is a promise that you will discuss certain ideas and not others.

You will not always use all the material you generated during the brainstorming step. In the sample that we have been discussing, you might have decided not to use material related to summers off or the encouragement of teachers. However, if you decide that there is some material you want to include in the body of your essay material which is not indicated by the thesis, you need to revise the thesis. Suppose you decide to include the information about summers off and the encouragement of teachers, how could you revise the thesis? Here is one possibility:

Revised Thesis: There are many reasons why I have chosen teaching as a career. The pleasure of working with children, the opportunity to make a contribution to society, the encouragement of teachers, and time during the summer to continue my own education and interests are a few of them.

You should understand that it is not necessary or advisable to give every reason why you would like to teach. Be selective. Choose reasons on which you can elaborate and ones you feel strongly about. This will make a more convincing essay.

OUTLINING

There are different ways of grouping brainstorming ideas. The traditional format is the outline. Here is one example, based on the thesis we have been discussing.

Thesis: There are many reasons why I have chosen teaching as a career; some of them are the pleasure of working with children, the opportunity to make a contribution to society, the encouragement of teachers, and time during the summer to continue my own education and interests.

   I. I enjoy working with children.
      A. All children have potential.
      B. Their responses are unpredictable.
      C. They are excited when they learn something.

  II. I will make a contribution to society.
      A. Many jobs have questionable social value even if they have high salaries.
      B. Teachers can help children develop a good self-image and give them necessary skills.

 III. Teachers have encouraged me.
      A. They say I can express myself clearly.
      B. They see that I am enthusiastic about learning.

  IV. Summers will be time to continue my education and interests.
      A. Teachers must be lifelong learners.
      B. Intensity of teaching requires time for pursuing other interests.

CLUSTERING

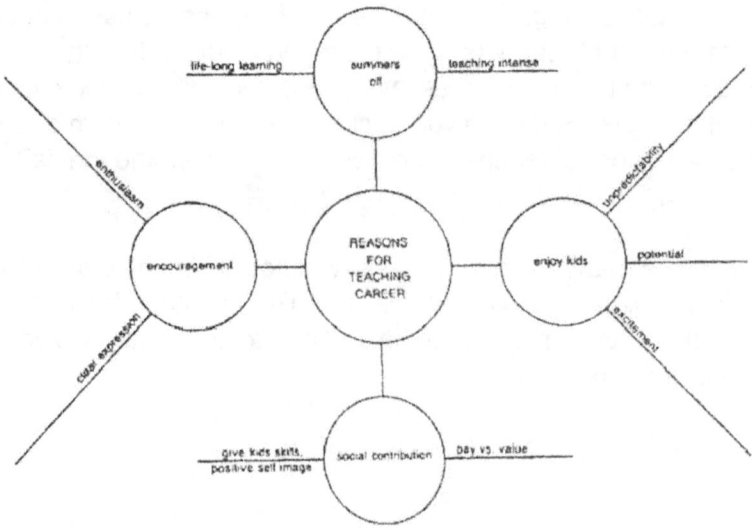

FLOW CHARTS

Still another way to map ideas is with the help of a flow chart. The main idea is placed in a box at the top, and other categories branch off below.

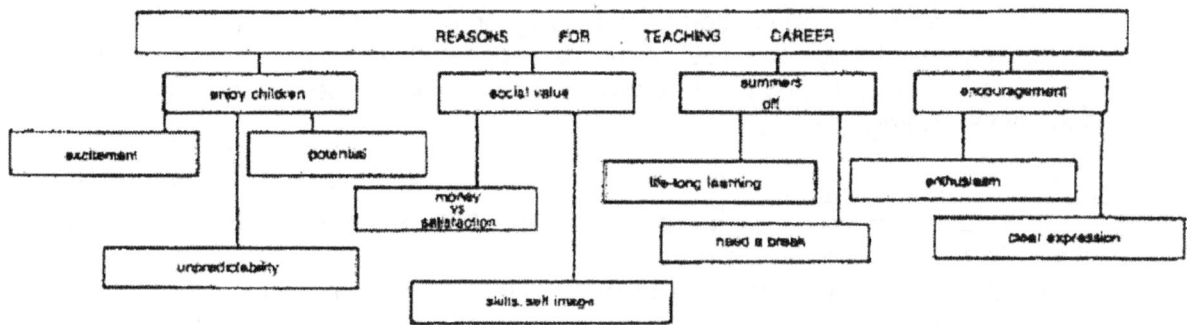

INFORMAL LISTS

An informal list is an easy way to group ideas.

My Reasons:

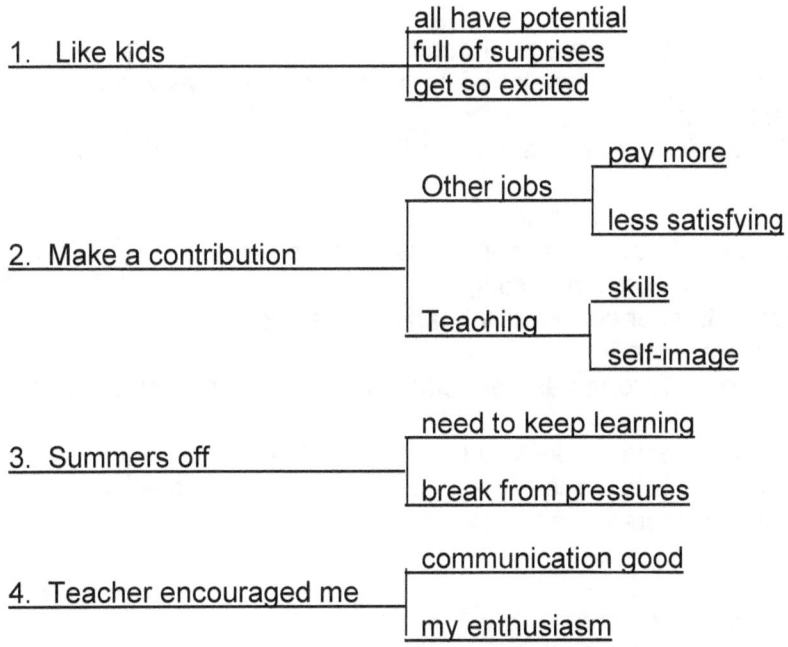

Regardless of which method you use to group your ideas, the goal is to pull together related bits of information and sketch the paragraph structure for your essay before you actually start writing your essay in the test booklet.

EXERCISE E

1. Go back to the material that you produced through brainstorming in Exercise D.2 and group the ideas by using one of the formulas illustrated.

2. Using one of the strategies mentioned previously, group the ideas given below in each set. For each set, read through the ideas in the set and identify or create a thesis statement; group related sentences; and find or create a sentence or phrase that will hold each group of sentences together.

   SET A.
   1. TV cartoons show characters recovering quickly from serious injury.
   2. Mr. Rogers never loses his temper.
   3. Ads associate happiness and good times with possession of a product.
   4. The ads show cereal boxes opening by themselves and dancing on the table.
   5. TV gives children a distorted sense of reality.
   6. Mr. Rogers always takes off his shoes when he comes inside.
   7. A character falls off a mountain top, shakes his head, and gets up.
   8. Positive role models, like Mr. Rogers, are unlike any real-life adult.
   9. Mr. Rogers never raises his voice.
   10. The ads are deceptive and manipulative.
   11. Characters who smash into walls are never badly hurt.

   SET B.
   1. I felt welcome when I went to see my math teacher during his office hours.
   2. The activity fair during orientation week had something to offer everyone.
   3. The counselors were helpful.
   4. Many teachers ask if students need help rather than wait for the students to get in trouble.
   5. The counselors helped with course selection.
   6. Resident advisors counsel students about adjustment problems.
   7. The counselors provided placement testing.
   8. Teachers talk to students after class rather than just rushing off.
   9. Students on campus are friendly.
   10. My experience at Winona College has been good, and I would recommend it to others.
   11. Teachers go over sample tests before you take the first test.
   12. The dorm council plans activities and projects to bring students together.
   13. The counselors offer minicourses on taking notes and tests.

   SET C.
   1. I don't belong to any organizations.
   2. I'm not involved in any special activities.
   3. I go to classes, work at the store, and see my friends on weekends.
   4. My job isn't special.
   5. I work at a supermarket.
   6. I need the job for spending money and college expenses.

7. I have learned some things from working.
8. It's not like school.
9. You have to be there to get paid.
10. The boss isn't always fair.
11. Sometimes she is impatient.
12. As a lowly clerk, you don't get any respect.
13. The boss seemed annoyed when I brought back the shopping carts.
14. There were long lines at the registers.
15. She told me to help bag groceries.
16. There's a pecking order in most companies.
17. My boss is under pressure from the manager.
18. I'm trying to stay on top of the situation rather than just reacting.
19. I ask the boss how things have been going.
20. I try to anticipate what she'll ask me to do and offer to do it first.
21. Sometimes I feel frustrated about being low on the totem pole.
22. The manager doesn't even know who I am.
23. There's not much incentive to do good work.
24. You can always be replaced by another minimum wage worker.

SET D.
1. DEATH OF A SALESMAN is a book that influenced me because of the connections between the play and my own life.
2. Each time I had a different reaction.
3. I read the play once in high school, again in college, and then saw it on TV.
4. In high school, Biff was a good-looking football hero.
5. The play is about a salesman named Willy, his wife, and two sons, Biff and Happy.
6. Happy was just an ordinary kid, living in his brother's shadow.
7. When Biff learned that his father was not perfect, he began to drift around.
8. I realized I was only hurting myself.
9. I had an older brother who was a star.
10. I was always trying to get my parents' attention.
11. I even tried to get their attention by doing poorly in school.
12. At first, I identified with Happy.
13. Biff had a big ego because of all the attention he received.
14. Biff became a bum because of all the attention he received as a teenager.
15. When I read the play in college, I sympathized with Willy.
16. He never received any respect from his boss.
17. I have been working at a supermarket.
18. Clerks are a dime a dozen, just like salespeople.
19. I want a career where a paycheck is not the only satisfaction you receive.
20. The TV version made me admire the mother.
21. She held the family together.
22. She was completely loyal to Willy.
23. We all want someone to stick by us like she did.

SET E.
1. Earning credit for my choice of courses and activities will give me a chance to integrate course work and real experience.
2. Reading Methods is a required course.
3. I'll learn how to assess a student's reading level.
4. I'll learn about various methods for teaching reading skills.
5. I plan to work as a literacy volunteer.
6. I want to know why people don't learn to read.
7. I'll learn about methods for teaching adults.
8. I'll learn how illiteracy affects a person's life.
9. I'll realize what's at stake if the education system fails.
10. I want to take either an advanced composition course or an independent study in composition.
11. I would like to keep a journal of my experience as a literacy volunteer.
12. I would like to write about the connections I see between the methods course and my tutoring experience.
13. I would like to write some feature stories about illiteracy for the college newspaper.

COMPOSE YOUR ESSAY WITH CLEAR SIGNALS FOR THE READER

Your essay is judged on how well the essay communicates a whole message. If you keep the reader in mind, your essay is likely to communicate more effectively. The most important signals to use are topic sentences to state the main idea of each paragraph and transitions to link sentences within the paragraphs. One basic pattern you might use in composing your paragraphs is the five paragraph essay. Here is one example of such an essay written in response to Prompt 1, Exercise B. Study the way in which the topic sentences give the reader a preview of what will be discussed.

Paragraph I.	Lead and thesis statement.
Lead	Some students may have time for sports, clubs, or volunteer organizations. Unfortunately, my schedule of classes and part-time work does not give me much time to devote to other activities. However, my job has been quite a learning experience.
Thesis	<u>Although I am just a supermarket clerk, I have gained insight into the demands of a job, the behavior of supervisors, and my ability to influence a situation.</u>
Paragraph II	Topic sentence developed with sufficient detail.
Topic Sentence	<u>I realized that the demands of a job re not always like the demands of school.</u> Maybe that is something that other people know from the start, but it did not work that way for me. In fact, I can remember how the equation between work and pay dawned on me; if I missed an afternoon of work, I missed an equivalent amount of money in my paycheck. The connection between work and rewards is not quite so clear in school. A student can study hard for a test and do poorly. On the other hand, a student can sometimes bluff through a test and get a good grade.

Paragraph III.	Another topic sentence with supporting detail.
Topic Sentence	<u>I did not work for very long before I also realized that bosses can be difficult.</u> At first, my supervisor seemed like a nice enough person. However, I had a look at her other side one day when I returned to the store, pushing a long line of shopping carts which she had told me to gather from the parking lot. Lines had formed at all the registers, and she snapped at me to bag for one of the cashiers. It was as if it my fault that she had sent two of the cashiers out for supper just as it was getting busy in the store.
Paragraph IV.	Another topic sentence followed by detail.
Topic sentence	<u>After my initial anger at the boss's behavior, I decided to try to influence the situation rather than just reacting to it.</u> I realized this approach might work as I was bagging groceries. I saw the store manager peering down at my box from her office window. My boss had a boss who had a boss who had a boss. She was part of the pecking order just like me. Now I try to make small talk with her, ask how things have been going, and so forth. Also, I try to anticipate what she might ask me to do and then offer to do it first. This gives me the feeling that I can be an actor rather than just a puppet.
Paragraph V.	Conclusion with restatement of thesis.
Thesis Restated	Sometimes I still get frustrated at work. As a lowly clerk, I do not get much respect in a large, impersonal company. <u>However, my job has shown me that even the most ordinary parts of my life can give me an opportunity to learn something about myself and other people.</u>

Topic sentences do not always occur at the beginning of paragraphs. In fact, at times it seems stilted to put the topic sentence at the start of a paragraph. You may need a sentence or two that makes a bridge with the preceding paragraph. For example, the fourth paragraph in the sample essay above might have been written more chronologically, following the sequence of events more closely.

Example:	After my initial anger, I noticed the store manager peering down at my boss from the upstairs office window. I realized that my boss had a boss who had a boss;
Thesis Statement	She was just a part of the pecking order like me. <u>I decided to try to influence the situation instead of just reacting to it.</u>

Placing the topic sentence at the start of a paragraph gives the clearest signal to a reader, but it is not always essential to place the topic sentence at the beginning. It is important, however, to have a sentence that holds the rest of the paragraph together. It can come at the beginning, the middle, or the end of the paragraph. Here is a paragraph without a topic sentence:

Ms. Rodriquez always had a word of encouragement on each test she handed back. Furthermore, she taught me the difference between an intelligent mistake and a dumb one. An intelligent mistake occurs when a learner applies a rule or procedure to a special situation where it does not apply. For example, if a young child says, "I taked the book," she is applying the rule to use a "d" sound for a past action. Ms. Rodriguez also had a way of making math problems exciting mysteries. We watched her solve equations on the board like Sherlock Holmes in pursuit of a suspect. The work was never easy, but she always made us feel that it was possible to succeed if we put in enough time.

One way to phrase a topic sentence for the paragraph above would be:
Ms. Rodriguez was one of the best teachers I ever had.

Even if you think that the point of the paragraph is perfectly clear without a topic sentence, put one in. You are now writing this essay for a sophisticated magazine; you are taking a test to show that you can get an idea across clearly to a reader.

EXERCISE F.

1. Each paragraph below lacks a topic sentence. Create a topic sentence for each paragraph and decide where best to place it.

    a. I would be happy if I could make some difference in the lives of the students I will teach. It might just mean making them more curious about the world or more accepting of themselves. I realize that it is difficult to reach each student, but that does not mean that I will not try.
    b. Mr. Wright began every class by putting the homework on the board. Then he would announce what we were going to do that day. Usually, we went over the homework problems first. Students were asked to put their solutions on the board. After discussing them and making necessary corrections, Mr. Wright would turn to the new material. Using three or four pieces of colored chalk, he illustrated and commented on the examples in the book. Finally, if we finished all of the scheduled lesson, there was time at the end of class to start on the homework.
    c. Every teacher spends a minimum of 35 hours in school. In addition, teachers must often supervise activities such as the drama club or school newspaper. Conferences with parents, staff meetings, and required professional development activities also add to the total hours required. A teacher usually has three different course-related preparations, each of which may take an hour or more, depending on the teacher's experience. English teachers who have 25 to 30 students per class may assign a short piece of writing each week, and may spend 4 to 5 minutes reading each paper. This may add 13 hours of additional work per week.

2. Go back to the material that you brainstormed and organized in Exercise D. Pick at least one batch of material and turn it into an essay following the pattern of the five-paragraph essay described previously.

TRANSITIONS

Transitions are signals to your reader about how your ideas are connected. Certain words and phrases prepare the reader for what is to follow. Examples of important transitions to use in your essay are:

1. Words that indicate sequence of events or ideas: first, second (etc.), finally, last, ultimately, eventually, later, meanwhile, afterwards;

2. Words that indicate examples: for instance, for example, specifically, in particular;

3. Words that indicate addition of similar ideas: and, also, furthermore, moreover, similarly, equally important, another;

4. Words that indicate addition of contrasting ideas: however, but, on the other hand, on the contrary, still, yet, in contrast, nevertheless.

Transitions between sentences can also be achieved by repeating key words, using synonyms, or using pronouns.

1. Example of a repeated key word: *Literacy* is not just a matter of learning the ABC's, *Literacy* means having sufficient control of the language to function in one's society.

2. Example of use of a synonym: *Literacy* is not just a matter of learning the ABC's. One's ability to read and write must be equal to the demands of one's society.

3. Example use of a pronoun: *Literacy* is not just a matter of learning the ABC's. It means having sufficient control of the language to function in your society.

EXERCISE G.

1. Look at the paragraphs you wrote in Exercise F and underline all the transitions.

2. Go back to the essay you wrote in Exercise F. Underline any transitions you used. Find places where you might insert additional transitions.

PROOFREAD FOR WORD CHOICE, GRAMMAR, AND MECHANICS

Under ideal conditions, you would complete a first draft and then evaluate it for content and structure. However, a subtest, lasting approximately one hour, does not allow time for true revision. You may want to think of your brainstorming as a type of first draft and your focusing as a type of revision. As you focus and compose your essay, you will do a certain amount of revision, deciding to change the order of paragraphs, inserting or deleting details, trying out sentences in your head before you put them down on paper. Once you have completed the essay, you need to proofread to make sure you have used words correctly and avoid errors that will detract from your essay and subsequently from the score you receive for your essay.

WORD CHOICE

In choosing words to express your ideas, keep in mind that the directions on the examination writing subtest are likely to specify an audience that requires you to use a professional tone. You should avoid slang and cliches. On the other hand, don't go overboard and complicate your essay with fancy terms and inflated language. Aim for a clear and direct expression of your ideas.

Here are a few examples of the kinds of words and expressions to avoid:

1. One activity that I've really *gotten into* lately is sailing. (Substitute *became involved in, become interested in, become enthusiastic about*).

2. The person sitting behind me talked *a lot* during the class. (Try to be as specific as possible about what *a lot* means in the sentence where you are tempted to use it. Here, you might use *continuously* or *incessantly*, but at other times, you might want to substitute *a great deal* or *often*.)

3. My first class was *awful*. (General words such as *awful, perfect, beautiful*, etc. are acceptable if you are going to follow up with more specific description. However, it is almost always better to use specific language. In what respect was the experience or the person awful, perfect, or beautiful? In the example above, was the class dull, disorganized, too demanding?)

4. I was faced with a *number of alternatives*. (Strictly defined, an alternative is a choice between two things. If you mean more than two, use options *or* choices.)

5. Computers are a *new innovation* in the classroom. (Innovation means *new*; therefore, the phrase is redundant. The same would be true of expressions such as *personal friend* and *advance planning*.)

Our language is constantly changing. At any period in history, some words and expressions are considered suitable for formal writing while others are considered colloquial and appropriate only for informal settings. As you prepare for the writing subtest, you might want to use a dictionary or a glossary of usage in a handbook. These references will provide guidance in currently acceptable choices. You might also want to keep in mind that no references will be available during the test. Therefore, if you have any doubt about the appropriateness of a word or phrase, you might want to avoid using it, and choose words about which you feel more confident.

Excess words are as much a problem as inexact words. When people don't know what to write, they often try to pad the paragraphs with sentences that say the same thing in slightly different words or fill up the sentences with empty phrases. Superfluous words and sentences may bore, frustrate, or even confuse your reader. You will be spared these problems if you practice brainstorming for relevant and interesting details before you compose your essay. Here are some examples of padded writing:

Wordy: Education faces a crisis today. At the present time, a number of problems are troubling concerned citizens. Not a day goes by that you do not hear about one problem or another.

To the Point: Many problems in education call for our attention.

Wordy: Due to the fact that a problem arose concerning the time our committee should meet, we decided in the final analysis that it would be best to postpone our decision until the new chairperson took over.

To the Point: Unable to agree on a meeting time, our committee postponed the decision until the new chairperson took over.

EXERCISE H

1. Find places in your own writing where you could eliminate words without losing meaning.

2. Trim unnecessary words from the following sentences and rewrite.

   a. The aspects of teaching that I imagine I will most enjoy are the diversity of students and the freedom to organize my own classes.

   b. The problem that I foresee causing the most difficulty in the future is that a few years from now we are going to have even more non-native English speaking students than we do now and people don't understand the need for bilingual education.

   c. In conclusion, the final point that I want to make is to say that the productivity of our economic system will decline unless we do something to tackle the problem of illiteracy among the many people who can't read at all or who can barely read.

EXERCISE I

There are a number of commonly confused words. Use a dictionary or handbook to check the correct choice for each of the sentences that follow.

1. I _____ your invitation to the party. (accept, except, expect)
2. I _____ to do well on my math exam. (accept, except, expect)
3. Everyone is going _____ Susan. (accept, except, expect)
4. I went to my guidance teacher for some good _____. (advise, advice)
5. I always _____ my students to take French literature. (advise, advice)
6. The _____ of the hurricane was horrendous. (affect, effect)
7. Does this test _____ my grade? (affect, effect)
8. _____ never too late to try. (Its, It's)
9. The committee reported _____ decision. (its, it's)
10. Please place the books over _____. (there, they're, their)
11. _____ my brother's friends. (There, They're, Their)
12. The boys have lost _____ shoes. (there, they're, their)

13. Most of the students could not choose _____ the four answers. (between, among)
14. Mary is trying to decide _____ two majors: History and French. (between, among)
15. John arrived at the game, _____. (to, too, two)
16. Please place _____ books on this corner. (to, two, too)
17. David gave the ball _____ Mark. (to, two, too)
18. Peter ran the mile _____. (bad, badly)
19. I feel _____ when it rains. (bad, badly)
20. Teachers often have to _____ packaged materials to the special needs of their students. (adopt, adapt)
21. Our school would like to _____ a dress code for all students. (adopt, adapt)
22. This corner will be the _____ for the reading materials. (site, cite)
23. Students must learn how to _____ source materials in a research paper. (site, cite)
24. Individualized activities are needed to _____ group activities. (compliment, complement)
25. Teachers should _____ children often on the work that they successfully complete. (compliment, complement)

GRAMMAR AND MECHANICS

An occasional error in grammar or mechanics in an essay written without access to a dictionary will not result in failing the writing portion of the exam. However, frequent errors will detract from the effectiveness of your message and can cause failure. There are so many possible errors, that they cannot be covered in this brief guide. A discussion of the most serious errors will be followed by a set of sentences you can use to test your proofreading skills.

1. <u>Sentence Boundaries</u>: Running two or more independent clauses together without linking words or proper punctuation violates basic rules. A grammatically incomplete sentence is equally distracting.

    a. Run-on, fused sentence, or comma splice: Teaching is not an easy field, the rewards aren't always there. (A comma is not sufficient to separate two independent clauses. Substitute a period, a semi-colon, or a linking word, such as *because* for the comma.)

    b. Fragment: The best example being the difference between the way we see a character on TV and the way we visualize a character in a story. (The *ing* form of the verb creates a fragment. Substitute *is* for *being* to correct the sentence.)

2. <u>Agreement of Sentence Elements</u>: Verbs must agree with their subjects; pronouns with the nouns to which they refer. Similar elements must have parallel structure. Parts of the sentence must fit together grammatically.

    a. Lack of subject-verb agreement: The problems that young readers have seems to come partly from the environment. (*problems* calls for the verb form *seem* not *seems*. In sentences where several words come between subject and verb, it is easy to lose track of the elements.)

b. Lack of pronoun agreement: Everyone wants to achieve their potential. (*Everyone* is singular and calls for *his/her*, not *their*.)

c. Lack of parallel structure: I learned to operate the computer, write some simple programs, and the fundamentals of word processing. (*Operate* and *write* set up a pattern which calls for a similar word. Therefore, the last part of the sentence should be rephrased to include a verb; for example, *...and use the fundamentals of word processing*.)

d. Lack of grammatical fit: While taking an elective course in design my freshman year sparked my interest in art. (The introductory phrase, *While taking an elective course*, calls for a subject to come before the verb. This sentence could be revised in at least two ways:
While taking an elective course in design my freshman year, I became interested in art.
Taking an elective course in design my freshman year sparked my interest in art.

SELECTED CAPITALIZATION RULES

A few of the rules governing capitalization are reviewed below. Consult a dictionary or handbook for more complete coverage of this topic.

1. Capitalize proper nouns and adjectives.
   Example: Capitalize: *Judy Blume* and *Southington High School*.
   Do not capitalize *the author* or *my high school*.

2. Capitalize titles when they precede proper names, but not when they follow proper names or are used alone.
   Example: Professor Kent Curtis
   Kent Curtis, professor of history
   the history professor

3. Do not capitalize the names of academic years or terms.
   Example: spring semester
   my sophomore year

4. Capitalize the names of specific courses, but not fields of study unless they are languages.
   Example: Capitalize *English, Spanish,* and *Math 101*
   Do not capitalize *math, physics,* or *education*.

5. Capitalize the important words in titles of books and underline the titles.
   Example: Catcher in the Rye
   Grapes of Wrath

PUNCTUATION

Punctuation is another area that you should review with the help of a good handbook or dictionary. One simple rule to remember is: Do not use the dash as a substitute for the proper punctuation. Example of a punctuation error: Although I took up swimming—the doctors said it would be good exercise—but I found that I did not have the ability to make the team

(The problem with relying on dashes is that, as in the example, dependence can lead to sloppy sentence construction. The sentence above should be revised: I took up swimming because the doctors said it would be good exercise, but I found that I did not have the ability to make the team.)

EXERCISE J

1. Proofread the following essay to identify errors in grammar, mechanics, and word use. Underline or cross out all errors.

2. Rewrite the essay, using correct grammar, mechanics, and wording.

The extent of illiteracy in the Country is documented in Illiterate America—a book by Jonathan Kozol. When I read this book and realized the extent of illiteracy gave me a shock. Kozol claims that 25 million people can not red warning labels or a simple news story, another 35 million do not read well enough to survive in the Modern Age—Like being able to follow printed instructions. For someone who can't read and has to support himself or a family could be a real disadvantage.

The problem of illiteracy will be difficult to solve. There being many causes that go deep into our society. Schools have failed to halt the problem and may be contributing to it. My parents say that the problem with schools today are a lack of respect for authority. Years ago, everyone know what would happen if they disobeyed a teacher. Today, teachers must contend with students who are often bored, rarely prepared and frequently they defy the teacher. Some respect and discipline is needed to create a learning environment.

Another problem with the schools is poorly prepare teachers. Students graduating from college without being able to read or write well. During the 1960s was the decline of strict academic standards. Students failed to learn what they should of learned. The decline may be ending, new tests and requirements are in place. For example, the college of arts and sciences at Northeastern State University changed their requirements because entering students were so poorly prepared. Some of them unable to identify Sophocles or locate spain on a map.

Kozol's book interested me in the larger issues of literacy—it is more than learning the ABCs. Literacy is when you can read and write well enough to survive in a complex technology and making informed opinions about government policies. Teachers can help to create a literate America. After reading about the problems of illiteracy facing this country, I want to become one,

19

PUTTING IT ALL TOGETHER

PRACTICE TOPICS

You will not know in advance the topic on which you will be asked to write an essay for the examination. However, the topic is likely to involve your education, education in general, or your choice of a career.

The best way to prepare for the writing subtest is to practice the skills presented in this book and to write whole essays under conditions similar to those found in examinations. Below are several topics you may use for practice.

Practice Prompt 1

The Academic Standards Committee of your college is considering changes in the current grading system and they have asked you to write a statement about the impact of the letter grade system (ABCDF) on learning. You may want to consider how the letter grade system affects certain types of students, how it is viewed by students, teachers, or prospective employers, whether there is a practical alternative, or whether modifications should be made. Write a statement of your opinion of the letter grade system and the reasons for your opinion.

Practice Prompt 2

A screening committee is reviewing your application for a teaching position and has asked you to submit a statement of your strengths and weaknesses for the position. Imagine a specific teaching position for which you might apply and write a statement about how well you qualify for that particular job. You might want to consider how your educational background, work experiences, internships, or special interests make you a suitable candidate. You might also want to consider whether there is anything about the position, the type of students you might face, the location, or the responsibilities that might be a challenge to you. Describe the teaching position for which you are applying and explain why you would be a good candidate for the position.

Practice Prompt 3

The committee considering your application to enter a teacher training program wants to learn about your awareness of students' non-academic needs. They have pointed out that a teacher must often do more than teach subject matter. Consider the psychological, physical, social, and economic problems that affect a student's ability to learn. Describe your understanding of the ways in which the role of a teacher goes beyond teaching academic subjects.

Practice Prompt 4

Your college is hosting a conference for state high school teachers to address the problem of the inadequate preparation of the average student for college work. The conference is focusing on the average student because college teachers are concerned about the many students entering freshman courses who are unable to meet the demands of college. You might want to describe how serious the problem is, whose problem it is, and to what extent high schools should consider changing what they are doing. Use your experience, observations, and knowledge to write a statement which gives your perspective on the gap between the academic requirements in high school and those in college.

POST-TEST

Writing Subtest Directions

This part of the examination consists of one writing exercise. You should allow approximately 60 minutes to complete this assignment. You may NOT use a dictionary during the subtest. Make sure you have time to plan, write, review, and revise what you have written.

Before you begin to write, read the topic carefully and take some time to think about how you will organize what you plan to say. Your writing exercise will be evaluated on the basis of how effectively it communicates a whole message to the intended audience for the stated purpose. Your writing exercise will be judged on the success of its total impression by a panel of language arts experts. When evaluating your ability to communicate a whole message effectively, the scorers will also consider your ability to:

1. state and stay on the topic;
2. address all specified parts of the writing assignment;
3. present your ideas in an organized fashion;
4. include sufficient detail and elaboration to statements;
5. choose effective words;
6. employ correct grammar and usage; and
7. use correct mechanics (spelling, capitalization, paragraph form).

PROMPT

The screening committee considering your application for a teaching position is concerned about teacher stress and burn-out. They would like to learn about your awareness of this problem and your susceptibility to it. You might want to discuss how you have handled stressful situations in the past and any techniques that you use to cope with stress. Describe in writing how you would confront the problem of stress and burn-out in the teaching profession.

NOTES/OUTLINE

21

KEY (CORRECT ANSWERS)

In some cases where there is no one right answer, possible answers are given. If your answer is significantly different, discuss it with a teacher or tutor.

EXERCISE B

1. I must describe an activity and tell the committee why it is important to me.

2. I must explain to the superintendent why I want to teach and how an experience or subject helped me make this decision.

3. I have to select three courses or activities and justify why they would be worthwhile.

4. I have to write a letter to the director of admissions at the college of my choice and explain why I want to go there.

5. I have to describe to the committee a significant book and concentrate on what I got out of it.

EXERCISE C

   Answers will vary.

EXERCISE D

   Answers will vary.

EXERCISE E

1. Answers will vary.

2. A. An ideal wheel:

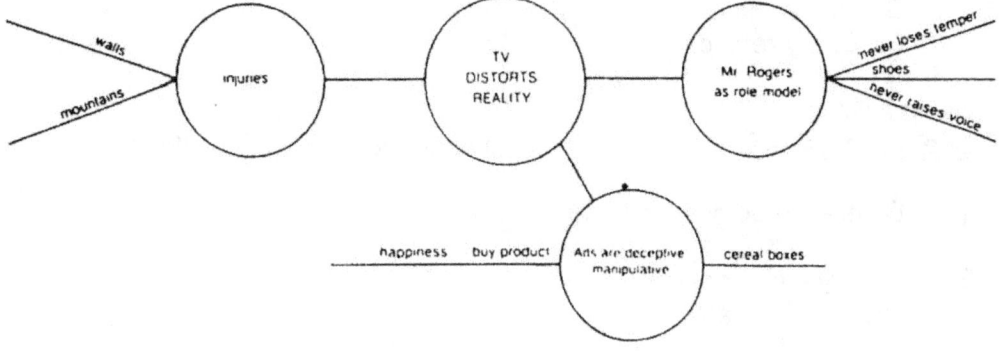

247

B. A flow chart:

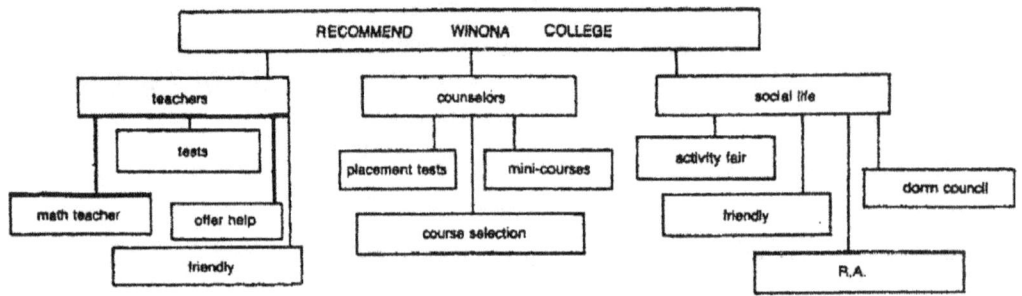

C. Using an outline:

Thesis: My job as a clerk has taught me about the reality of work and how to get along with supervisors.

I. I don't have time for special activities.
   A. School
   B. Need job
   C. Friends

II. Work is not like school because if you don't work, you don't get paid.

III. Boss is not always fair.
   A. No respect for clerks
   B. Gets impatient
   C. Got annoyed about lines

IV. I'm trying to get on top of the situation rather than just reacting.
   A. Boss is part of pecking order
   B. Make small talk
   C. Anticipate orders

V. I am still frustrated.
   A. No recognition
   B. No incentive
   C. Easily replaced

D. Using a list:
Death of a Salesman – connections between the play and my life

1. Different readings – different reactions

2. Describe characters
   Willy: salesman
   Linda: wife
   Biff: good looking, football hero breaks with Willy, drifts around
   Happy: ordinary, shadowed by Biff

3. Identified with Happy
   My older brother
   Wanted parents' attention
   School troubles
   Realized I was hurting myself
   Attention hurt Biff

4. Sympathy for Willy
   No respect from boss
   My job as a clerk, dime a dozen
   Want more than a paycheck

5. TV version – admiration for Linda
   Held family together
   Loyal to Willy
   Want someone like her

E. Another list:
   Choices: integrate courses and experiences

   1. Reading Methods Required – would choose it
      What I'll learn; assessment, skills

   2. Activity – literacy volunteer
      Why don't people learn
      How to teach skills
      Effect on a person's life
      Failure of system

   3. Course or individual study in writing
      Keep journal
      Make connections
      Write feature stories for newspaper

EXERCISE F

1. Answers will vary.

2. A. One benefit of teaching is personal satisfaction.
   B. Mr. McGrath ran a tightly structured class.
   C. Many teachers work harder than people realize.

EXERCISE G

1. Example: furthermore, for example, also, like, but
   A. but
   B. then, after, finally
   C. in addition, also, another

2. Answers will vary.

EXERCISE H

1. Answers will vary.

2. A. I will enjoy the diversity of students and the freedom to organize my own classes.

   B. The failure of people to understand the need to provide bilingual education to the increasing numbers of non-native English speaking students will be our biggest problem.

   C. Finally, failure to tackle the various forms of illiteracy will cause a decline in our economic productivity.

EXERCISE I

1. accept
2. expect
3. except
4. advice
5. advise
6. effect
7. affect
8. It's
9. its
10. there
11. they're
12. their
13. among
14. between
15. too
16. two
17. to
18. badly
19. bad
20. adapt
21. adopt
22. site
23. cite
24. complement
225. compliment

25

EXERCISE J

The extent of illiteracy in this ~~C~~country is documented in <u>Illiterate America</u>~~,~~ a book by Jonathan Kozol. When I read this book and realized the extent of illiteracy ~~gave me a~~ shock, I was shocked.

Kozol claims that 25 million people can~~~~not read warning labels or a simple news story; another 35 million do not read well enough to survive in the Modern Age; ~~Like being~~ because they are unable to follow printed instructions. ~~For~~ Someone who can't read and has to support himself or her or a family is at ~~could be~~ a real disadvantage.

The problem of illiteracy will be difficult to solve. ~~There being many~~ Its causes ~~that~~ go deep into our society. Schools have failed to halt the problem and may be contributing to it. My parents say that the problem with schools today ~~are~~ is a lack of respect for authority. Years ago, ~~everyone~~ students knew what would happen if they disobeyed a teacher. Today, teachers must contend with students who are often bored, rarely prepared, and frequently ~~they defy~~ defiant of the teacher. ~~Some~~ Respect and discipline ~~is~~ are needed to create a learning environment.

Another problem with the schools is poorly prepared teachers. Students graduate~~ing~~, from college without being able to read or write well. During the 1960s ~~was the decline of~~ strict academic standards declined. Students failed to learn what they should ~~of~~ have learned. The decline may be ending because new tests and requirements are in place. For example, the ~~c~~College of ~~a~~Arts and ~~s~~Sciences at Northeastern State University changed ~~their~~ its requirements because entering students were so poorly prepared. Some of them were unable to identify Sophocles or locate ~~s~~Spain on a map.

Kozol's book interested me in the larger issues of literacy. Literacy means more than learning the ABCs. It means reading and writing well enough to survive in a complex society and making informed opinions about government policies. Teachers can help to create a literate America. After reading about the problems of illiteracy facing this country, I want to become a teacher.

TESTS OF STANDARD WRITTEN ENGLISH (ESSAY)

QUESTIONS AND MODEL ANSWERS

TABLE OF CONTENTS

		Page
1.	Excellence in Education	1
2.	Meeting the Needs of All the Children	5
3.	Motivating Learning	9
4.	United Community Action	12
5.	Lengthening the School Day and Eliminating Homework	16

TEST OF STANDARD WRITTEN ENGLISH *(ESSAY)*

QUESTIONS AND MODEL ANSWERS

QUESTION I - EXCELLENCE IN EDUCATION

The modern school is a cooperative venture in education, involving the child, the parent, the school administration, and the community.

In a well-organized essay of *at least 450 words,* discuss the ways in which each of the four mentioned above may contribute to the objective of excellence in education.

ANALYSIS OF THE QUESTION

1. Your composition is to be a *well-organized essay.* Since the question itself gives you the four major areas to be discussed, a good arrangement is to have an introductory paragraph, four middle paragraphs devoted to the topics stated, and a paragraph of conclusion.

2. The beginning paragraph should restate and comment on the *objective of excellence in education* and indicate that each of the areas will be analyzed and developed.

3. In developing the four middle paragraphs, be sure to include logically reasoned concepts and to link them all together with skillful transitions. You are asked to see each area in itself and in its relationship to the others in a *cooperative venture.*

4. The concluding paragraph should reaffirm the central idea of *cooperation* and indicate its importance.

5. Although it is stated that the paper will be rated ONLY for written English, be sure to deal with the matter of the question DIRECTLY AND SPECIFICALLY. You may lose much credit by wandering from the point, because you would then not really be answering the question.

6. Arouse and maintain interest in each of your central paragraphs by using topic sentences and clincher sentences which vitalize the concept.

7. Do not talk vaguely of the child, the parent, and such. The question asks for *ways in which they contribute to excellence in education.*

8. In meeting the requirement of length, plan carefully to include all designated areas.

PLAN OF THE ESSAY

The overall plan of the model below consists of:

1. An opening paragraph which goes directly to the topic, the components of excellence in education.
2. A body which devotes separate paragraphs to the:

a. child, his interests and aptitudes;
b. parent, his role in school matters;
c. school administration, its plans and programs;
d. community, adjunct to the school and cultural resource.
3. A brief statement of conclusion which stresses the idea of balance among all cooperating forces.

MODEL ANSWER

POINT-SCORING ELEMENTS	PARAGRAPH NUMBER
Statement of theme suggested in question	(1) The goal of excellence in education is an objective that calls for united effort. The important ingredients in this endeavor are four vital forces, each of which must make its contribution -- the child, the parent, the school administration, and the community. Each has its own <u>role</u> to play, and all must work together cohesively in the <u>drama</u> of the educational process.
Interesting diction: use of metaphor	(2) The child occupies the <u>center of the stage.</u> It is the child whose trials and successes indicate the value of our schools. When the child responds to the lure of learning, he is well on his way to the development of his potential. It is most important, therefore, that the child do all he can to learn essential skills, increase his store of learning, and strengthen attitudes and traits of character.
Note varied types of subordinate clauses	
Parallel structure	If, for some reason, the child is out of tune with the purposes of education or reluctant to apply himself to the tasks placed before him, there is a serious obstacle to be overcome. One might say that in a very real sense all education is self-education. The willing participation of the child is basic.
Pointed summary sentence	(3) Behind the child is the parent. In the modern world, the parent's function is clear. Aware that the primary concern during the childhood years is success in school, the parent undertakes to prepare his offspring for the daily tasks. He develops tactfully in the youngster the habits of punctuality and readiness which are the foundation of good performance. He helps him to obtain and care for his materials of learning. He inquires about his progress in school. He supports him in difficulty. He meets with the teacher in order to share information which will be helpful in motivation and correction. Without an active parent on the scene, a strong strand of guidance is missing. The parent's cooperation is vital.
Transition	
Introductory modifer	
Effectivenesss through repetition of "He...."	
Summary	

POINT-SCORING ELEMENTS	PARAGRAPH NUMBER
Simple sentence	(4) Within the school building, the contact between pupil and teacher is at the core of learning. The teachers are devoted to the task in their personal ways, but it is the school administration which performs a special <u>function</u>. The school leadership provides direction in laying out the whole scheme of activities in the various subject areas. It groups students in <u>interpersonal patterns</u> calculated to stimulate effort. It uses testing procedures to diagnose aptitudes and to gauge achievement. It arranges guidance services for those who need special help. A well-run school is, <u>in a word,</u> the perfect <u>environment</u> for education.
Compound sentence	
Mature diction: "function," "interpersonal patterns," "gauge," "environment"	
Summary	
Examples	(5) More and more, in our time, the community is a powerful factor in the educational setting. The resources of the community -- its library, its museums, its public services, and its citizens -- are <u>avenues of instruction</u> which the school wisely utilizes. The community represents the <u>segment of the world</u> which gives breadth and reality to the ideas found in books. It is the <u>classroom outside the school</u>, to which students go for motivation and application of skills and knowledges learned.
Imaginative diction	
	(6) The balance established among these four essential factors is evidenced by the cooperation shown by each element. All must work together in cooperative venture to make and to stabilize the school as an effective social institution basic to democracy.

QUESTION 2 - MEETING THE NEEDS OF ALL THE CHILDREN

Great emphasis in recent years has been placed on the training of teachers for a role particularly attuned to the needs of children in large-city schools.

In a well-organized essay of *at least 450 words,* discuss the specific needs of children in an urban environment and the various approaches the classroom teacher might use in meeting the needs of all the children.

ANALYSIS OF THE QUESTION

1. You are asked to write an *essay.* Be sure then that you observe the requirement that your composition have a beginning, a middle, and an end.

2. The beginning should address itself directly to the question, considering it broadly, reflecting on its importance, and leading to various aspects to be developed in the middle or body. What is called for here is a picture of urban education in our times and its relation to contemporary life.

3. The middle of the essay should rightly be concerned with a detailed analysis of pupil needs, teacher skills and attitudes, and teacher training objectives.

4. The conclusion should leave the reader with a reinforced emphasis on the heart of the matter, namely, the role of the teacher in the advancement of our society.

5. Although it is indicated that the paper will be rated ONLY for written English, be sure to deal with the matter of the question DIRECTLY AND SPECIFICALLY. You may lose much credit by wandering from the point, because you would then not really be answering the question.

6. Note that *specific needs of children in an urban environment* and *various approaches the classroom teacher may use* are called for. Arouse and maintain interest in each of your examples through the introduction of varied concepts and through skillful transitions.

7. In meeting the requirement of length, plan carefully to include all important aspects of the question.

PLAN OF THE ESSAY

The overall plan of the model below consists of:

1. An introduction which goes directly to the topic, the problem of education in today's cities.

2. A body which devotes separate paragraphs to the:
   a. needs of children, as shown in their family heritage, language background, class attitudes, and way of life.
   b. skills teachers should have in teaching basic subjects, in remediation techniques, and in guidance orientation.

3. A conclusion which summarizes the essentials of the problem and reaffirms the concept of teacher training as a prime requisite.

MODEL ANSWER

POINT-SCORING ELEMENTS	PARAGRAPH NUMBER
Direct attack on the nub of the question	(1) In recent years, the problem of educating children in large-city schools has been the object of much inquiry. <u>These schools</u> reflect in a marked degree the major social developments of the postwar world, such as the influx of migrants from Puerto Rico and other areas of the world, the move toward an integrated society, and the phenomenon of poverty amid prosperity. As legislators attempt to come to grips with the implementation of civil rights, with traditional practices in housing and employment, and with the improvement of health and welfare standards, educators must deal with the children of families whose lot in life cries out for betterment.
Cohesiveness with previous sentence	
Parallel structure	
Question for interest *Key sentence directing division within paragraph*	(2) What are the needs of these children? Specifically, there is great need for such important learning factors as remedial instruction, broadening of horizons, and guidance-oriented teaching. Remedial instruction in the basic subjects of reading and arithmetic should be used to raise achievement levels up to grade. These skills may have suffered as a result of a language barrier, such as the use of Spanish at home, or because of an impoverished background. <u>They must be improved. Then, too,</u> horizons should be broadened. It is a known fact that big-city children are largely provincial in experience and outlook. Their world is bounded by their own neighborhood; they have not had contact with the cultural resources of the city. <u>Lastly,</u> the teacher finds that many of these children are not responsive to the ordinary classroom situation. They need the understanding treatment which could come only from teachers who recognize the impairments resulting from environment and can and want to deal with them.
Short sentence for effect Connectors then, too; lastly	
Semicolon between coordinate clauses	

POINT-SCORING ELEMENTS	PARAGRAPH NUMBER
Topic sentence, connecting with previous paragraph and leading to new aspect	(3) It is indeed the teacher who is vital here. The teacher of big-city children must be skilled in teaching reading and number skills; he must be able to diagnose each child's problems in these areas of study and select tools and methods to move the child on to remediation and further development. He must be able to interest the child in making progress in book subjects. He might do this, <u>for example,</u> by taking his class on trips to community facilities, such as the firehouse, the post office, and the museum. These excursions from the school proper should be conducted in such a way as to provide not mere entertainment but real learning experiences, <u>for instance,</u> the construction of an experience chart. <u>Finally,</u> the teacher should be able to approach each child knowing enough of the family background to <u>elicit</u> from the child his very best effort toward learning. This can mean a knowledge of home conditions, the degree of <u>rapport</u> within the family, the <u>value, level</u> on which the child operates, and the personal, social, and economic factors which influence his life. In this way, the teacher uses the best of guidance techniques to stimulate and encourage learning.
Use of examples introduced by for example, such as, for instance, finally	
Mature diction, elicit, rapport, value level, focal point	
	(4) The training of teachers for this challenging task has become a <u>focal poin</u> of teacher education, a fact which the colleges clearly recognize. Because of his disadvantaged background in basic skills, in community contact, and in personal orientation, the big-city child poses a problem of serious dimensions. The teacher who holds the key to this problem must have the special aptitudes that can bring about quality education in every potential member of our democratic society.
Interesting conclusion: summary and application	

QUESTION 3 - MOTIVATING LEARNING

Advertising firms have been interested in motivational research. Teachers, too, are interested in what will make learning attractive to children.

In a well-organized essay of *at least 450 words,* discuss interests of children that may be utilized by a teacher in the approach to learning, giving specific illustrations in any or all subject areas.

ANALYSIS OF THE QUESTION

1. Note that the piece of writing called for is an *essay.* Be sure that your composition is an orderly succession of paragraphs with a beginning, middle, and end.
2. Although it is indicated that the paper will be rated ONLY for written English, be sure to deal with the matter of the question DIRECTLY AND SPECIFICALLY. You may lose much credit by wandering from the point, because you would then not really be answering the question.
3. Strive for correctness in all details as indicated, namely, sentence structure, grammar, spelling, idiomatic usage, etc. With respect to sentence structure, be sure every sentence is a complete one and meets the requirements of formal style. Do not use the run-on sentence or the fragment permitted in informal style and fiction.
4. Give some maturity to your style by using varied sentence patterns, both simple and complex.
5. Note that specific illustrations in subject areas are called for. Do not make this a mere factual listing in your essay. Arouse and maintain interest in each of your examples through the introduction of varied concepts and through skillful transitions. In this connection, too, the most important factor is the clear reference to a pupil interest which leads to, or may be involved in, a subject field.
6. Be sure to conform to the requirement of length. Do not be careless about this.

PLAN OF THE ESSAY

The overall plan of the model below consists of:

1. An introduction which goes directly to the topic, that of motivation in learning.

2. A transitional paragraph which opens up the idea of pupil interests.

3. An enumeration of recommended devices, each paragraph dealing with one device, and showing its usefulness in a particular subject area, viz.:
   a. story-telling - reading and language arts
   b. pupil experiences - arithmetic
   c. projects and constructions - social studies
   d. trips - science, music, art
   e. holidays - general achievement

4. A brief statement of conclusion with a short reference to the advertising practices mentioned in the question.

MODEL ANSWER

POINT-SCORING ELEMENTS	PARAGRAPH NUMBER
Sentence pattern: complex, simple, compound-complex	(1) Teachers know that their task is to effect a pleasant and profitable meeting between the child and learning. This is the daily challenge. To meet it, they think in terms of *motivating* the pupils, and they are agreed that the best stimulation is an attractive learning experience.
Use of question *Transitional sentence*	(2) How can the educative act be made appealing? There are a number of pupil interests which may be utilized to bring about this result.
Mature and precise diction: device, imaginative, venture, sure-fire, compensations	(3) Children like well-told stories. Oral story-telling is, therefore, an effective <u>device</u> in the teaching of reading and the language arts. The experienced and <u>imaginative</u> teacher stores up accounts of personal experiences and uses these at the appropriate time, usually at the beginning of a new reading <u>venture.</u> In addition, she has a fund of <u>sure-fire</u> tales to read to the class. Her enthusiasm for reading leads the pupils to explore library resources and to find similar <u>compensations</u>.
Parallel structure in phrases of a simple sentence *Note semi-colon*	(4) In any field, the best approach is usually made through the use of pupil knowledge and experience. In arithmetic, number concepts and computing operations are concretized in terms of what pupils know from daily living. Problems deal with money, with store purchases, with game materials, with houses and home living, with the division of pies and cakes into fractional parts, and the like. The fundamental principle here is the use of an apperceptive basis for learning; in other words, that which is to be learned must be related to that which is already known.

POINT-SCORING ELEMENTS	PARAGRAPH NUMBER
Transitional word, another	(5) Another writing path to new knowledge is provided by means of projects which call for construction, for the use of the visual and the tangible. At the start of a unit in social studies, for example, pictures, reproductions, and various realia may be exhibited to stimulate interest. What child fails to respond to a colorful illustration such as a scene from history, a map or portrait of a hero? Consider the appeal of real Indian arrowheads, old coins, battle equipment, and antique household articles. With such stimuli as these, the child plunges into the past and roams in far places. He is lead eventually to draw his own maps, to compose his own Indian book, or to build his own pioneer cabin or canoe.
Note commas	
Question for interest, followed by imperative "consider"	
Note diction: trip, excursion, visit, bus ride *Use of capitals*	(6) An occasional trip gives great impetus to the search for knowledge. An <u>excursion</u> to the Museum of Natural History or to the Hayden Planetarium opens up the world of science; a <u>visit</u> to the Philharmonic nurtures the seeds of music appreciation and skill; a <u>bus ride</u> to a zoo or to an arboretum kindles love of nature and lays the groundwork for experiences in art. This kind of linkage of the world of the school with the outside world gives meaning and inspiration to pupils' classroom lives.
Summary sentence to round out paragraph	
Key word: lastly	(7) <u>Lastly,</u> the big events of the school year are centers of natural interest. Thanksgiving and Christmas spur activities in choral music; Lincoln's Birthday encourages brotherhood themes and learnings; Decoration Day offers opportunities for patriotic fervor and for appreciation of our country's history. On the local scene, Open School Night and the preparations for it lead to the kind of bee-hive activity which keeps the children engrossed in studies and eager to show themselves at their best.
Compound sentence with three main clauses	
Idiomatic and imaginative presentation	
Direct and simple sentences	(8) Such motivational devices as these pave the way to successful learning. Good teachers are good ad-men.

QUESTION 4 - UNITED COMMUNITY ACTION

In an article in a recent publication of the Board of Education, the following statement was made: *"The united efforts of all agencies in the community are needed if the school is to achieve the goals for which it has primary responsibility."*

In a well-organized essay of *at least 450 words,* explain in detail the part played by community agencies in developing the child as a social and moral being and as a healthy, useful, and productive citizen. Include in your discussion a consideration of any or all of the following: the home, the church, community groups, communications media, industry, labor, and government.

ANALYSIS OF THE QUESTION

It should be noted that this essay is to be an expository one *explain in detail* -- setting forth the *part played by community agencies* in education CONSIDERED BROADLY. Although this is a question in a test for a specific license or certificate, its terms are NOT LIMITED TO THAT LEVEL.

The quotation from the recent publication of the Board of Education indicates that the efforts of all agencies should be *united.* The model essay recognizes and includes this idea.

Note, too, that *the goals for which it has primary responsibility* are detailed later on in the question: social competency, moral strengthening, good health, personal development according to ability (useful and productive), good citizenship.

PLAN OF THE ESSAY

The agencies themselves are listed and provide the framework of the essay. The model which follows adopts a simple plan of paragraphing:

- Par. 1. Introduction, stating the relationship of the school and other agencies
- Par. 2. The influence of the home
- Par. 3. The church
- Par. 4. Community agencies (clubs, teams, services, etc.)
- Par. 5. Communications media
- Par. 6. Government
- Par. 7. Conclusion, containing summary

MODEL ANSWER

POINT-SCORING ELEMENTS	PARAGRAPH NUMBER
Mature thought and vocabulary *Direct reference to main theme of the question*	(1) It is a truism that education is the business of the school, but this statement is also an oversimplification. The school cannot handle all the concerns of education. While it assumes primary responsibility for clearly recognized goals, it depends markedly on other community agencies for success.
Point No. 1 - the home *Sentence variety; simple introductory sentence followed by complex sentence with a multiple subject and an interrupted construction*	(2) The home is certainly a heavily influential factor in a child's educational development. The stature of parents and siblings, the level of the cultural milieu, the maintenance of standards of dress and deportment, the attention given to matters of health the extent to which these elements conform to praiseworthy criteria will determine the readiness of the child and his attitude toward the educational approach provided in the school.

Transitional sentence links previous paragraph (home) to this one (church)
 	
 Point No. 2 - the church.
 	
 First three sentences of this paragraph are:
   1. simple
   2. complex
   3. compound
	(3) The church (synagogue) adds to the contribution of the home in its own particular way. While it is an accepted fact that parents imbue their children with moral and spiritual values both by instruction and example, it is the church (synagogue) which gives added emphasis by virtue of its superior knowledge and inspiration. Its representatives relate codes of conduct to deep moral and theological concepts; moreover, they activate these through religious ceremony and planned social action. The activities of the church and the synagogue develop the character of the child in a functional pattern.

Transition to Point No. 3 - community agencies <u>*Thus*</u> *introduces illustrations* *Parallel structure in clauses separated by semi-colons*	(4) Still, other community groups lend their support. Clubs provide outlets for a variety of talents and thereby help in their exercise and improvement. Thus, musical interests are discovered and cultivated; dramatics ability is perfected; scouting activities are given direction; hobbies are encouraged.

POINT-SCORING ELEMENTS	PARAGRAPH NUMBER
In addition provides transition within paragraph *Examples answer request for <u>details</u>*	Neighborhood teams and "Little League" organizations contribute their benefits in the area of health, sportsmanship, and character building. In addition to these well-known instruments, there are the family agencies, such as the Jewish Family Service and Catholic Charities, which take it upon themselves to give relief in cases of hardship and social maladjustment
Point No. 4 - communications *Identification of media and their concomitant elements.* *Three simple sentences varied in structure* *Maturity of judgment indicated* *Balanced structure*	(5) The impact of our ever-present communications media is certainly a potent force visited upon our young. They learn about life through television, the movies, the radio, and the newspapers. In these media, mixed in with the factual are the many imaginative creations of artistry, the lure of entertainment, and the blandishments of persuasive advertising. The quality of this kind of influence is often regarded as debatable, but an influence it most certainly is. As such, a responsible nation must have a constant concern that it plays its role well, setting forth truth rather than error, excellence rather than shoddiness, worth rather than waste.
Transition to Point No. 5 - government *Answering direction to be specific*	(6) Last consideration of all, but not least, is the hand that government plays in education. It provides museums and parks, its police give direction in living amid the unavoidable hazards of traffic and crime, it sends its firemen to counsel concerning the dangers of fire, its sanitation department pursues a policy of active education in the maintenance of clean streets and neighborhoods, its hospitals stand ready with emergency services and clinics to preserve bodily health.

Final paragraph providing summary	(7) The union of all such agencies as these cited here can give fulfillment to the broad objectives of education. The home, the church, clubs, centers, teams, family services, the media of communication, government itself each has its own contribution to make. Working and planning together provides the best product honest, healthy, useful, well-educated citizens.
Return to the main theme: united community action for a definite goal	

NOTE: If you elected to describe, in addition, the part played by industry and labor, you would specify the following: the influences of steady employment upon family living, the suggestions given by industry for the improvement of curricula in line with technological advancement, the protection of rights, and the prevention of exploitation.

QUESTION 5 - LENGTHENING THE SCHOOL DAY AND ELIMINATING HOMEWORK

Among proposals for increased utilization of school facilities and extension of educational guidance is the suggestion that the school day be changed to an eight-to-four o'clock schedule and that no homework be assigned.

In a well-organized essay of *at least 460 words,* discuss your reactions to this proposal for a lengthened school day. Consider advantages and disadvantages for both pupils and teachers.

ANALYSIS OF THE QUESTION

The question deals with two educationally provocative problems of perennial interest -- the lengthening of the school day and the elimination of homework. In this question, the two are co-joined. Be sure to include both of these items in your answer.

Your answer should be a *balanced* one -- the advantages and disadvantages of each course advocated should be given temperately in respect to BOTH pupils and teachers.

Select and present only the most general and outstanding outcomes and features for the topic can be (and has been) engaged at great length and in a variety of expositions.

PLAN OF THE ESSAY

- Par. 1. The proposal for a lengthened school day is stated succinctly in the opening sentence. The idea of *advantages and disadvantages* is used as the *division* of the topic.
- Par. 2. Discussion of *advantages to pupils:* more time for instruction in basics; provision for special subjects.
- Par. 3. Discussion continued: a *varied program* possible through related experiences; the homework activities improved through supervision.
- Par. 4. *Advantages to teachers:* guidance services, clerical responsibilities; reduction of tension.
- Par. 5. Transition to disadvantages to both pupils and teachers: danger of over-long sessions; personal factors.
- Par. 6. Discussion of disadvantages continued: possibility of poor planning because of limited facilities for play; teacher programming a real consideration.
- Par. 7. Concise conclusion, summarizing main theme and calling for wise study before implementation.

MODEL ANSWER

POINT-SCORING ELEMENTS	PARAGRAPH NUMBER
Use of question for interest *Complex sentence*	(1) Shall the school day be lengthened from six to eight hours? Before such a proposal is put into effect, it would be wise to consider what advantages and disadvantages would be present for both pupils and teachers.
Complex sentence with that clause *Complex sentence with which clause* *Transitional expression, In addition* *Complex sentence starting with since clause* *Simple sentence*	(2) It is clear that in some ways the proposed plan would be profitable for pupils. They would have more time in which to receive instruction in their studies. There would be greater opportunity for the full development of skills and concepts in the basic areas of reading and arithmetic. In addition, provision may be made for science, social studies, and foreign language instruction. Since these areas have grown in importance in recent years, they should be included in the elementary program. The additional time of the longer school day would make their inclusion feasible.
Use of also as transition *Compound subject for variety (use of dash before all)* *Attractive diction:* <u>aspects</u>, <u>rich</u>, <u>ample</u>, <u>quota</u> *Balance phrase*	(3) An eight-to-four day would also allow for a more varied school program. Assembly programs, remedial instruction, visual aid activities, art and music, physical fitness training all these, and other, aspects of a rich school experience can be realized when an ample quota of time is available. Even the ordinary homework responsibilities may be planned within the school day. Thus, the work can be done under expert supervision and with the aid of classroom libraries and reference materials.

POINT-SCORING ELEMENTS	PARAGRAPH NUMBER
Moreover as transition *Reference to examples found in question*	(4) Teachers would also find some advantage in the longer day. They would find additional opportunities for guidance services, studying pupil problems and working out solutions. Moreover, they would have more time for the performance of clerical duties, such as the collection of milk money, the keeping of school records, and the handling of reports and correspondence. The pace of the day's activities would be relieved of undue tension, and happier personalities might result.
Contrast (comma after introductory phrase) *Variety in use of gerund as subject* *Commas before and after parenthetical expressions:* too, as a result *Sums up the idea of the paragraph*	(5) On the other hand, there may be real disadvantages for both pupil and teacher. Long sessions in school may be excessively tiring. Starting as early as eight o'clock can impose a further burden on the family which is sending its child (or children) off to school. Teachers, too, may have considerable traveling to do before reaching the classroom. It is conceivable that, as a result, neither child nor teacher may be in the best frame of mind for the work of the day.
Further as transition *Simple sentence* *Simple sentence* *Complex sentence starting with if clause*	(6) Without careful planning, further disadvantages may eventuate. Pupils may not be given opportunities to participate in a varied program and to enjoy free play out-of-doors. Teachers may be expected to devote an excessive amount of time to contact with pupils in the classroom. If the concept of the longer school day means an extended teaching day, one wonders about the effect on teacher morale and physical resources.
Final summation Use of infinitive phrase, set off by comma	(7) All in all, there is much to be said on both sides of this stimulating question. To devise the perfect-school day, one must seek to incorporate every advantage and plan to avoid every possible defect.

TEST OF STANDARD WRITTEN ENGLISH *(ESSAY)*

QUESTIONS AND MODEL ANSWERS

CONTENTS

TOPIC	Page
1. Cultural Enrichment	2
2. The Non-Teaching Assignment	5
3. Extending The School Year	8
4. Softness in American Education	11
5. Soviet and American Education Compared	14

TEST OF STANDARD WRITTEN ENGLISH *(ESSAY)*

QUESTIONS AND MODEL ANSWERS

QUESTION 1

In an experimental project in selected schools in low socioeconomic areas, it was found that when the children were taken to theatres, museums, and other places of cultural enrichment and were given special help in school to develop latent interests and to express special talents, marked improvement resulted. Many of the children developed greater interest in academic subjects and began plans to continue their education in college.

In a well-organized essay of *at least 450 words,* discuss the advantages, and possible disadvantages, of extending such a program to other schools in the city. You may include in your answer one or both of the following aspects of the topic:

1. The role of community resources in carrying out a program of this type.

2. A plan for determining the degree of success in attainment of the desired goal of such a program.

ANALYSIS OF THE QUESTION
The response to this question may well emphasize the many advantages of the cultural enrichment opportunities in a city like New York. The item of *possible disadvantages* may be slighted since the implication is that they may not be great. The model essay takes this tack. Moreover, it slights the plan for determining success since, according to the instruction, it is not necessary to deal with both aspects.

PLAN OF THE ESSAY
Par.
1. Topic an important and interesting one. The program, of enrichment identified through various examples. Fine effects noted.
2. Brief, transitional paragraph.
3. Opportunities in the arts.
4. Science: natural history, astronomy.
5. Literature, the newspaper, the theatre.
6. The business world: manufacture, automation, commerce, transportation.
7. Summary of advantages: knowledge, experience, interest in study, personal traits of good manners, responsibility, civic-mindedness. A few dangers dealt with.
8. A yardstick for judging the value of extra-school visits: pupil interest.

TOPIC: CULTURAL ENRICHMENT

POINT-SCORING ELEMENTS	PARAGRAPH NUMBER
1. *Puts topic in perspective* *Two simple sentences* *Relates closely to the question by using its terminology* *Compound sentence* *Short transitional paragraph* *Discussion of the role of community resources (aspect #1 of the topic): The arts* *Note commas* *Complex sentence-noun clause introduced by how series* *Use of example* *Use of capitals for specific orchestra* 2. *Science* *Two simple sentences* *Examples* *Complex sentence (adjective clauses)* *Effective diction: wonders, fascination, learning process*	(1) The problem of the culturally deprived child has been one of absorbing interest in the last decade. Among possible solutions, the direct provision of programs of cultural enrichment has proved most worthwhile. Through the education attained by means of out-of-school visits to museums, theatres, and the like, pupils have developed greater interest in their school subjects and they have even begun to prepare themselves for college training later on. (2) Varied community resources may be used to effect the desired result. In a city as large as New York, there are a tremendous number of such resources. (3) First, in the field of music and art, concert halls, theatres, and museums play a major role. The pupil may be introduced to the works of the masters, both classic and modem, in the areas of painting, sculpture, tapestry, and ceramics. He may see for himself how these arts have originated and developed down through the centuries. As for music, special trips may be arranged to the opera house, the ballet performance, and the concert orchestra. It is even possible to see a rehearsal of the Philharmonic Symphony under one of its outstanding conductors. (4) Science education, a field of increasing performance, may also receive an impetus through visits to places of cultural enrichment. Two favorite objectives in recent years have been the Museum of Natural History and the Planetarium. The wonders of living things and the fascination of the universe fill the child's mind with impressions he carries back to school, where the learning process goes forward with growing interest and intensity.

POINT-SCORING ELEMENTS	PARAGRAPH NUMBER	

3. Literary
   a. libraries Complex sentence Simple sentence
 	
   b. newspaper plants Complex sentence
 	
   c. theatre Simple sentence
 	
4. Business Simple sentence
Complex sentence
(adjective clause)
Use of examples
 	
Effective use of imperative
<u>Think</u>
 	
Summary and transition
Advantages
Simple sentences
 	
Balanced infinitive phrases
 	
Possible disadvantages
 	
Effective alliterative expression, <u>pure profit</u>
 	
States reasoned preference for the advantages
 	
Apt diction: <u>diminution, runs off-course</u>
	(5)	The world of books and the printed word may be examined at close range, too. The neighborhood library is often a source of pleasure, which when once experienced becomes a continuing source of intellectual development and delight. A visit to the great library at 42nd Street and 5th Avenue is an unforgettable experience of the same type. In addition, trips can be arranged to newspaper plants, where the excitement of the daily press fills the onlooker both with knowledge and with inspiration. The great world of the theatre is but another sphere in which the word becomes a concrete, living thing.

	(6)	Even the industrial, and commercial areas of the city contribute to the child's education; A plant which contains a multi-phased process, such as the assembly line of the Ford Motor Company, or which makes use of the machinery of automation, such as the Sperry-Rand Corp., becomes an informative experience. Think, too, of the breadth of vision which New York harbor or JFK Airport can provide.
	(7)	The advantages of this type of introduction to learning are clearly many. The pupils gain knowledge and experience. They are stimulated to return to school with an increased appetite for book learning. Moreover, they have an opportunity to develop and exercise good manners in public, to accept responsibility, and to grow in civic appreciation and loyalty. The only dangers to be avoided are lack of relatedness to the school program of studies and loss of time from basic subjects. With good planning, the *trip* can become pure profit.
	(8)	To judge the success of such a program, the teacher should concentrate on the determination of evidences of growth, both personal and social. If the program

runs off-course, a diminution in pupil response and behavior will be obvious. The chances of success, however, are great, for there is a clear connection between experience and education.

QUESTION 2

Criticism has been levelled at the schools because of time taken from *regular* work for such activities as school banking, milk distribution, class trips, book fairs, bazaars, evening dance or song festivals, and operettas. Teachers, too, have complained of feeling frustrated by the encroachments of such non-teaching duties on the teaching day. They feel that their energies are dissipated with bus firms, the collection of money, and the keeping of records.

In a well-organized essay of *at least 450 words,* discuss the problem of non-teaching assignments referred to in the above passage. Express clearly your own thinking on the subject, touching on one or more of the following aspects:

1. The burden of non-teaching assignments upon the teacher
2. The point of view that non-teaching activities are *frills* which encroach upon the teacher's real work of teaching the basic skills
3. The value of using voluntary or paid assistants to take care of non-teaching duties.

ANALYSIS OF THE QUESTION

In this question, you are invited to express *your own* ideas and you are required to *touch upon* one or more of the suggestions given. Thus, it would be sufficient to develop a whole composition on *frills* (1) or on the use of assistants (3) as long as you stay on the general topic of *the problem of non-teaching assignments*. The essay which follows makes use of all the aspects presented.

PLAN OF THE ESSAY

Par. 1. Presents the topic in the light of the *heatic* life of the teacher. Cites the need of determining who will best perform the *non-teaching* assignments.
2. Refers to the history of modern educational development. Raises question of necessity of the extra responsibilities mentioned; justifies their inclusion with reasons for each; banking and thrift, milk sales and health, book fairs and reading, etc.
3. Moves to consideration of the relative value of the teacher and the specialized assistant; the inherent authority of the teacher; the peculiar knowledge and interest of the special teacher or expert. The attempt to make efficient use of both.
4. The reaction of individual teachers to demands and opportunities; the cry for equality of treatment; the malcontent; factors in faculty morale.
5. Comparison of the teacher's day with that of the present-day worker. The role of the budget-maker and the administrator in solving the problem.

TOPIC: THE NON-TEACHING ASSIGNMENT

POINT-SCORING ELEMENTS	PARAGRAPH NUMBER	
Presents topic as having two sides; some ...... others ...... Balanced structure of that clauses *Suggests solution broadly*	(1)	One hears much these days about the hectic day of the elementary school teacher. Some say that it is too busy and call for a re-appraisal of the situation with lessening of the load a prime objective. Others feel that the teacher is the best one to handle the many activities which flow in and through the normal day's work. Perhaps it is all in the point of view.
Discusses (2) at length *Complex sentence with when clause* *Question lends interest* *Compound sentence (four independent clauses)* *Note use of semi-colons* *Commas for words in series* *Conclusion of (2)*	(2)	At one time, it was thought that the only concern of the teacher was that of teaching the basic skills. When other duties, such as school banking and milk distribution, were added, these were regarded as *frills*. But are they? School banking is a way of developing the necessary habit of thrift; milk sales and accounting make a contribution to health and number work; book fairs stimulate interest in books and leisure reading; bazaars develop loyalty to the school through a building-wide or, at least, grade-wide activity. Dances, songs, festivals, and operettas promote their own special kind of learning in the form of culminating long-range activities, chiefly in the arts. There are few educational theorists today who would deny the value of these co-curricular interests.
Discusses (3) at length *Compound question* *Simple sentences* *Note connecting words (underlined)* *Compound complex sentence* *Simple sentence*	(3)	The question is, Shall the classroom teacher be expected to handle all the details of such activities or should assistants of some sort be employed to take care of non-teaching assignments? In some schools, the PTA or a hired monitorial staff performs eating and lunchroom chores. <u>Such</u> an arrangement may work well. It is a fairly common experience, however, to find that there is a loss of authority in some cases: pupils may not respect the casual employee as much as they would the teacher. Another device, of course, is to have the specialist instruct in such areas as music and dance. Book fairs and bazaars may

POINT-SCORING ELEMENTS	PARAGRAPH NUMBER	
Simple sentence with compound subject		be run by the representatives of companies especially skilled in such enterprises. When such an arrangement is set up with proper scheduling, and safeguards, the complaints about excessive burdens tend to diminish
Complex sentence (adverbial indicating time)		
Discusses (4) at length *Complex sentence*	(4)	No matter what assignments are given to the various teachers on a school staff, there is bound to be some inequality. This is inevitable in the nature of things. There are malcontents here and there who feel that this is an evidence of favoritism or prejudiced planning. If faculty morale is low generally because of other factors of wide and great importance, such a charge may be an incisive blow to school administration, but in a normal situation where the principal enjoys good relationships with the staff because of broad and sympathetically conceived principles of cooperative action, the cries of the unhappy few should fall on deaf ears. Actually, the extra assignment given to a teacher is best taken as a sign of trust and confidence and as a stepping-stone to promotion.
Simple sentence *Complex sentence with adjective clause* *Complex sentence (conditional)*		
Compound element introduced by but		
Effective diction: <u>*sympathetically conceived principles*</u>, <u>*unhappy few*</u>, <u>*deaf ears*</u> *Balanced phrases*		
Compound sentence *Brief summary reference to (1)* *Effective close*	(5)	We are living in an age of shorter working days and lighter responsibilities, but the work of the teacher has appeared to grow in intensity and complexity. Wise attention to this situation on the part of the budget-makers and the school administrators should result in the best possible day-to-day performance in the classroom.

QUESTION 3

In recent discussions of American education, many suggestions have been made for enriching and accelerating education. One proposal which has had a warm reception among educators and the public is to lengthen the school year to permit full-time use of school facilities and to eliminate the alleged education *waste* of the long summer vacation. As a prospective member of the educational profession, you will have some reactions to this proposal.

Write an essay of *at least 450 words* on the advantages and disadvantages of the all-year school. You may include in your discussion consideration of some of the following aspects of this topic:

- A. The effect of such a program upon
  1. intellectually gifted children
  2. slow learners
  3. children with special talents in music, art, or dramatics
  4. children who do not adjust well to school.
- B. The effect of such a program upon traditional summertime activities, such as travel, camping, etc.
- C. The advantages and disadvantages of shortening the twelve-year period normally required to prepare for college
- D. The economy of using educational facilities on a full-time basis
- E. The effect upon present and prospective teachers of a possible curtailment of the traditional vacation period
- F. Possible effects of *voluntary* summer service upon basic salary schedules of teachers.

ANALYSIS OF THE QUESTION

This question calls for the reaction of a prospective teacher. Many such reactions are, of course, possible. Full-length essays could be written on any one of the suggestions given or on several of them combined, such as A, E, and C since they deal with the effect on children, or E and F since they concern teachers. The sample essay given attempts to consider the topic in all aspects and sets up a criterion for making a decision between the advantages and disadvantages — certainly an acceptable collating of ideas.

PLAN OF THE ESSAY

Following are the pertinent lines of development:

Par. 1. Introduces topic, relates it to traditional schedule, raises question as to advantages and disadvantages
2. Advantages: maximum use of plant (D); effect on children (A); acceleration (C); teacher compensation (F).
3. Disadvantages: need for change of routine (B); shortening of college preparatory period (C); curtailment of teacher improvement (E); effect on plant (D).
4. Consideration of possible motives for a change to the twelve-month scheme. Call for caution. Citing of a recommended criterion: the service to children.

TOPIC: EXTENDING THE SCHOOL YEAR

POINT-SCORING ELEMENTS	PARAGRAPH NUMBER	
Striking diction: <u>staple, envision, revolutionary</u>	(1)	The summer-long vacation has been such a staple of American education that it is difficult to envision the revolutionary idea of the all-year school. Nevertheless, this concept is being widely discussed. What are the advantages and the disadvantages of keeping our schools open for twelve months of the year?
Complex sentence Leads easily to the main topic and its two-fold division *Brief simple sentence Question*		
Discusses advantages 1. plant (D) Compound sentence with semicolon 2. children (A), (C)	(2)	Some advantages are immediately identifiable. The school plant, an expensive construction, is put to maximum use; it does not stand idle for two whole months. In addition, the talents and skills of children need not lie dormant during this period. They may blossom and grow under expert supervision, as in art and music. At the other end of the spectrum, children who need special remedial help in basic subjects will receive instruction. The slow learners and maladjusted may find within the pace of the new summer school period the kind of opportunity they need to improve themselves. <u>Finally</u>, some pupils may utilize the summer time to move ahead in basic subject areas and in this way accelerate their progress through school. As, <u>for the teaching staff</u>, the year-round school should mean more pay, an outcome all critics will applaud.
Simple sentence		
Complex sentence (adjective clause) *Complex sentence*		
Note connectives from sentence to sentence (underlined)		
S. teachers (F)		
Transition to disadvantages, Topic (B)	(3)	On the other hand, it is possible to cite a number of disadvantages. Many feel that a full vacation during the summer is a needed change of pace. After he has spent ten months in daily classroom routine, the pupil is ready for travel, for rest, for camping, in short, for the activities that will restore and refresh his physical and mental powers. A summer program which would make these activities difficult or impossible to actuate may be detrimental to education in the long run. Again, continued application to school tasks and resultant acceleration may
Complex sentence (adverbial indicating time) *Comma for series*		
Complex sentence		
Connective (underlined)		

POINT-SCORING ELEMENTS	PARAGRAPH NUMBER
Apt diction: acceleration, propel	propel the pupil at an immature age into the advanced studies of college and eventually graduate school. The life of the teacher would also be affected adversely by the newly proposed plan. Opportunities to travel and to take summer courses for personal enrichment would be fewer, since the young teacher may rightly feel the need of making money rather than engaging in study. Even the school plant may suffer from constant use. The daily traffic of hundreds, maybe thousands, of youngsters takes a toll of the physical structure which cannot be obliterated in a weekend or even a week. The building custodian usually requires a much longer period of time for repairing, painting, floor polishing, and cleaning.
Topic (C) *Use of also as connective*	
Topic (E) *Complex sentence (causal, clause)*	
Use of even to move to next idea *Effective diction; traffic, toll, obliterated, weekend, week* *Citing of specific tasks relevant to (D)*	
Summing up and leading to conclusion *Noun clauses in parallel - a mature style*	
	(4) Where does the wisdom of the situation lie? Those who fear the Russians and wilt under their claims of superior education, those who feel they may squeeze the most return out of the taxpayer's dollar, those who consider that teachers have too easy an existence at present — all these may advocate the twelve-month school. But we should be most discerning in weighing both their motives and their arguments. The best criterion is surely that of the advantages which may accrue to the children; that is, whatever suits them best by answering their needs, abilities, and interests. Applying such a criterion will test the knowledge and skill of educators everywhere.
Simple connective	
A key to resolution of the discussion *Complex sentence*	
Use of gerund as subject *A sense of conclusion*	

QUESTION 4

Everybody has heard in past years that the schools are *soft*. The children do not work hard, or long enough. Schools must be toughened up and speeded up or *the Russians will get us. Now it is the Japanese.* As someone has said, *The responsibility for national survival has been placed squarely upon the shoulders of the children.*

The barrage of destructive criticism of education (and of children and their supposedly soft-living and indulgent parents) has put great pressure upon the schools. In some instances, this pressure has resulted in unwise practices.

In a well-organized essay of *at least 450 words,* discuss the current controversy over *softness* in American education. You may include in your discussion personal experiences, case studies, or recent books and articles on the subject to substantiate your opinions.

ANALYSIS OF THE QUESTION

The answer to this question must deal with the impact of adverse criticism, stimulated first by *the Russians* and now by the Japanese upon our schools. You are directed to discuss the alleged *softness* of American education. You are free to include personal experiences, case studies of specific areas, and books and articles. These will help to *substantiate your opinions.* The model essay makes use of all these briefly as space permits.

PLAN OF THE ESSAY

The scheme of development is as follows:

Par.
1. Introduction of the topic, a broad picture of the rise of recent criticism as related to modern scientific developments. Gradual arrival at key point of *softness*,
2. A prominent area of controversy-reading instruction. The battle between the *whole word* and *phonies* methods. Books projecting the attack.
3. Effects of this criticism: theories compared; methods and materials examined; the view of practical educators; recognition of importance of reading standards and reading achievement
4. Briefer references to other areas: two new subjects added to elementary curriculum to *beef up* the program; namely, science and foreign language; impact on the program
5. Value of the controversy: our faith in free discussion and eventual improvement of the schools.

TOPIC: *SOFTNESS* IN AMERICAN EDUCATION

POINT-SCORING ELEMENTS	PARAGRAPH NUMBER	
Complex sentence with adverbial clause	(1)	Ever since the Russian Sputnik blazed its trail through the skies, American educational patterns and practices have become the object of sustained critical appraisals. The reason is a compelling one. We who had always considered ourselves supreme in science found that we were outstripped and outsmarted in the race into space. Where did the fault lie? Inevitably, the accusing finger was pointed at the schools. From elementary to college grades, the whole system has been adjudged by some to be too full of mistaken theories, too lacking in direction and purpose, and, fundamentally, too *soft*.
Short effective simple sentence arousing interest		
Complex sentence with adjective and noun clauses		
Question for interest		
Simple sentence with directness		
Climactic series reaching central point		
Simple transition to prime example		
Complex sentence with adverbial and noun clauses		
Complex sentence with noun clauses	(2)	One of the most violent areas of attack has been that of basic reading instruction. The opening gun was fired even before Sputnik when the book WHY JOHNNY CAN'T READ made the charge that the phonics system should be restored to its proper place in the primary grades. The allegation was made that this method of teaching reading has been supplantet in the last few decades by the *whole word* method and that this latter method was erroneous in its assumptions and unproductive in its results. In subsequent books came the inevitable comparison between American and Russian techniques as in WHY IVAN KNOWS WHAT JOHNNY DOESN'T, and the quality of our educational output was denoted even in the title of a book, TODAY'S ILLITERATES.
Note balanced predicate phrases		
Inverted structure		
Compound sentence		
Transition through question	(3)	What has been the result? There has been a concentration of attention on the whole problem of reading readiness, methods of instruction, materials, and remedial techniques. Sharp differences of opinion have been delineated and defended by the theorists; the practical educators have done their best to choose wisely from all that research can offer. Parents have become alerted to
Simple sentence		

POINT-SCORING ELEMENTS	PARAGRAPH NUMBER
Simple sentence with compound verb	the situation and have become more cognizant of the standing and progress of their children. School administrators have set minimum reading grades as absolute standards for promotion. Special reading teams have been added to school staffs to care for revealed needs. In all this, it is apparent that the need to cope with the written and printed word has been underscored. Despite the rise of radio, television, and other forms of oral communication, the place of reading has retained its importance. It will remain basic and will receive more and more emphasis in the schools.
Simple sentence	
Simple sentence with infinitive phrase *Complex sentence with noun clause*	
Simple sentence, effective because of periodic structure	
Simple sentence, conclusive in tone	
Transition through <u>also</u>	(4) Science and foreign language study have also received a tremendous amount of attention. Statistics revealed that in most schools these were hitherto unknown in the lower grades. Now, syllabi in science call for the introduction of simple concepts and experiments very early in the educational program. Common branch teachers have had to learn how to teach this kind of material. In addition, outside the city, as I know from personal experience, teachers of foreign language have been added to elementary school staffs, and *oral-aural* instruction begins as early as the fourth grade. The need for communicating with the other peoples of the world has been recognized.
Complex sentence with noun clause	
Simple sentence	
Simple sentence with infinitive phrase *Compound complex structure*	
Simple sentence	
Effective diction in this final paragraph *Inverted order in this noun clause*	(5) Our country has always distinguished itself by preserving the individual's right to free discussion. It is our faith that out of the exchange of knowledge and opinion comes the most perfect instrument. In education, we look forward with the hope that out of stern criticism will rise stronger schools, with better teaching techniques and materials, and with an improved educational product.
Optimistic prognosis	
Effective climax in series	

QUESTION 5

In Russia, before the overthrow of communism in 1991, the State attempted to decide through its planning mechanism what skills were needed and in what proportion they were needed for the most efficient development of the State. For example, the State decided that a certain number of ballet stars were needed to entertain the people. In turn, aspiring children throughout the USSR competed for enrollment in the few ballet schools. Of those permitted to enroll, only those judged best according to Soviet standards survived the years of study and practice necessary to become stars for the State.

Similarly, exacting admission requirements applied to the university or the engineering institute, the excellence of whose graduates was considered to be fundamental to the advancement of the Soviet State both economically and militarily. Whatever the type of training or whatever the kind of school or educational program the individual was permitted to enter, it was his duty to contribute his maximum to the State in return for State-provided education.

Soviet education aims at education for excellence with freedom of choice resting with the State to the end that the State may be developed to the optimum.

Taken from *Education in the USSR*
U.S. Department of Health, Education, and Welfare

In a well-organized essay of *at least 450 words,* discuss the above passage, pointing out how the principles set forth therein differ from those which are fundamental to our system of education.

ANALYSIS OF THE QUESTION

The excerpt from the document *Education in the USSR* provides a bird's-eye view of the fundamental tenets of Soviet education. You will note the elements of this doctrine: strict planning by a totalitarian State, limitation upon human aspiration, control of the individual by the State, the ultimate functioning within a Communist dominated society. In answer, the American creed must be detailed and illustrated

PLAN OF THE ESSAY

Following are the pertinent lines of development:

Par. 1. Broad contrast between the USSR and the USA, mentioning various differences in education and proceeding to the heart of the matter: the purpose of education. This is then related to the State and society.
2. Russian objectives and principles, developed as in the excerpt explained above. At the end, a preparation for transition by reference to the effect on the individual qualities we in the USA esteem.
3. American beliefs and goals: education for all according to potential; an informed public the basis of democracy; personal freedom of choice in life and work; the ultimate value of man in society.
4. Concrete demonstration of the American philosophy in action: free schools; scholarship aids; types of schools and courses; varying standards of achievement according to interest and ability.
5. The contrast drawn again in terms of ultimate conflict.

TOPIC: SOVIET AND AMERICAN EDUCATION COMPARED

POINT-SCORING ELEMENTS	PARAGRAPH NUMBER	
Broad approach to topic *Complex sentence with noun clause*	(1)	In the competitive spirit of today's world, it was inevitable that our system of education would be compared with that of other nations and, particularly, with that of Russia. A finger has been pointed at contrasts in curricula, in materials, in teaching techniques, and even in the length of the school year. Beneath these considerations, however, lies the fundamental idea of purpose. How did the schools of the USSR and the USA differ in purpose? The answer to this inquiry is imbedded in the political theory of the State and the relationship of the individual to society.
Contrasts in the schools - an effective series		
Simple sentence stressing main idea		
Question to elicit interest *Indication of broad lines of inquiry*		
Simple-direct statement *Compound-complex sentence*	(2)	The Russian idea stemmed from its concept of totalitarianism. The State was the all-important element and all individuals were subject to the service they may contribute to the government. Thus, as authoritative sources revealed, the schools were permitted to produce only the number of engineers, of lawyers, of technicians, and of artists, that the State could have utilized. Rigid examination procedures limited sharply the number of aspirants in each skill area. The rest were forced into occupations as the need indicated. This sort of planned preparation for life had a natural concomitant. Once trained for a particular niche in society, each growing citizen devoted all his talents, training, and energy to the development of the State. The whole process is a kind of mathematical equation in which people become numbers and symbols, losing the qualities of personal freedom, ambition, inventiveness, and interest which we, of the Western world, hold so dear.
Introducing examples *Complex sentence with adverbial and adjective clauses*		
Simple sentence		
Short complex sentence		
Long, well-developed simple sentence		
Use of figurative language		
Complex sentence with an effective series		

15

POINT-SCORING ELEMENTS	PARAGRAPH NUMBER
Transition	(3) Our fundamental belief in the value of each individual results in school patterns quite different from that of Russia. We subscribe to the theory of full education for all to the best of each one's ability. Out of <u>such</u> development will come the informed citizenry that will make a success of our democratically functioning society. <u>Moreover,</u> we urge each person to select the way of life which appeals to him and suits his talents and interests, — the profession, the occupation, the goals that he envisions for himself. <u>This exercise</u> of freedom will engender respect for the country which provides opportunity for self-advancement and will elicit that participation in society which is characterized by good-will and cooperation.
Simple sentenoe	
Complex sentence with adjective clause Note coherence in such, <u>Moreover,</u> and <u>This exercise</u>	
Summary in effective diction and parallel predicate elements	
Simple sentence	
Compound sentence without connective	(4) To implement these ideals, we have educational programs for all: the bright, the average, the slow. Education is free up through the high school; many concessions and grants are given to the deserving to go on through college and advanced study. Both academic and vocational courses are provided, depending upon interest and ability. The slow, and even the handicapped of all kinds, have the opportunity of progressive schooling at their own rate and according to their own potential. Remedial helps are offered at every level to salvage those whom sickness and adverse fortune have kept from successful participation earlier.
Simple sentence	
Complex sentence with adjective clause	
Complex sentence with conditional clause *Question* *Echo of condition but now given as answer*	(5) If the opposing forces of society are eventually to clash, the weapons are being forged now. Shall we be free or slaves? If our schools do their job well, the processes which give man his full stature of dignity, worth, and freedom, will triumph over those which deny him these fundamental rights and desires.

www.ingramcontent.com/pod-product-compliance
Lightning Source LLC
Chambersburg PA
CBHW082031300426
44117CB00015B/2446